AMERICA FROM TH

AMERICAN LAND CLASSICS

Charles E. Little
Series Editor

George F. Thompson
Series Director

American Land Classics makes available to
a new generation of readers enduring works
on geography, landscape, nature, and place.

*Published in cooperation with the Center
for American Places, Santa Fe, New
Mexico, and Staunton, Virginia*

America from the Air

AN AVIATOR'S STORY

Wolfgang Langewiesche

edited and introduced by
Drake Hokanson and Carol Kratz

with a foreword by William Langewiesche

THE JOHNS HOPKINS UNIVERSITY PRESS

Baltimore and London

Chapters 1–14 originally published in Wolfgang Langewiesche, *I'll Take the High Road*. New York: Harcourt, Brace and Company, 1939.
Chapter 15 © 1951 McGraw-Hill, originally published in Wolfgang Langewiesche, *A Flier's World*. New York: McGraw-Hill, 1951.

The Johns Hopkins University Press
2715 North Charles Street
Baltimore, Maryland 21218-4363
www.press.jhu.edu

Library of Congress Cataloging-in-Publication Data

Langewiesche, Wolfgang, 1907–2002.
America from the air : An aviator's story / Wolfgang
Langewiesche ; edited and introduced by Drake Hokanson and
Carol Kratz ; with a foreword by William Langewiesche.
p. cm. — (American land classics)
ISBN 0-8018-7819-5 (pbk. : alk. paper)
1. United States—Aerial photographs. 2. Landscape—United
States—Pictorial works. 3. United States—Description and travel.
4. Aerial photography—United States. 5. Landscape photography—United States. 6. Langewiesche, Wolfgang, 1907–2002.
7. Air pilots—United States—Biography. 8. Airplanes—Piloting.
I. Hokanson, Drake, 1951– . II. Kratz, Carol, 1954– . III. Title.
IV. Series.
E 169.L2725.2004
917.304'91'0222—dc21

2003013849

To the memory of Myron J. Kratz, who flew

"There's nothing like it, you know."

Contents

91   Chapter 8: Pilot's-eye View

102   Chapter 9: Neurosis in Miniature

115   Chapter 10: The Poor Man's Airplane

128   Chapter 11: You Must Beware of Hatteras

146   Chapter 12: Key West with Lady

160   Chapter 13: Adventure in the Forest

178   Chapter 14: My Kind of Flying

193   Chapter 15: American Air

*Photographs taken by Langewiesche during
his circa 1939 flights follow page 90.*

Foreword

William Langewiesche

My father was an extraordinary man; I knew this even as a young boy. For one, he was so old when I was born, nearly fifty, that throughout our long life together people mistook him for my grandfather. For another, he was deeply and impressively intelligent, with a mind that encompassed a wide range of understanding, from history to science, engineering, and math to modern philosophy and the aesthetics of poetry in (as best I can reconstruct) about six languages. He was quiet about all this. He was not just smart but also well educated—the product of the sort of high European education that reached its zenith in the generations just before his, and then crumbled in the ruins of the First and Second World Wars. But he disliked academic pomposity, snobbery, or intellectual pretentiousness of any kind. And having come to the United States as much to escape the conventions of family and class as the growing horror of fascism, he discovered a land without constraints, and a people of astonishing creativity and courage—a raw and fundamentally egalitarian place, which, on the scale of the whole continent, he gladly made his home. He also, of course, discovered the airplane, and the revolutionary, incomparable view of home, which is the view from above.

Though he became a test pilot, flew F4U fighters for the U.S. Navy during World War II, and within aviation circles became fa-

mous for his technical work, the airplanes that he loved best were to
the end of his life the egalitarian ones—the Piper Cub and its de-
scendants among Cessnas, Aeroncas, and Beechcrafts—that could
be flown slowly, cheaply, and at low altitude. To him the small airplane was an expression of the freedom that this country offered to
ordinary citizens, many of whom, by scraping together their savings
as he did, could find it within their means to fly. More important, the
small airplane served as the perfect vehicle for his explorations, a
machine that allowed him to float above the treetops and facades
and to look down in fascination on the endlessly changing patterns
of his adopted land. He was by nature and experience a skeptical
patriot, but until the end of his days he was driven by the question,
"What is this place called the United States?" It was the airplane
that helped him find answers.

Me too, I suppose. I grew up in his cockpits, an apprentice pilot
with a marked tendency to suck my thumb when things weren't
going well. For years I was too small to see outside, and so I flew as
pilots must when flying in clouds, by reference to the instruments
only. It must have been frustrating to my father; he didn't care about
training me for a career in aviation (yet another airline or fighter
pilot); he took me along because as a father he was ambitious and he
wanted me to see the world as only flying would allow. After I grew
taller, he had me sit on stacked magazines or boating cushions, and
though I was still too small to see ahead, he weaned me of the
instruments and insisted that I fly by looking out the side windows.
When he flew, if I tried to read to pass the time, he would grow angry
at my stupidity and insist that the only thing worth reading while in
flight was the view of the earth from above. In my teenage years, I
resisted of course. By then I was tall enough to see over the nose,
and all I really wanted to do was go fast and high and push into
weather far away, inside the sky. At times it was difficult to fly with
this wise and meditative man, with his monk-like asceticism, who so
clearly cared nothing about my yearnings for glory. But even then, at
my most rash and impatient, I realized that he was right when he
told me to get over my heroics and to remember that the first rule of
being in the sky is simply to open one's eyes.

Introduction

Drake Hokanson

Back in the early 1930s, Wolfgang Langewiesche sold his car, took the cash, went to what is now Chicago's Midway Airport, and began flying lessons. What lured him there was the song of two conspiring sirens: the heady appeal of airplanes in the Air Age and the desire to use one to explore America. He explained the idea to Carol and me a few years ago in his high-windowed office in Princeton, New Jersey: "I had the very strong idea that the small airplane was a great geographic and sociological tool for looking at the landscape. The point—or a main point—of flying is that you can go anywhere and look at any piece of the earth, and you see more or less all that is on it, and often even what is underneath, and what's on top of it in the way of weather. The whole thing is crystal clear." Flying, he said, is simply "a superior way to look around."

What began in those Depression days for Langewiesche led to a career of fifty-some years of flying and writing that included these essays, which were first published in book form in *I'll Take the High Road* (1939) and *A Flier's World* (1951). What we have in these works of a prolific writer and eager pilot is a remarkable and early aerial perspective on the American landscape. Langewiesche, who died in early 2002, was unusual among pilots then, and is unusual among them now, in that he always attended to the earth below.

Wolfgang Langewiesche, as you will see in the essays to come, is not only a pilot who *flew through the air* but also a pilot who *flew above the ground.* As it turns out, he was a scholar of landscape studies long before the thing had a name.

We first heard of Wolfgang Langewiesche while earning our pilot's wings in the mid-1970s. A friend had given us a copy of Langewiesche's well-known and perpetually in-print *Stick and Rudder: An Explanation of the Art of Flying* (more than 200,000 copies sold). Here was a fellow who could explain how things work, we said. Sometime later a geographer-acquaintance mentioned some interesting material about viewing the land from the air by the same writer. Copies of those books were rare, even in good research libraries, but a search paid off when we were eventually able to read *I'll Take the High Road* and *A Flier's World.* This fellow knows about more than just airplanes, we said.

We decided we'd like to meet this fellow. A couple of queries led nowhere, but then we discovered a letter to the editor, signed Wolfgang Langewiesche, Princeton, New Jersey, in a fresh issue of an aviation magazine to which we subscribe. Directory assistance did the rest, and we soon found ourselves on our way to Princeton to interview a man who thought the world had altogether forgotten these two early books.

We were welcomed by a thoughtful, precise, and dryly funny man who confessed to being a bit mystified by our interest—and perhaps a bit flattered. In his office, over sandwiches, over wine, through several long days, we talked of airplanes, of flying "cross-country," of Midway Airport in the 1930s, of the land and how it's changed. Through hours of conversation, we ultimately came to know something of the peculiar perspective that an observant pilot can have of the landscape. Indeed, perspective is a central idea in the essays herein—not just the "view from on high" but a flier's particular understanding of the world below, seen through a pilot's sensibility.

In his essay "The Beholding Eye: Ten Versions of the Same Scene,"° geographer D. W. Meinig offers a key concept. He writes

---

° In D. W. Meinig, ed., *The Interpretation of Ordinary Landscapes* (New York: Oxford, 1979).

of taking ten people of "varied company" to a prominence overlooking city and country—an aerial view of sorts—and having them describe what they see. He says that one viewer will see landscape "as nature" (the Sierra Club member, perhaps); another will see landscape as problem (the planner); another as aesthetic (the painter), and so on. "We may certainly agree," writes Meinig, "that we will see many of the same elements—houses, roads, trees, hills—in terms of such denotations as number, form, dimension, and color, but such facts take on meaning only through association; they must be fitted together according to some coherent body of ideas. Thus we confront the central problem: any landscape is composed not only of what lies before our eyes, but what lies within our heads."

What would a pilot such as Langewiesche see standing with these ten spectators? What makes up a pilot's "coherent body of ideas," especially those of a pilot who flew in an era when navigation information came from the ground underneath and not from flickering gauges and cockpit displays?

Because pilots rely on landscape in ways others do not, they regard it first in a practical fashion. A pilot must be able to find the way and be able to find the airport in the clutter below. A pilot must read the mountains and their winds for turbulence. And in Langewiesche's early days, pilots, nagged by the constant fear of engine failure, had to evaluate landscape for its suitability as an emergency landing field. Accordingly, Langewiesche found Illinois more comforting than Maine.

During those early days of flight, pilots also made their way across the country by means of landmarks, and those landmarks were often very different from those of the ground traveler. What is obvious to the pilot is often hidden to those on the ground and vice versa. While an auto driver might use posted route numbers, directional signs, and landmarks like truck stops or the big red house to mark trip progress, pilots looked for the tank farm, the big loop in the river, or the railroad yard, all hidden from the highway but evident for miles in any direction from the air.

But Wolfgang Langewiesche saw more than the practical. He was in a sense an "attached observer." For example, he used passing

towns to describe for the groundling something of the pilot's understanding of the earth: "Flying," writes Langewiesche herein, "you
tell these towns apart as you tell stars—by constellation. This one, of
about the fourth magnitude, with a smaller one to the north of it—
that must be this one on the map. Those three-in-line, that's those."

Langewiesche knew that to fly, to look down, and to analyze carefully what he saw was to help make plain the complex muddle of our
earthbound existence. For example, he understood that foreground
and background, so important to our pedestrian and auto-centered
lives, become continuous landscape from a few hundred feet above
the ground. Those things that seem so important from an earthly
perspective take on their rightful proportions when seen from above.
Of 1930s New York City Langewiesche writes: "What's it all about?
On the ground, why you know: *Time, Life, Look, Quick,* and *Harper's;* Batten, Barton, Durston and Osborne; Merrill Lynch, Pierce,
Fenner and Beane; NBC, CBS, ABC; words, ideas, paper of all sorts.
But, from the air, I regret to state, New York looks like a place where
steamships tie up to piers. The piers catch your eye, not Radio City or
the Wall Street skyscrapers. Manhattan, with all those tentacles sticking out into the water, looks like some biological exhibit—some organ
specially developed to draw nourishment from the sea."

Here, then, is what lies in this particular pilot's head: a genius for
analyzing what he sees of the earth, and in his writings, a way of
explicating the land as seen from his chair in the sky. His eagerness
and clarity become an invitation to the student of landscape to ride
along and look down with him. Pilots did (and occasionally still do)
navigate using towns constellation fashion, but it takes someone of
Langewiesche's caliber to help us understand the makings and
markings of the pilot's landscape, and even more important, to sug-
gest how this perspective might be useful for scholars who spend
most of their time looking at the world from eye level.

In the 1930s when Langewiesche began flying, the very idea of
looking down on the ground from an airplane held great novelty.
Aircraft of the era—including airliners—flew low and slow, and the
few Americans who had flown marveled at the view churning slowly
past at what seemed like steamboat speed. It was the Air Age after

all, and the whole world was dizzy with airplanes and what they could do. Thus, Langewiesche's impressions carry a freshness that is antidote to today's numbing frequent-flyer leaps across whole continents and entire oceans at altitudes of 30,000-plus feet, where, if you were to bother looking out the tiny window at all, you'd notice that the earth has turned into a map of itself.

Perhaps this is why so few landscape scholars consider the aerial perspective. If the only view from above we've ever enjoyed is of an acre of wing and a sliver of landscape seen through a scratched window from the stratosphere—well, we can be forgiven for missing the possibilities. By contrast, Langewiesche flew low—sometimes very low. He once flew much of the Florida coast with the wheels of his Cub just inches above the beach just to see what the landscape looked like blistering past. But don't try this today.

Of course there is little need for every scholar with a bent toward landscape—much less the ordinary traveler—to sell the car like Langewiesche did, take the cash, and start flying lessons, but the study of the land is poorer for the fact that few have. Anyone studying, for example, the proliferation of suburban outlet malls, the disappearance of Pennsylvania barns, the changes in strip mining practices, or the habits of rivers, would do well to take to the air for a few hours with a camera and notebook. There are things to be seen from the air that cannot be glimpsed from below.

Langewiesche told us how he made this discovery for himself after taking a Danube steamer trip in the 1920s. He had found the boat trip rather dull and decided to try it by commercial aircraft the next time. The aerial excursion over the same territory brought him a revelation: "It struck me how clearly you could see the old courses of the river, those from recent geologic times. I was fascinated as hell. When I got to Vienna, I was almost ready to throw up, but I was really fascinated. It was quite possibly the first time I saw something from the air which could not have been seen any other way—not by walking, not by swimming—you had to be above it. It confirmed in me the idea that one ought to look at places from the air."

Langewiesche's perspective on the American land was fresh—and still is—for another reason: the United States was new to him.

Born and raised in Germany, Wolfgang Langewiesche immigrated to the States in 1929 as a "self-help" graduate student, and like so many people in that era, was fascinated by all things American. "I came here to look at the country and to know what America was really like," he told us, "rather than to know it by reading books written by Germans and edited by Germans. The first year I was here, I was pretty damned busy just looking at how people ate lunch! I was always fascinated by America. I used to think that if I ever got to a place called *El Paso,* by God, I will be able to say that I am a well-traveled man!"

An outsider can bring to a new place an appreciation for the things that are too common, too ordinary for the locals to notice— things like how people eat lunch. But unlike the travel writer whose myopia blurs everything except that which can be seen through the refractive lens of home, Langewiesche used his clear eyes not to compare America to Germany, but to learn deeply and write simply about what he experienced in a new land that was fast becoming his home. On going west from New York to Chicago, Langewiesche said, "Oh, yes, I had the advantage that I was totally ignorant of the Midwest. I discovered section lines almost right away."

For most square-minded Americans, it is hard to imagine the section line as something novel enough to be scrutinized and analyzed, but for Langewiesche, such straight lines running to the four points of the compass were spectacular examples of American pragmatism.

Wolfgang Langewiesche was not the first to fly and look at the land and then write about it, but he has done so here with a grace, simplicity, wit, and perspective seldom found. An ordinary man with extraordinary sense, he was motivated by a simple idea: "When you mix America, and the air, and an airplane, you get a mixture that makes an ordinary person talk about it for a long time afterwards."

At dinner not long ago, after an afternoon of conversation, we sat over noodles at a Japanese restaurant talking of river meanders, of seeing Oregon Trail ruts from the air, that particular glint of sun on distant lakes so well known to fliers.

"The most unknown thing in the United States," said Langewiesche after careful thought, "is the United States."

A Life in the Air: Wolfgang Langewiesche, 1907–2002

Carol Kratz

During an interview a few years ago, Wolfgang Lange-wiesche described with great affection "the turn" in an airplane. As he spoke, his hand demonstrated this smooth, complex, even maneuver; fingers held tight together, wrist, hand, and forearm in a geometric plane. His hand banked in a satisfying arc to cut through the air, and his smile revealed his lifelong appreciation for the event. It was not a technical explanation he was offering, nor the sharing of a recent experience. This was a recollection of his second ride in an airplane, and the first time he consciously experienced a turn, nearly seventy-five years in the past. His vivid description provided not merely an image of the event, but the physical sensation as well.

It was in a Fokker passenger airplane. My mother took me as a Christmas present or something. I think it had four in the cabin, and two pilots in the front, though you couldn't see them. That man flew very nicely. He suddenly banked in a perfectly coordinated manner. You felt nothing, no forces of any kind. One had only the side windows, like now in an airliner, with little forward vision. Suddenly, the world tilted, and there was this strange event. I had not known that the turn involved perfect coordination such that 'down' always stays where it belongs, and that it is the world that seems to move. At that time, the whole thing, being more strange than it seems now, was a strong sensation, a pleasure, and I understood instantly.

This experience reveals much about Wolfgang Langewiesche; it speaks to his intense and early love of flying, and his power to observe, analyze, describe, and remember. This passion and these skills lie at the heart of his writings, his life works. And they are well expressed in the chapters republished in this book.

Langewiesche is best known as the author of the classic aviation text, *Stick and Rudder* (McGraw-Hill). Continuously in print since its first publication in 1944, *Stick and Rudder* is well known to pilots across the country. It has sold more than 200,000 copies. One pilot in our acquaintance says reading the book saved his life. The subtitle, *An Explanation of the Art of Flying*, hands it to the reader in the straightforward language that characterizes all of Langewiesche's writing. In chapters entitled "The Rudder," "What the Airplane Wants to Do," and, of course, "The Turn," Langewiesche synthesized detailed, accurate, and logical explanations useful to both novice and experienced pilots who seek a better sense of practical aircraft operations. So clear and accurate were his explanations that even today, sixty years after its first publication, the book is unchanged, and pilots everywhere are still drawn and directed to this now-Bible of aviation.

In one of our 1996 interviews, Langewiesche explained how he came to write: "I am hereditarily burdened in my soul, in the brain, by [the idea of] the book. I was born into a frame of mind in which almost anything is not real until it is written about and printed."

If not genetic, there is at least a familial tendency to write and publish books. Langewiesche's father Wilhelm Langewiesche and his mother Helena Brandt founded a publishing house, Langewiesche-Brandt Verlag. His uncle also published; his sister was a travel writer. His son William continues the tradition, having authored four books, and is today a national correspondent for the *Atlantic Monthly*.

This literary heredity compelled Wolfgang Langewiesche to

write five books during his lifetime that express both the very practical, as in *Lightplane Flying* (1939) and *Stick and Rudder* (1944), and the deeply experiential, as in *A Student's Odyssey* (1935), *I'll Take the High Road* (1939), and *A Flier's World* (1951).

The chapters republished herein are excerpted from the latter two books. In these chapters Langewiesche shows the reader the view from above, the feel from the pilot's seat, and gives us a peek into the pilot's heart and mind. He expresses deep appreciation for the sensations and observations this privileged position affords, the techniques it requires, and the miraculous nature of it all. If *Stick and Rudder* tells us how to fly, these works tell us *why*.

Langewiesche's memories of early life reveal his interest in the airplane and the land over which it flew. Born in Düsseldorf, Germany, in 1907, his publisher parents moved the family to Ebenhausen, south of Munich. There in 1912, at the age of five, when other children his age might have been looking at the ground and their marbles, Langewiesche's gaze was turned upward. "Flügel!" he would call out, "Flügel!" To this child, the years of World War I meant more airplanes overhead. Though he was recounting the sensation of the turn from his second ride, his very first ride, taken in an open cockpit biplane, left an equally indelible impression on him: "The thing had no stick in the back cockpit. They put you in a big fur coat. The man took us for a little low altitude ride of fifteen minutes, but it was a tremendous experience for me. It was incredibly noisy. In the open cockpit, you saw people's lips move, but you could not hear a thing. I looked and had the certain pleasure of seeing the trees go under you. It was a nice low altitude flight across the exurban area to the local river, and across the river."

He surfaced from the reverie for a moment and expressed the thrill he still felt for an experience that many have but few appreciate in the way he did. For many of us, our airline-acquired familiarity with flight has left us indifferent to what Langewiesche reminds us is the miracle of flying. "It is always an event when an airplane first crosses water, right? I always let my passengers fly, and when we come to the little lake, they ask, 'now when I get to the

lake, to that water, what do I do?' And I say, nothing! That is one of
the moments when you know you are flying!"

The story of his first airplane ride, his first look at the land from
the air concludes: "It was an absolutely decisive event in my life. Of
course, I was all primed for great sensations, and there they came.
After that there was no holding me." ·

When he was sixteen, he spent a summer as an apprentice at the
Junkers airplane factory in Germany. But working on airplanes did
not afford Langewiesche much satisfaction. "I said to my father, 'I
don't want to become an engineer and build airplanes; I would
much rather write about them.' "

Langewiesche wanted to be a writer, and felt that Germany
needed "a new, sharper, and corrected view of the countries surrounding us." He felt confined by the provincialism and isolation of
his country and the tradition-bound rules and roles of his culture.
After attending two German universities and the London School of
Economics, Langewiesche sought liberation in America. "I decided
to come over here, much against my parents' wishes, and study for
awhile and have a good look at the so-called United States. So I was
here with the attitude of being a writer of something of the world,
originally destined for German readers, you see, the people with
whom I had grown up and whose thinking I knew. America itself was
a very big subject on people's minds, in all respects, many of them
connected with money, but some actually connected with liberty. A
place with big distances, glamour, climate. I think it was the most
interesting country in the world at that time."

In 1929, at age twenty-two, he came to New York City as a "self-
help student" where out of necessity he interspersed his graduate
studies in economics at Columbia University with odd jobs to earn
his keep. The shoestring on which he had come to America frayed in
October 1929 when the stock market crashed. "I was in the Columbia University bookstore and heard people talking about the market
collapsing. I said 'What do you guys care? It's the stock market; it's
no worry of yours.' Well, I found out."

American life and landscape were ripe for his observation and analysis. His first book, *A Student's Odyssey* was translated from the German and published in 1935. Two years later it was published in its original language as *Das Amerikanische Abenteuer*. In it the ever-enterprising Langewiesche tells of graduate study and the jobs he held in his early years in America. His first job, which he held for twelve long nights, was to make sandwiches assembly-line fashion "so that the pretty stenographers in the city at midday may have a good selection for lunch." He went on to work as a busboy in the university cafeteria, as a window cleaner, a subway courier of boxfuls of croaking bullfrogs (for the biology laboratory), an electrician, and janitor in an apartment building where he lived.

Exploring America meant going places, too. Where others might have found such a poor financial situation an obstacle to travel, the young Langewiesche was liberated by it. In *A Student's Odyssey* he writes: "After the great stock market crash there was no sense at all in staying in New York over vacations in order, perhaps, to chase dollars for the new school year in advance. Dollars had become very fugitive. The best that I could have hoped for would have been just to exist, and just to exist was possible for me in other ways too." In the summer of 1930, with fifty dollars in hand, he joined an expedition of three other young adventurers in a old four-cylinder Dodge with 150,000 miles on it, and traveled from New York to California. His observant eye and mind gathered notions about the land and the people's ways.

His ride to California turned out not to include a ride home, so Langewiesche exploited another aspect of America's automobile culture. As a hitchhiker he absorbed more of the road, the culture, and the dust of his new country.

The summer after receiving his master of arts degree, the stricken economy continued to limit his summer job possibilities. Through correspondence with the university, Langewiesche landed a job as a ranch hand in Wyoming. With that, his ideas of America expanded to include fence building, cattle roundups, haymaking, all under the shade of a "handsome great five-gallon hat No. 2463, suitable to my rank." When the cowboy summer was over, the high price of a train ticket spurred him to hop freight trains for his trip back East. And so he had begun his study of America, on foot, by auto, and freight train, but not yet by air.

Langewiesche returned briefly to Germany to attend to some business. He sold a few stories to German newspapers, straightened out his visa, and returned to America in the fall of 1932 to continue his graduate studies at the University of Chicago. The money in his pocket empowered him: he took a commercial flight in a Ford Tri-motor from New Jersey to Chicago. At that time, such a flight was seen by most as risky. Only a few months earlier, in July of 1932, Franklin Roosevelt had been viewed as a daredevil when he traveled in a Tri-motor from Albany to the Democratic National Convention in Chicago. These were the coming-of-age days for aviation.

"When I landed at the airport in Chicago [now Midway]," said Langewiesche, "the place was lousy with various kinds of small planes, and I got a good sniff at the atmosphere and decided I would go back there after I arranged my affairs and talk to somebody. That is exactly what I did." Langewiesche returned to the field with the business card of a fixed-base operator (whom he calls George Adams in these chapters) and a ten-dollar bill. George showed him the Travel Air biplane he used for flight instruction and had the pilot-hopeful climb into the rear cockpit, the pilot's seat. It was a persuasive place to sit. "Below, when you looked over the side, were the wings, and below them, the airport grass; but it was easy to imagine, instead, forests and fields and cities." He didn't have to imagine long; he didn't even have to climb out. This first encounter with the plane soon became his first lesson.

He continued to buy his "Time" in this ship, first "dual," with George in the front cockpit, then solo. George taught by "flying much and explaining little," according to Langewiesche. Though "he knew his theory well enough," he rarely used explanations to advance a student pilot's knowledge. To George's way of thinking, you had to "feel it in your hand and the seat of your pants."

His time accumulated in half-hour segments. He soloed in 1934, and for two years Langewiesche flew the same plane around and around the same field practicing landings. He dreamed of taking an airplane on a cross-country trip; in pilot's parlance, a trip that would take him to an airport, say, fifty or more miles away from the home field. He writes: "Cross-country: it sounded so matter of course. What else would one do with an airplane but fly it cross-country (unless it be stunting) or across what else would one fly it but country (unless it be oceans)?"

It seems that cross-country flight beckoned him the same way the trip by auto from New York to California had a few years earlier. It was a logical extension of his desire to see America, and promised another perspective and another sort of liberation. It cost him the sale of his car, an argument with George, a few for-hire parachute jumps to earn some money, but he finally got his chance.

There were many cross-country trips to come in the following fifty-plus years Langewiesche flew airplanes. A scant few are revealed in this slim volume.

Not reported here is his continent-crossing September 1939 trip in a rented Cub (this machine was a "hot" one according to Langewiesche; it had a 55-horsepower engine instead of the standard 50) from New Jersey to New England around through New York, Pennsylvania, and to the Midwest. He followed the route of the Union Pacific Railroad across Wyoming and toward the West Coast. He talked not long ago about the drama of the route: "I was very happy and in my element, but the Rockies looked like death skulls."

In Nevada, Langewiesche glimpsed a herd of wild horses; they panicked at his low pass. East of Sacramento, at Blue Canyon, Langewiesche remembers pulling the throttle to idle and flying the Cub as a glider in the updrafts over the Sierra.

Homeward bound, the Cub proved its short-field stuff when he flew into (and, then remarkably, out of) a high-elevation, short strip used by forest fire fighting aircraft. In Montana, he landed on a sandbar where he met a gold prospector, who in his isolation was surprised to learn from Langewiesche that World War II had broken out.

Once back in the Midwest, Langewiesche flew the length of the Mississippi River to New Orleans, explored the delta, then flew along the Gulf Coast to Texas. He then returned home to New Jersey, three months after setting out and two hundred flight hours later.

Langewiesche kept no diary of this trip, but he did carry a camera. Until a few years ago, the black-and-white 35-mm negatives remained securely, if not cryptically, wound in rolls, safe in screw-top aluminum canisters. Few if any of the images had ever been printed, and he offered us these aerial time capsules. By the time we made prints, the sixty years intervening had taken a toll on Langewiesche's vision and memory of details of these flights. Consequently, the captions of these photographs, which we include in this volume, sometimes are shy on desired detail. But the images speak loudly, and give new dimension to the stories of his early cross-country trips in the late 1930s.

There are photos taken through the windshield at altitude, of mountain passes, river meanders, the Cub posed on the salt flats of Utah. Other photographs show the wild horses on the Nevada desert, galloping to escape the noisy, mechanical bird. One image, not used due to poor quality, shows the Cub pulled up in some now-forgotten town at Jautney's Drive-In (the airstrip must have been nearby) and Langewiesche being waited on by a young carhop in a captain's hat. She serves up Lone Star Ice Cream on a tray that hangs on the Cub's left side, the window swung up under the wing.

And one photograph perfectly embodies the spirit of the cross-country. Under the wing of the Cub, ready to be loaded, waits Langewiesche's equipment for the journey ahead. Gas cans, a bedroll, an axe, odd pieces of luggage are inventoried and soon to be stowed. His overcoat hangs over the wing strut. The image captures that moment when an adventure is about to begin.

Wolfgang Langewiesche flew across this country countless times. On one trip he ferried a Cub on floats from Wall Street to Seattle, and Langewiesche tells of landing it on the Missouri River in Mobridge, South Dakota. Many years later, in a conversation with a man from Mobridge, Langewiesche acknowledged that he knew the town, and that he had landed a seaplane there years ago. The man excitedly responded that he remembered that incident because it had "created so much attention to see a seaplane on the prairies." A bit later on the same trip, the reception was not quite as enthusiastic when he landed on a lake, against regulations, in Glacier National Park.

From very early on, Langewiesche believed in the democratiza-
tion of flying, that it is not a heroic activity, but can be enjoyed by all.
In his *Lightplane Flying*, he proclaimed, "The good news contained
in this book is that any man or woman who wants to fly can now fly.
To be a pilot is a right no longer reserved for the soldiers, the
daredevils, the millionaires, and the professionals."

Aeroncas, Cubs, Taylorcrafts and other new planes in the early
1930s were "simple, light, inexpensive, and safe." Some called them
flivvers of the air, likening them to the Model T Ford in which
America took to the road. In those days there were boosters in
aviation who imagined the same trend in the air. Langewiesche
expressed the excitement of early flying in the United States much
the way early transcontinental automobile travelers had in travel
journals a decade or two earlier. "So, deep in the twentieth century,
air age and all, you personally met this continent: its mountains,
plains, rivers." He speaks of "getting the country with one's nerves
direct," and his sensing of the country from the air parallels the
observations and travails of the early motorists.

But the dangers of flying, both real and perceived, were a barrier
in those days to every man and every woman learning to fly. Leighton
Collins was a Harvard-trained insurance man, then Aeronca sales-
man, who early on used a personal airplane for business travel. He
was eager to promote safety in flying, and so started a small magazine
called *Air Facts* in which he analyzed reports about airplane mishaps.
Understanding cause might lead to prevention; explaining technique
was a key to avoidance. At a fall Cub convention in 1940 in New
Jersey, Langewiesche and Collins met and began to talk about flying,
leading to a lifelong association and friendship. Langewiesche's articles about technique appeared in *Air Facts* in 1941 and 1942, and
some articles were later adapted to *Stick and Rudder*.

From his first decade of flying and observing the behavior of an
airplane, Langewiesche synthesized detailed explanations of good
techniques of flying in *Stick and Rudder*. What he had learned from
his instructor and pre–World War II books on flying was at odds
with what he experienced when he flew. Explanations in pilot education seemed to him to be missing, frequently dismissed by his own

instructor's declaration, "You have to *feel* it." In other cases, theories put forward seemed inadequate or even wrong-headed. Again, he was compelled to write. "I knew something which I did not know before, and I wanted to communicate this new view of old things.

"A good many people *did* it quite well in reality, but did poorly on the explaining side. I thought what the art needed was, and still is, is simple, clear explanations that should preferably be true." But his iconoclastic ideas weren't immediately accepted or universally liked. They conflicted with then-current theories of flight held by the government and most flight instructors. Nonetheless, time has borne out the validity and usefulness of his theories: *Stick and Rudder* is now in the canon.

In the early years of World War II, he spent a year teaching ground school at an Army flying school. Although he aspired to more aviation involvement in the war, he was initially thwarted by holding only a private license and by having less-than-perfect vision. Eventually Cessna hired him as a production test pilot, during which time *Stick and Rudder* was conceived. He moved on to test-fly Chance Vought's F4U Corsairs. In 1950 the Kollsman company put Langewiesche to work experimenting with an angle of attack indicator and a celestial navigation device.

His lifetime list of planes flown includes early biplanes (Fleets and Travel Airs), the Stinson Voyager, Beech 18, F4U Corsair, Cessna 140, Cessna 182, high-performance gliders, and, of course, his favorite, the Cub. By the time he stopped flying around age eighty, he had accumulated more than 15,000 flight hours. Throughout his writings, we experience his affection for his varied aircraft through endearments like *sky-buggy, air yacht, putt-putt, big noise,* and most commonly, *the ship.*

His flights carried him around the United States and then beyond. After World War II he flew a Beech 18 to Europe, the Middle East, over the Indian subcontinent, and on to New Guinea. In 1949 he made a shakedown flight in a Cessna 140 from the East Coast to Gander, Newfoundland, then shipped the plane to Europe and flew it to Africa, where he and his wife Priscilla plied the skies for two years while he wrote as a *Saturday Evening Post* correspondent.

He contributed to magazines as varied as the places he visited and the planes he flew. He wrote for *Travel, Holiday, Life, The Sportsman Pilot, Science Digest,* and *Flying.* "I was anointed [in May of 1940] by having a piece in *The Saturday Evening Post,*" he said. When speaking about the monthly articles he did for *Air Facts,* he modestly stated he didn't know how he "kept it up so long—there isn't that much to it." Langewiesche wrote for *Harper's* over a thirty-year span, from 1941 to 1971. Working with a group of experts in several fields, he authored a long series of articles in *House Beautiful* about regional differences in U.S. climate and how they might influence home architecture. He worked as a roving editor for *Reader's Digest,* retiring in the mid 1970s after twenty years.

Readers get to know the authentic Langewiesche through his writings. Upon meeting him a few years ago, we discovered that his books and magazine articles reflect him: his humor, his modesty, his charm, and most evident, his gift of understatement and his power to observe and describe.

His analogies not only enliven the descriptions, but are instructive as well. In *I'll Take the High Road,* he offers that the fabric on a Cub downed in the forest, was "as vulnerable in most spots as an umbrella"—an image vivid enough to cause readers to reflexively lighten their grip on the book. On another trip he debates his approach to an impending storm: "I was confident that I could fly out along the beach in front of the storms, like a car beating a train to the railroad crossing; if I could not make it I might still let a storm go out to sea first, and fly through behind it, like a jaywalking pedestrian crossing a busy street."

Through his flying experiences and with this aerial perspective, how and what did he see? In these writings Langewiesche demonstrates his remarkable ability to see below the surface and reveal the hidden details. With equal skill he steps back—or up—reducing the broad and complex into a satisfying, understandable entity. In his observing eye, he carries a close-up lens, a telephoto, and a wide-angle. And a looking glass, too.

He sees in the landscape the simple and the beautiful, as in the aerial view of porpoises playing off Cape Hatteras. He translates the large and complex into an image we are bound to understand and remember. Hoover Dam becomes just a rock jammed into "this stream at just the right spot." He observes geography as "East changes to West." He finds history in the dunes at Kitty Hawk, the testing grounds for the Wright brothers. His analysis of section lines and the American landscape speak of his sociological observations. And while he looks outside the ship, he looks inside himself as well, especially when he writes about being suddenly mapless when his chart blows out of the plane, and when he tells us how it feels to fly out over open sea.

Wolfgang Langewiesche died on February 9, 2002, in California, with his family near, at the age of ninety-four. When we first met him six years earlier, he sat at his desk in his Princeton, New Jersey, apartment, where he had lived for many years. He was surrounded by books and was still writing. Though it had been several years since he had piloted a plane, his remembered sensations, observations, and analysis still made for fascinating conversation. His pleasure in talking of "the turn" had not been dampened by the innumerable times he and the ailerons and rudder had coaxed an airplane into one.

Always the observer, the student and author, by Cub and Cessna, from Mobridge to Manhattan, Wolfgang Langewiesche lived a life in the air. Through his writings, we can ride along.

AMERICA FROM THE AIR

I. Aerial Beachcomber

I am no helmeted, begoggled hero of the skies; picture me bookish, bespectacled, unable even to hold a teacup without rattling it. As a pilot, I am merely an amateur, and I know it. The air itself has a way of reminding me of it once in a while. When I am sitting up there high over the rivers and forests, I sometimes cannot quite suppress a small voice that says: "Come, come, Langewiesche, you know damn well you ought to be sitting in some library. What are you doing up here?"

I am only an amateur, and I shouldn't be talking.

But I can't help talking. For you take the air: the thin, substance-less air that can be made to bear a man; you take America; and you take an airplane, which of all the works of man is the nearest to a living being—you take those things and mix them up, and they will act as a drug which will knock all proper reticence right out of you.

And so, here I go talking.

The time was when the sound of airplanes used to torment me. It came down to me where I sat, deep down in the innermost recesses of the university library, where the bookstacks were, and where the more serious students did their work.

I was making my living there, a research assistant to a professor at a Middle Western university. I had a pilot's license. I had earned it the hard way, taking half-hour lessons at a time, two or three of them a month. It had been foolish, and everybody had warned me that it was foolish, both at the airport and on the campus. It was during the Depression, and amateur flying had almost disappeared completely; besides, I had no ship of my own, and no prospect of being able to buy one. The obvious way out—to get a commercial flying job—was closed to me: at that time, one could not get a commercial license if one was short-sighted.

Thus I was in a fix; it seemed that I should never be able to use my license the way it was intended: for travel. Flying Time on a training ship cost fifteen dollars an hour, and merely to keep my hand in took all my money. Yet if I stopped flying altogether to save up money, I would lose both my license and my flying ability. It was a case of having a white elephant by the tail.

I tried hard to forget about flying. But wanting to fly is like hunger and like love: the harder you try to forget it, the worse it gets. It got so that I could spot an airplane on the cover of a magazine on a newsstand clear across the street.

Every afternoon at three, the sound of the transcontinental mail ship came down to me in the library, plaguing me. The line running that ship had the name of Transcontinental and Western Air, Incorporated, and the mere name seemed to me absurdly proud and exciting: they had conquered the air, they had sewed the continent up in a bag and they have incorporated it; but meanwhile I had never even flown out of sight of the airport. The afternoon ship was eastbound; it was fresh from the West, only a matter of hours, and that too tormented me; for out there was the country I liked, the part of America I had cut my teeth on. I had driven cattle over it and ridden on the freights through it and dug fence-post holes into it for a living; I had slept out there on the bare mountain sides hundreds of nights; but now I was feeding myself by reading books in a cellar.

Every afternoon at three, I was thus tormented, and one afternoon at three, something snapped: I put some markers into my books and put on my hat and drove my old car to the nearest used-car lot. It fetched exactly seventy-five dollars: five hours of ship time.

Out to the airport, on the airport bus, once more stripped of my

worldly goods, a happy fool. I was going to fly cross-country. I was
going to make this thing work, or give it up.

The Metropolitan Airport lay on the dreary edge of town. You got
the drone of the motors from far away; it infused into the traffic
along the boulevard a sense of airfaring. Its six hangars rose out of
the messy industrial landscape, all six alike, concrete-and-steel.
Even from the bus stop one could see the airplanes sitting in the
grass. They were, of course, just ordinary airplanes parked along the
edge of an ordinary airport; but if only you knew, i.e., if only you had
soloed a ship once, they were more beautiful than the loveliest
beauties on a bathing beach: glamorous, graceful, haughty; you
spent a lot of time thinking of them, and drawing dream ones.
　"Spectators Not Permitted Inside the Fence," said a sign. But I
was no spectator, I belonged; and was proud of it. Instead of walking
on the road behind the hangars, I let myself in by the little gate and
walked up the Line, that long strip of pavement that ran between
the field proper and the hangars. The Line was the water-front quai,
translated from the nautical into the aeronautical, lined with hangars
and work-shops on one side and with parked ships on the other.
Only insiders were tolerated there because there were running propellers and one might have to step aside for an airplane taxiing down
the Line.
　At the administration building, an airliner was taking on passengers, its blunt nose arrogant above the attendants, a crowd of
spectators crowded behind the fence; the loud speaker was chanting
the names of faraway cities.
　The airline hangars, the National Guard Hangar, the post office
shack: that was impersonal aviation, big organizations. My own hab-
itat was further along, at the nonairline end of the field. For the
Metropolitan was a port of many ships, both the liners and tramps of
the air and the fishermen and its yachts: small red gay ones, large
gray far-traveling ones, a hard-working one just in from a long run,
its flanks streaked by exhaust smoke. At the nonairline end, the
instructors and the charter pilots kept their ships standing on the

Line all day ready to fly, and the sight-seeing ships were hangared, and the smoke writing outfit and the aerial survey people were based. I knew every one of those ships by that time: who owned it, and who flew it, and also—most important—how it earned its keep.

"Sky Harbor Café, Open Day and Night": a bunch of the boys were hanging out there, pilots and mechanics talking about ships, about girls, about the dangers of the air. I knew the fliers, and no longer stood in awe of them: I had found out the secret of what a man does when he flies. But I had a lot of liking for them. They were ordinary Depression Americans who wore sweaters with holes, and spoke ungrammatical English, and worried about money; and acted as if all they wanted was to make another dollar; while all they really wanted was to fly—just as I did.

The radio shop, the weather bureau, the compass adjustors, the parachute rigging service, the approved repair station: that was what had served as my ground school; there, if you were on good terms, you could poke into the insides of engines and ships and gadgets. There was that sign advertising "Pilot's Supplies, Maps and Protractors, Helmets and Goggles," and I had a vision of a man sitting high over the country, staring out, map on his knee, waiting for some landmark to emerge out of the distance-haze: myself, very soon now.

I sought out my instructor. He was in the hangar, giving his ship a 20-hour check, tinkering with the engine. Excited, I told him the news. I had money. I wanted to hire the ship for Sunday morning and take it out cross-country for five hours. I would not waste any time, just land at some airport and refuel quickly and turn right around and bring it back by noon: but for once I was going to fly out into the distance and see.

But no.

The ship was busy. What about Sunday after next? The ship would be busy.

"You're trying to stall me along."

"Well, frankly," he said, "you're not ready yet to go cross-country. The way you fly now, you'll break your neck if your engine quits. You need more practice on approaches. You need more Time."

There it was again.

The ship: shiny and taut-skinned, well-kept-up. All my money had gone into that ship for two years: a quarter-dollar for each and every minute of flying. For two years now, all money had meant Time for me, Flying Time on this very ship. I had gone around in an old suit, without fun, without dates; this ship had swallowed my camera, and my books, and a decent car I'd had, and a middling car I had had later, and now even that last jalopy. For two years I hadn't traveled because one day I had meant to fly and now there it was again: I needed more Time.

My nerves snapped, and I tried to fight.

"You have been telling me that for three months now."

"You haven't made headway. I've been telling you to take your Time faster. Half an hour a week is not enough."

"You know damn well I can't take my Time faster. You shouldn't have taken my money."

He answered that he had warned me. That was true. He had said to me more than once, "Even if you've got a license, what have you got?" I wanted to tell him I could always find some other instructor and fly some other ship. But he was my flying teacher; he was the nearest thing to a God; I was only railing.

I told him he had better give up flying if he couldn't trust his engines to keep running for five hours. He turned thoughtful and said, "That just goes to show, Red, you haven't any judgment yet; you know better than that, you can't ever rely on any engine."

I was excited, and he was calm; the ship was his, and in addition, he was right. I was frazzled, and he was businesslike; he had gone through this sort of scene before; it was part of his job as a flying teacher. I might as well have butted my head against a padded cell.

I had been shouting; mechanics were beginning to stand around and listen, a bunch of people to whom flying was business. I was making a fool of myself with romantic ideas. I stamped off.

It was almost sundown now, and ships were coming out of the evening sky in rapid succession: pilots planned their cross-country flights so as to come in before dark.

There I was again, a man without a ship; almost two years after my first solo flight, and still stuck in port.

Cross-country: it sounds so matter of course. What else would one do with an airplane but fly it cross-country (unless it be stunting) or across what else would one fly it but country (unless it be oceans)? At first, I had thought so myself. I had decided I would see America by air, and I had thought that all I'd have to do would be to let someone show me how to take one of those things up and put it down again, and then I'd take out my license, and then I would go.

But at the airport, one was soon taught much more respect for the air. One had duties; training was for a sort of captaincy rather than mere working of the controls. Even if you were not carrying passengers, you had a responsibility that transcended the mere financial value of the ship; the time was far past when it was all in a day's work for a pilot to crack up a ship, and when a man wasn't considered quite seasoned until he had been in the hospital a few times. Now a pilot must be matured slowly, carefully; he must be cured thoroughly with that sour ingredient, Experience; he must be aged expensively, at two bits a minute, quarter-hour after quarter-hour. Meanwhile, he must be kept where his instructor can keep an eye on him even while he is flying solo, where he can't lose his way and can't get into trouble with engine failure or bad weather. Thus for two years now—some seventy hours—all I had done was to trace precise patterns into the sky for my instructor's eyes, all within the same few cubic miles of air immediately surrounding the airport.

Anything beyond had become a mysterious region which was forbidden, something like what Life used to mean to us at school, something exceedingly earnest for which one was not yet ready. Only now it was called cross-country. Down on the ground, it might be quite familiar to you; it might be Wisconsin, Illinois, Indiana, Missouri, civilized, kindly country with not even a trace of wildness left; but by air, it was called cross-country, and it was full of dangers. By air, your own father and mother's house would be called cross-country, and would be as awesome as the high seas.

I'll be damned if I do any more practice, I thought. But I knew I would. I knew all along that I would practice and eventually fly cross-country, even if it were to be the last thing I would ever do.

My instructor stopped his car beside me. He was on his way home, and he wanted to make peace; not because he cared, but because that, too, was part of his job of handling his students. "All right now, Red, when are you coming to practice approaches?" Just as soon as I had once made three perfect approaches in a row, he said, he would let me take the ship cross-country.

I knew that by that time my money would be used up; for perfect with him really meant perfect. But I made an appointment for the next morning at daybreak.

2. The Mysterious Factor X

It was still dark when I arose the next morning.

In those years, flying was still flavored with frequent crashes and sudden death, and I remember how I shaved with special care, and how I selected my newest and best shirt; not with any strong feelings, but simply as a matter of being prepared and looking decent.

I rode to the airport over boulevards still lighted in the dawn. At the field, the first ships were being pulled out onto the Line. Up on the control tower, the officials were standing glumly behind their glass panes. They had watched all night, and now were waiting for the morning ship from the coast. From the Sky Harbor Café came a nice smell of scrambled eggs. But flying ranked before breakfast.

Up the Line, in front of Hangar 5, an engine shattered the quiet of the morning. George had seen me and had started warming up his ship for me.

That prelude to flight: the ship stands on the ground, chocks before its wheels to hold it back, and roars at the sky, its head upraised, its flanks vibrating, working itself up like a Homeric hero before battle.

It was too noisy to talk; we simply nodded at one another, and I clambered into my cockpit and took over the throttle.

It was an open cockpit. At that time, such ships, already obsolete for most other purposes, were still used for training; and thus at that time, one still had to wear helmet and goggles. The ship was flown by many students, and the last man to fly it always left helmet and goggles hung on the control stick to be worn by the next man. While I kept an eye on oil temperature and oil pressure gauges and listened to the engine, I strapped them on.

A uniform: the uniform of a soldier, or the white coat of a physician, or the helmet and goggles of the aviator; with a uniform there goes a whole lot of other things: a knowledge of what is expected from you; a certain style of doing things; a certain bearing and outlook on life; even an etiquette; and an insider's view of things. By this time, I was an aviator; I had been broken in over two years of airport life, and I knew the flying mind. Here is what went with helmet and goggles.

As for crashes and sudden death and a need for courage, there were no such thoughts now; not when I was at the airport, in the pilot's cockpit, not while I had a stick and a throttle in my hand and pedals under my feet to help myself.

As for power dives and other breath-taking flip-flops, they were never even mentioned at the airport, let alone done; if one wanted to see that sort of flying, one had to go to the movies. Once during practice period I had sneaked away behind a cloud and looped myself a loop, but my instructor had seen it and had not been impressed: "You are only wasting your time."

As a matter of fact, it is easy enough to throw yourself around up there in the emptiness where there is nothing to hit; an airplane, like a cat, always finally comes out right side up if there is only enough space to fall through. Thus, that kind of flying proved nothing and did not count.

What the mind of a flier was actually concerned with was something else entirely. It was something of which few ground people have ever heard, though it is the very essence of flying; the one thing in the whole art of piloting that can't be learned in a few hours of practice and the one reason why pilots are not mere aerial chauffeurs. It is something which is hard for the terrestrian to grasp because it can be experienced only in the air.

I found at the time that my campus friends simply refused to believe that it existed: "That sort of thing may bother you," someone might say, "but I don't think *I* would have any trouble." It cannot be photographed and shown in the movies, and it can hardly even be described in words, though I shall now try.

It is a purely psychological thing. There is something in the air that befuddles a man's mind, his vision, his sense of space. An airline passenger gets an inkling of it when he first finds out that one does not get dizzy in the air, and when he first is amazed that he cannot sense his own speed. For the airline passenger that is wholly pleasant, for it allows him to feel at home in an element where—take it from me—he is not at home at all. But for the pilot, the same effect means trouble. Regardless of how good his eyes may be in the terrestrial sense, they fail when pitted against tremendous depths and distances of the air. Just like the passenger, he sees all there is to see: the ground, the horizon, the clouds. But just like the passenger, he cannot gauge decently that which he most needs to gauge: his own motion and his own height. And so he staggers through the heavens like a drunken man.

Strangely enough, this befuddling power of the air has no official name; call it the factor X of flying. Yet it was the most important thing in the mental climate of the airport.

It occurred constantly, though only in negative fashion, in the talk of the pilots; they were always talking of precision; precision was the biggest virtue in a pilot; not courage, not presence of mind, not engineering knowledge, not steady nerves, not any of the things which a young boy would have imagined would make a good pilot; but simply the ability to go where you wanted to go, instead of staggering.

One was very much concerned with it, though only obliquely, at the flight surgeon's consulting room in the back of the National Guard Hangar, where they gave you your medical tests; the Doc talked about "depth perception," and had some elaborate gadgets by which to test it.

The Government inspectors—veteran pilots themselves whose offices were in the administration building—were conscious of this factor X above all else; when they tested you for your license, they gave you a lot of completely unspectacular and seemingly mild things to do, such as spot landings and figure eights, much as a police surgeon might make a drunken man walk a straight line.

It furnished the inner sense to all that airport activity which to a casual visitor might have seemed exceedingly dull: airplane after airplane taking off, flying counterclockwise around the field, landing, taking off again, all to no apparent purpose: actually they were training their vision by making stab after stab at the airport, just as a three-months-old infant might make grab after grab at some toy dangling over its crib.

And it was the bane of a student flier's life. It was the thing that a flying student kept chewing on from his first solo hour to his two hundredth. Everything else was simple. The maneuvering of the ship, take-offs, turns, glides, landings—they were in feel and inner sense much like the maneuvering of a sail boat. Navigation, the art of finding one's way from A to B—it was simple geometry and was all written up in textbooks and one studied it at home in bed.

But against that factor X one had to go through long series of exercises, a whole manual of arms, as it were, of the air, precise convolutions whose very names were cold and mathematical: the "one-eighty," the "three-sixty," the "seven-twenty," the figure eight, and so forth. And not until you could do them with precision were you fit for the freedom of the air.

This factor X is never as noticeable as when you want to come down. The landing itself is simple enough to make, but first you must make your approach to the landing field. Out of the mile-wide spaces of the air, you must bring your ship down to the intended spot, within feet exact, and at a slow speed: and that is exasperatingly difficult. This time the drunken man is trying to put a key into a keyhole. Yet if your engine ever quits in flight, you have to do it in earnest, and you have only one try. At first, when you have just soloed, you miss the whole mile-square airport itself; then you are glad if you manage to touch down on the first half of the runway, then on the first third. For the license test, you must touch down within 100 feet of a chalk mark. But for my instructor, even that wasn't good enough; before he would entrust me with his ship, I must be able to hit a spot half the size of a tennis court.

That was the sort of thing that went with my helmet and goggles.

I warmed up the engine, gave it a wide-open test for a few minutes, letting its sound reverberate gloriously from the wall of the hangars all over the field, and waited for my instructor to give me my orders and to kick the chocks away from under my wheels.

My orders were laconic: do two "one-eighties" and two "three-sixties": those were two different ways of bringing an airplane down to a landing.

Mine was the first take-off of the morning. I taxied away and thundered out across the line of hangars into the cool morning air, my first job being to get into position at exactly a thousand feet, exactly over the airport. . . .

It should have been like a bird seeking the heights and all that sort of thing; but actually it was hard work, and quite different from the popular image of a flier in action; there were those goggles, and there was that roar; but there was not even a trace of exultation, fear, courage, excitement—merely cool attention to the machine.

I had to get the throttle set just so, and the rate of climb indicator to read 500 feet a minute, and the air-speed indicator at 80 m.p.h., and the stabilizer set, and pay considerable attention with my feet to flying a straight line: for my instructor was standing behind me in the field, looking up, and he wanted to see nothing wobbly; he wanted to see a sovereign, well-planned flightpath.

That is one of the strange things about airplanes: they look so free, and able to move through space with no restrictions whatever; but actually an airplane's motion is almost as restricted as that of a pawn in a chess game. A pilot who wants to be in one place at one time must have planned to get there a minute or two beforehand, and planned it right—for an airplane cannot be turned on the spot; it can turn only in wide curves almost like a railroad train. It can climb only so fast and so steeply without stalling; descent, too, must be shallow, careful not to pick up undue speed, which speed would

mess up the next maneuver, especially a landing; thus while climbing I engineered my path much as if I were planning the track of a
mountain railroad up to the top.

Upstairs, in the morning sun, the view of the city and the prairies
was tempting, but there could be no looking except on business.
Look around idly, and before you knew it, you were "messed up."
The ship's nose pointed at the wide green horizon, and I would have
liked to hold it thus and let it roar straight ahead; but my next job was
to let it swing off again, cut my power, and plunge down at the
airport that lay deep below me, a star of concrete runways; I must go
down there, and hit it where the chalk mark was, engineering my
flight track as I went.

That would be the first test.

I humped myself, and for the next two or three minutes excluded
all foreign matter from my mind. I trimmed the stabilizer back so
that the ship would glide slowly, with the nose pointing not very
steeply down, and I took a new hold of my ship. Down I glided,
silently almost, feeling out the ship's buoyancy with my hand on the
stick, listening for its speed in the humming of the wires, feeling for
its balance with the seat of my pants, and steadying its direction with
my toes on the rudder pedal, and somehow with my whole body
sensing its flightpath (which I could not see because of factor X):
whether it was sinking away under me or holding up well under me.

Thus I gauged my way down through the ungaugeable air, judg-
ing my approach as best I could by the many small clues by which
one judges: the perspective slant of the airport, the angle at which it
lay under the horizon, the size in which it appeared to the eye; flimsy
clues, if compared with an automobilist's solid highway lined with
trees and made gaugeable by other cars. As I came down, the horizon itself came down, sank behind the skyscrapers of the city and
then behind the gas towers and let them rise into the sky: and then
finally as the perspective became almost terrestrian, the horizon
sank behind the trees: while I at the same time was sinking down
onto the runway. Down at very low altitude the bane is off, you can
see again the way you are accustomed to see, you can watch yourself

sliding onto the runway as a ferry boat slides to a landing. But I had come down too short: my wheels touched before I had reached the chalk mark; I had undershot.

If you overshoot a landing, that's bad enough; if it had been an actual forced landing, it would have meant that you would have touched down too far forward in that cow pasture, and rolled into a fence or a ditch, and probably wrecked your ship. You are now theoretically several thousand dollars poorer, and possibly in the hospital. But if you undershoot a landing, that is aeronautical sin: in an actual forced landing, with the engine dead, it would have meant that while still in full flight, you would have hit the trees surrounding that cow pasture, and theoretically, you and your passengers are dead.

Up again for the next try.

The next one was overshot by 200 feet; up again for the third try; the third one was undershot; up again, for the fourth one: it was overshot.

Up once more—but from the hangar, my instructor waved me in. My forty-five minutes were up and I mustn't waste money by flying when I was stale. "Try again," he said, "in a couple of days."

I clambered out, inordinately tired, yet all keyed up.

I spent the rest of the morning at the field, standing around watching ship after ship make its approach and come in.

That was actually a psychological trick they applied to you. It was like those laboratory experiments one reads about on rats in cages: the accepted method of teaching a man to fly was to jerk him out of the ship just when he felt he might now begin to hit his stride—and thus they produced in him a nervous state that was unique. From the outside, scientifically, one might describe it as pathologically over-excited interest; from the inside, when you had it, it felt like a mixture of frustration, greed, hope, wanderlust.

It made you unreasonably reluctant to leave the airport and go home. You spent hours and whole days standing around at the hangar or sitting on the ground in the shade of an airplane wing, or hanging about at the airport café three hours or so for every hour of flight; if you did leave, you came back in the evening, to hang about some more. And every time an airplane landed or took off you watched it the way sailors watch a woman walking by the pier.

In my memory, that airport waiting is all merged, two years of it, and it is almost more vivid than the actual flying I did as a student pilot: those endless days of standing around on the Line. The field itself was a piece of desert, a far cry from the meadowy flying fields of old. Most of the grass had long since been torn up by many tailskids and blasted away by many propellers, and had been supplanted by runways and aprons and taxi strips of concrete which gave it a climate all its own. Every kind of weather was fiercer there. The winds blew across the open field more stiffly; photographers had to stop down their lenses to values which are ordinarily prescribed for the brilliant light of the open sea. In summer during the heat waves, the airport readings made local headlines—108°, 110°, 112°, and in winter, the icy blasts were twice as icy. That is where I seem to have spent all my time for two years, watching the endless counter-clockwise droning of the ships, standing around under the fierce beating of the sun until I could stand no more.

Two days later I decided to use another forty-five minutes of my time. The first approach was overshot. I went up again, determined to do my utmost in concentration. There isn't any hope of making the field, let alone the intended spot on the field, by simply barging down; you must sneak down in curves.

It takes a little more than two minutes to come down from 1500 feet; the critical moment always comes at about 400 feet. All the maneuvering above that height merely serves to put you into the correct position for this moment. Here, then, is the way a pilot brings his ship in to a landing.

The field is on my left because I put it there by careful maneuvering. I am gliding so that I neither get nearer to it nor farther away from it, I am losing altitude, about ten feet every second, and I am waiting for the moment when altitude and distance will be just right (that is to say, will seem just right) for this particular ship in this particular wind. Then I shall turn toward the field, make a glide for it, and arrive on the spot.

Not yet; the angle is still wrong, the field still lies too steeply below me. I swerve a bit away from the field, and wait another second: two; three; while the field takes on a more slantwise perspective. *Then*—well, not quite yet, wait still a little longer; but *now.* (Meanwhile my instructor, down at the field, is thinking: the fool, he has turned-in too soon, he will overshoot. Or perhaps he is thinking: the fool, why doesn't he turn-in, he will undershoot. I wish I knew which it is he is thinking, for his trained eyes can tell from down there what mine can't even tell while I am doing it.) And so I turn.

Then comes the proof; the airport runway now stretches in front of the ship's nose, drawing nearer, coming up, getting larger. I seem to be a little high, but I can't tell yet, I must wait and watch: I am too low, no, I am too high; yes, no, *yes:* I am a little too high and am overshooting.

The temptation now is to drop the nose a bit, and simply point the ship more steeply down at the field; but that wouldn't help. It is the chessman trouble again: to an airplane, speed and buoyancy and altitude are intricately interconnected (in the theory of flight, they are really the same thing in three different forms): as you kill one, up pops the other, and as you kill the other up pops the first again. If I killed altitude now by nosing down, I would pick up more speed; and if I then, before landing, tried to kill the speed, I would balloon away from the ground and get altitude again. That's why I have nursed my airspeed indicator carefully all the way down. It stands at sixty-five miles per hour, which is slow for an airplane such as this; at fifty-five, all her buoyancy would go suddenly pfft—like a flat tire; when I arrive at the ground, that's what I want to happen: I want her wings to go dead in a stall and want her to sit down; and, therefore, dropping her nose now would not help.

Or, I could tilt her on her side and let her slide off sidewise, thus killing height without picking up speed; but George won't allow side slipping; it would make it too easy; it is a trick I must keep up my sleeve as a reserve for a real emergency landing.

Thus instead I pull the ship's nose up a bit. First she balloons, then she slows down her glide and kills her buoyancy; I may make it yet. I float across a golf course with people looking up, a boulevard with traffic, then across a hangar roof, propeller wind-milling slowly, the nose almost level, dangerously slowed up, one eye on the air-speed indicator which is wavering just below sixty. I wonder what is keeping me up: the controls feel slack, like the tiller of a sail boat that is becalmed; a little less speed, and her wings will stall, she will suddenly drop out from under me and crash. Anxiously, I probe her buoyancy with my hand, feeling out the controls with slight motions; it is all going soft, her buoyancy is almost gone. I must drop the nose again and pick up some speed, or crash.

Now the runway is under me, like a highway, ready to take my wheels, and the spot is coming, but I am still floating. The spot is rushing at me now, I am slowing her up again. It is nip and tuck: how much buoyancy there is left in the ship versus the distance still to go. I am using up her buoyancy as fast as I can, pulling back on the stick as fast as I can without letting her balloon back into the air; she is still floating two feet above the ground, a magic automobile that refuses to touch the ground. There is no point in letting her wheels touch while she is still buoyant, it would only bounce her nose up and she would balloon; first I must squeeze the last bit of lift out of her: I must get the stick all the way back against my stomach. There is the chalk mark now, flashing past a few feet under me at sixty m.p.h. while I still float. And there, at last, she goes and settles to the ground, and I can feel the three points of a three-point landing, two bouncy wheels and a grinding tailskid making contact; and within a few feet of the spot!

Up again. Perhaps I could pull off the series of three today.

The next one was 100 feet off, overshot; not good enough. The one after that was far overshot; the wind had died down, and in the still air, glides were shallow and fast; everyone else, too, was over-shooting a bit and landing deeply into the field.

There was the factor X for you. I gave up and went to the airport café.

At the café, flying talk trickled unendingly. There were large glass

panes toward the field, and a full view also of the approach lanes.
The crowd was expert: pilots, mechanics, students. To them, flying
was not just flying. They had keen eyes for the fine points. "Look at
Al," says a mechanic. "He brings that ship in like a 20-hour student."
"What do you mean, like a student?" "About ten miles per hour too
fast. She is going to float halfway across the field before she'll settle."
And float she does. "Here comes Chicago, trip number four," says
one of the pilots: there is a lull while everybody watches an airliner
make its approach. "Must be Eddy flying it today." "How can you
tell?" "By the way he handles the ship. Look at the way he's goosing
her." Goosing, that means coming in undershot, and then blasting
your engine to pull you in: you can't do that in a forced landing with
the engine dead. Another pause, and more observation. "Hey, he
seems to be mad at something." All I see is an airliner, taxiing across
the field.

Another ship was coming down, one of those glossy jobs for
wealthy amateurs. There were three of them at the field. "Here
comes Doc Jones," predicts somebody, maliciously. "Watch him
bump." And sure enough, the doctor bumps, and bumps again:
trying to let her touch down before her flying speed is spent to the
going-dead point.

They know the air: "The first thing I will do when I get my
license," says one fellow, "is to go to 15,000 feet."

"You won't like it—you'll be too damned lonesome."

Between two pilots:

"He undershot."

"The damn fool, I suppose he lost his ship?"

"Sure he lost his ship."

"Lost his job?"

"Sure he lost his job."

"Then what is he doing now?"

"He's pushing up the daisies."

In the back of everybody's mind, there is the crack-up. Far in the
back—so far that most of them would deny it; but deeply. In a
negative way, crack-up is the one thing they live by: mechanics,
instructors, pilots. Anybody could fly if he could risk an occasional

crack-up; but avoiding of crack-ups is what all aviation practice centers around and what salaries are paid for. Forgetting about crack-ups is what all aviation publicity tries to achieve. Even the aviation magazines don't mention them; and Article XXV of the Metropolitan Airport regulations says that damaged aircraft must be removed from the public view forthwith. Crack-ups are the forbidden thing. And crack-up stories are to these men what sex jokes are to ordinary men: a way to handle stuff which is too strong to be taken straight.

For instance, at the hangar, the phone rings and the flying service operator takes up the receiver. It's a pilot calling, long distance:

"Harry, I'm afraid I've had a forced landing."

"How'd it go?"

"Field was pretty small."

"All right, I'll drive out and fly her out."

"I'm afraid, Harry, I overshot a little."

"Propeller busted?"

"Yes, sir."

"All right, I will bring a new propeller."

"Harry, I am sorry but there seems to be a little damage on the wings, too."

"All right, take off the wings and put the fuselage on a truck and bring it back."

"The tail is kind of bunged up, too."

"Take off the engine and bring that."

"The engine is broken, too."

"In that case, unscrew the clock and bring it home as a souvenir."

Two days later I rushed to the airport to try again. I had done a great deal of soul-searching in the meantime, the way a flying student will between flights, and I thought I had the trouble by the ear: it might be my manner of looking.

It was Sunday morning, and the ship was busy—the whole field was busy. For there were several instructors at the airport, each operating one or two ships and each teaching one or two dozen students, all of whom had to do the same thing: the piano scales, as it were, of the third dimension, steadily from their twentieth to their two hundredth hours; stab after stab at the chalk mark. Even experienced pilots went up, between cross-country flights, and did a few one-eighties or three-sixties, to keep up their precision; and thus, from sunrise to sunset, the procession of ships seldom stopped, 'round and 'round the airport, up and down, up and down.

Toward noon, the ship was free, and I taxied out. The red light from the control tower held me for minutes while ship after ship swept in across me. Then there was a lull, and they were flashing the green light impatiently for me to take myself off and be gone from the runway, and I did.

Flying in heavy air traffic, you were not allowed to depend on your presence of mind even in that respect. The proper style in that case, too, was to be cool and systematic; you were supposed to keep methodical track of every ship that was flying from the same airport. Here is how it went:

Ship number one, the Standard School's new Travelair, is now taking off. A take-off is an amazing thing to watch from the air; the ship crawling slowly along the airport runway like some yellow-winged insect, and then crawling across the railroad tracks and across the canal; for from high up one cannot see his height. Ship number two, John Miller's Fleet biplane, is now at a thousand feet out over the gas towers, practicing turns; he's got a completely green student in there and is doing primary exercises—he is teaching him how to bank the ship around turns by the feel of the seat—and so he looks now like a red *accent aiguë* on the landscape, now like an *accent grave*. Ship number three, Doc Jones' red cabin ship, is doing figure eights out over a farm. I bet the farmer thinks that the airport boys are after his daughter—what does he know about the mysterious factor X and the need for precision training? Ship number four, the Standard School's Fleet biplane, is climbing towards 1500 and intends presently to turn-in and stab away at the airport. If I stayed a half mile behind him, I could guide myself in by him, but that would be cheating. Ship number five, the Midwest Air Service Waco, now crossing 500 feet under me, is also on his way up. I can look down and see the fellows sitting in their cockpit, as in a slender canoe with wings, floating on the farms.

Then you must check them all over again; for otherwise they could be upon you terribly fast.

Number one is in my neighborhood now, we are flying side by side, about a thousand feet apart, and can see one another's faces, but not our speeds: we are peacefully floating side by side, like two boats in a gentle swell; I can see how under him there is nothing but air, all the way down: he is without visible means of support. Then he rolls over into a curve and our speeds become visible: he is gone, swept far back as if jerked away by an angry hand. Ship number two has landed and is refueling at the gasoline pits; ship number three has come over to shoot landings, crossing under me at close range; our speeds in combination make it seem that he is sweeping sideways through the air. It is getting crowded up here. But ship number four is now well on the way down, and it is my turn now: and so I cut my power, and from now on I am the landing airplane and have the right of way and can try out my new hunch.

It has to do with watching the field; not looking where you are going at all as you curve down, but with your head turned so that you can always see the field. You watch the spot as a man would keep his eye on the ball, but a ball that comes through space infinitely slowly: so slowly that you can hardly see its motion. I watch it as a mother might study the face of a sick child, with a sort of long-drawn-out patience that was trying to read the smallest signs. It is quite different from my early visual gropings. It is actually a pose, it is imitating the way my instructor acts when he flies an approach but only since I am posing that way can I make my approaches at all accurate.

That time, my wheels touched within twenty feet of the mark: good enough. I didn't even roll to a stop, but blasted right through into the next take-off. Now two more accurate ones, and I can fly cross-country. The second one came out all right too. But the third one was undershot.

I sat at the edge of the runway for hours, a small heap of frustration, and worried.

Why could one never deal with this mysterious factor X in the manner in which one usually deals with trouble, either by brain, or by force, or by courage? Perhaps because it was nameless; its very essence was a vacuum, an optic vacuum. To our wings, the air is a fluid in which they plane much like surf boards; to our propellers, it is almost a solid in which it screws itself forward. But to our eyes, it was as nothing: empty space, a vacuum, nothing to hold on to. Psychologists can enumerate about seven different ways in which a man perceives depth: none of them could work in this optic vacuum. One gets an impression of depth because one's eyes are set a distance apart and each one sees the same view from a different angle; and the difference the brain interprets as depth. But that effect was good only for a few hundred feet at best; it might be all right for playing ball or for driving a car, but pitted against the depths and distances of the air, it was ineffectual; in fact some of the best pilots have only one eye.

Again, one might judge by the way in which familiar things are arranged behind one another in space as, for instance, cars on a highway. But in the air there were no things; at least not usually. Once in a while, there are, and then the optic vacuum is punctured, with startling effects. Near the Metropolitan Airport, there was a radio tower, about three hundred feet high. Once I had crossed over it at about eight hundred feet at the very moment when another student ship was also crossing over it at perhaps six hundred: some of us liked to fly exactly over it for just this effect. For one rare moment, there had existed an optic ladder: my own ship's wheels, the other student's ship, the tower's head, the tower's foot, the ground: and for that moment an attack of ordinary high building dizziness went through me like an electric shock.

In the evening, I went up once more, hoping perhaps to start my series anew. Three good ones would prove I was good, but only if they were in a row. Again the ground fell away, flattened out, slowed up; again my vision went numb, and I sat alone, a vibrating, roaring thing alone in the emptiness. And on the way down I missed.

Patience.

Three of my five hours were used up when things at last broke for me. That morning, I had done four approaches, two of them to the mark, two not far off. I was just peeling off my helmet and sticking my finger into my ear to kill the tickle of the pressure changes. It was eight o'clock now, and I would have to get going back to town. George Adams said, "Well, you overshot the last one, but, Red, you are getting hot." And then he said, "Mike has some proposition for you at the café."

Mike was an airplane dealer, new and second hand. I found him at the café, eating griddle cakes and sausages for breakfast; fat pig, he owned perhaps a dozen airplanes at that very moment, and to him they were mere merchandise.

"How are you, Professor?" he said; at the airport I was the Professor because I had to do with the university and was no longer a college student.

"Have a good breakfast on me, Professor," he said. "George tells me you been working hard." There was some conversation on approaches: yes, sir, if a man didn't know how to get down, he'd better not go up.

Then he opened up. A certain ship of his was out in the Southwest; it was to have been demonstrated and sold, but the customer had gone broke and the ship was now waiting at a small airport, five hundred miles away. It was a Travelair, the very kind I was trained on. How would I like to go out at my own expense and ferry it back?

"You mean, cross-country?"

"Sure, cross-country, what do you think, on a truck?"

He eyed me suspiciously: "George says you are getting hot, and you have good judgment."

Careful now. I must hold down this surge; I must behave like a regular airport guy. They don't want to trust their ships to high-strung people. "I guess that would be O.K., if I can do it over the week end."

It was agreed that I should come to his office the next day and we would send the necessary telegrams.

When we got up, he said, "That will be about five hours of flying time."

"I know," I said, and thought how that would boost the figure in my log book.

"That will be seventy-five dollars. Better bring that into my office beforehand," he said.

The surge in me turned around and was a big ebb. Apparently my airport manner was not yet authentic; I was not yet accepted as an insider. Seventy-five dollars plus the ground fare out, and my automobile money used up except for thirty dollars. But never mind; I would borrow the difference and give up flying for good afterwards if necessary, and pay it back. But I was going to fly cross-country at least once.

Friday night, I rumbled Southwest on the bus.

3. Dead Reckoning

I had become library-stiff and untraveled; now, even when I engaged a room in a small-town hotel I felt shy and clumsy. But I was going to travel cross-country by air. Incredible.

That evening in the hotel I had my bed all covered with maps. George had talked over the trip with me. He felt responsible. He wanted me to fly the careful way: follow the double-track railroad for a hundred miles to the river, then follow the river to the second bridge, and then head straight east until you intercept another double track, and follow that, and so forth. It is called flying by landmarks. It has the advantage that there is always something to follow, and in this case it also had the advantage that I would pass near several airports.

But the book said that flying by landmarks was bad style. I had taken along my textbook on air navigation. I had studied it for months; it weighed three pounds and was learned and full of tables and diagrams; it was going to ride with me in the cockpit. And the book said that one should fly by dead reckoning, which means bee-lines, calculating one's position by compass and watch. It is more difficult, but more sovereign. This was to be my first cross-country flight, but unless I could get the finance problem solved, it might be my last. I felt guilty, and my heart pounded, but I decided to fly by dead reckoning. Till late that night, I sat on my bed computing the compass headings, the distances, the times when I should arrive over the various points, marking my maps.

The important day started cloudy and cool.

At the airport they took me for a grown-up pilot. No one offered advice. I was not so sure about the weather; I didn't know how the various kinds of weather felt while you were out cross-country; I wanted someone to take the responsibility for dispatching me or not dispatching me. But no one did, except that the mechanic had the ship warmed up and the engine running, and the airport manager, who seemed also the sole pilot and instructor of the field, had taken down from his radio the "Winds Aloft" report and gave it to me. There was a ten-mile-an-hour cross wind blowing at two thousand feet, increasing to fifteen miles an hour at four thousand, and so forth. I stowed my tourist roll in the luggage compartment, and managed to throw the textbook into the cockpit while nobody was looking, and climbed in to test the engine on each of its two ignition systems. Then in the swelling noise, the manager stepped up on the wing and said into my ear: "Take it easy." Maybe he had been tipped off, after all. I gave him a dignified nod, and taxied away and took off.

I circled the field once to get altitude. There was no sun to give me an elemental sense of direction. There was only my compass. I circled once more, looking down at the small town, the main street, the hotel, the railroad line; then I struck out. I turned her northeast, sixty degrees by my compass. I held her there, hoping I had not mismeasured or miscalculated the night before.

The railroad slanted away at what seemed the proper angle.

With a certain solemnity I did for the first time the many small jobs to be done when you take your departure on a flight cross-country: set the fuel valves so that the engine runs on one tank only, instead of on all of them (thus the time it takes for the first tank—whose gallonage you know—to run dry, gives you a check on the fuel consumption). I leaned-out the mixture, carefully, watching the engine tachometer; I must not burn up my fuel unnecessarily quickly, for in an airplane, reserve fuel means safety. I wrote down the time of departure, for my dead reckoning. I set throttle and stabilizer so that the ship trimmed level with my hands off the stick, neither gaining nor losing altitude; and then I consulted my drift tables: for a wind of so many miles per hour, blowing at such-and-such an angle to one's intended course, in an airplane cruising at 100 miles per hour, one must allow a drift correction of (running a finger down a column of figures) six degrees. I must steer 54 degrees from now on, and I carefully tapped her around with my toes to her new course.

Then I looked around.

The town was gone. I was out, swimming alone on the endless plains.

I shall never forget the flavor of that moment.

The country was so much bigger than I had thought country could ever be. It was like a sea, flat, featureless, its cornfields and wheatfields, unnumbered and impersonal like the waves of the sea, all the way out to the horizon. There was nothing to steer by. The railroad had slanted out of sight. Behind one point of the horizon lay the Metropolitan Airport, a runway to catch me, the moment, hours away, when I would touch hard ground again. Behind all the other 359 points of the horizon, there lay trouble; there were plenty of other airports in the U.S. and plenty of big fields; but if I did mis-navigate, I'd get messed up factually and emotionally and they would be hard to find and hard to get into. One might even get into legal trouble. I had no very definite orders, and as the pilot, I was entitled to my own judgment. But I wondered what would happen if I missed and ran out of fuel and cracked up.

When you faced the wide horizon the way I faced it then, free to steer anywhere yet not free at all, it induced a peculiar sort of dizziness—not a fear that I might fall, but a half-pleasant fear scientifically called agoraphobia, the contrary of claustrophobia: a feeling that you must pull yourself tightly together or you would simply flow apart, like a chunk of butter on a frying pan.

"Take it easy."

The air was smooth, as it usually is on cool, cloudy days. In that ship, as in most of the old open-cockpit ships, the pilot's seat was well back in the tail, and one could see one's own wings. I watched her and I liked her. Broad wings over the broad country, sliding smoothly. There is nothing one can do with an airplane to make it go;

one cannot push it along, not even in the slight fashion in which one pushes an automobile along with one's foot on the accelerator; in an airplane, the throttle is set for cruising and stays set, and the ship travels at its once-for-all cruising speed, never more, never less, steadily for hours, much like an ocean steamer.

Once I had been a passenger on a freight steamer, spending whole days with the captain on the bridge. That captain had watched that ship the same way I was now watching mine: leaning on the railing of the bridge, looking down, just watching it slide through the water of the South Atlantic. Once in a while he would say:

"Das Schiff streicht durch die Wellen . . . ," which was, in rather highflown language, the statement that the ship was moving through the waves: to the captain, there could be a lot of delight in just that, and he could never tire merely watching it. But then he always would add quickly, and embarrassed:

". . . Der Koch backt Fricadellen . . . ," which rhymed, and meant that the cook was making hamburgers, and was designed to take the curse of emotionalism off the matter.

The same way with me. I spent one batch of time just watching her fly. When I looked down from an airplane in the ordinary manner I couldn't see my speed very well, because of factor X. But when I held my glance right downward—as one might hold a walking stick and trace a line in the snow—then I could see my 100 miles per hour. Next, I spent a batch of time watching her another way now, conning her sidewise drift. That again can't be done by simply looking. I picked some object below me, a group of trees, a crossroads, a house, and watched it as it drifts astern and a bit to the left, for the cross wind was setting me off steadily to the right.

Through the noise of the engine, something started to drum: the firewall—a sheet of metal between the engine and the rest of the ship. That occasionally happens when some resonance is set up between it and the engine vibrations, and it might have scared me green; I might have thought the engine was acting up. But I had had it before. "Good thing," I thought fatuously, "that they don't let students fly cross-country while they are still too green—I am, after all, quite seasoned." I changed the throttle setting by a hair's breadth to break the resonance.

The minutes went by, the beats of the engine cutting them up into little pieces.

One hour had gone when I noticed that my drift was increasing; a new wind was drifting me to the right, crabwise, off my course. There was another thing, I thought: I wouldn't have known if I had gone cross-country with less upbringing; to recognize those small inconspicuous matters of sidewise drift was a matter for the air-trained eye. But I must take action, or go astray.

Better not try any more advanced navigational stunts, but give up: this new wind must sooner or later drift me over a railroad track or some other landmark, and from there on I shall fly obediently by landmark.

I got out my map from under me, to look the situation over. I had the penciled line of my course, and I had stepped off in twenty-mile intervals the points where disregarding wind, I should be after twenty, forty, sixty minutes of flight—just as the book had said. I dug into my pocket for my watch, to check the time. My map was sucked up by the wind, and before I could catch it, it had blown away; it was gone.

I saw it float around behind me, slowly losing altitude. I banked around, and passed it closely. It was flapping, doing a "falling leaf," mocking me. Below were cornfields. Not sound policy to go on without a map; to turn around and fly back by compass, no good either; I cut back my power and kept circling down around. I thought I would land and pick my map up. The cornfields were rough and small, and I lost heart. I had never heard of anyone making a landing for that reason; it would be even less sound policy to land.

The best thing to do under the circumstances was to go on by compass and watch. From there on it was dead reckoning willy-nilly.

All I had now was my compass course and the memory of one fact: that the whole flight was to have taken four hours and twelve minutes.

I made my drift correction by eye judgment alone, allowing an angle of five additional degrees for drift and steering now 51 degrees, by compass. That ought to hold me on the original course, but it was purely a guess. There was no way to check. Before I would know, I would have to do two and a half hours of sitting tight.

Take it easy, I thought. Think of your textbook. You are Using your Best Judgment, Taking into Consideration all Known Factors. You have arrived at a Decision, and are Proceeding to Execute Same in Methodical Fashion. A Tendency to Undue Concern should be Firmly Suppressed.

Steering a compass course: of all the things a man can do one of the best. There is no other way of traveling quite like it.

There is no inner rhyme or reason in what you see of the country. You see it because it happens to lie on the exact straight line from A to B. Still it is not a bad way to see the country. For what you get is quite literally a cross section.

I had a roommate at that time, a mining geologist, who was working out a gadget by which to study sand—what kind it was and what it contained, gold, oil, fossils, or whatnot, per ton. You poured a bagful of the sand in on top, and out of the flow the machine took a part and let it run into a pail, and then you poured that in on top again and got back a part of it into a pot, and poured that in and got back a part of it into a cup, and so forth. At the end you had a hundred grains or so of sand which you then studied under the microscope. And because they had been selected so carefully at random, they were strictly representative of the whole sand. It is the same thing a compass course does to one's view of the country.

What was sliding by under me, with a rumble and a roar, was not spectacular; it was just ordinary Middle West. A railroad track, running from some city that is no concern of mine, to another city that has nothing to do with my flight: I glided across it. There was a river, and I slid across it, without a bridge. There was a fence line, and I slide across it, without a jar: straight across lots. A house, and its backyard, and a woman hanging up the wash, and then contemptuously across the corner of a small town, a baseball lot and then a cornfield, with a machine on it and a tractor and then slantwise across a swimming pool on the highway and a filling station and then again farms and farms, and a brick factory with a high cloud of smoke rising just on my course. I burst into it and out again on the other side and it goes on: a small town with a silver watertank on a tripod, and then more cornfields and fences and farmhouses, and on the fields the geometrical pattern left by the working of the agricultural machines.

I steered sharply; I must hit that airport, still hours away, or get into trouble. I split down that compass course of 51 degrees with utmost concentration as if I were the legendary archer, trying to split an arrow with an arrow.

After a while came rain.

From the distance, it was a gray curtain hung across the plains. When I went into it, it was invisible, except that my wings got shiny. I was going too fast to see the drops, and the drops hit much too fast to make a visible splash; only a glistening of water. I huddled up under the windshield; but in open-cockpit ships, the draught hits you from behind, and my back and shoulders turned damp.

My view was cut down now to a circle, a mile in radius, just underneath.

I would have liked to land. But where?

I might be passing within gliding distance of the most inviting airport that might be lying there by chance, somewhere in the rain, but I would not know it. The farmland below was still cut up in smallish parcels, and was slightly rolling, and there were many fences. It was hard to estimate whether they afforded enough runway. I had to fly on 54 degrees by compass, and to the Metropolitan Airport, or else, into trouble. I had chosen dead reckoning, and dead reckoning it was.

One hour and thirty-seven minutes after I had lost my map, I crossed a river. The river was on the wrong slant; according to my memory of the map, various rivers should have crossed my course, but at a different angle. It might be that this river was winding at this particular spot. But it might also be that my calculations made on the hotel bed had been wrong.

One degree of error in your navigation carries you astray one mile for every sixty miles of flight; if I had added some item that should have been subtracted, I would miss The Metropolitan Airport by sixty miles. It would be pure chance if I could find an airport to sit down on before I ran out of fuel.

Had I made a mistake the previous night?

Compass navigation is not quite simple. A compass doesn't show "true" directions, but "magnetic" ones; it points, not to the North Pole as it should, but to a place in Northeastern Canada, the magnetic pole. And this "Variation" from true directions differs from place to place so that in flying a new correction must be made every hour. They don't even show magnetic directions correctly; they have errors of their own, caused by the iron of the engine; and this "Deviation" differs according to the way the ship is headed. Thus, calculating a compass course from a map is like trying to compute Railroad Time when all you have is a watch running in Daylight Saving Time and when that watch is known, moreover, to be slow on Monday, Wednesday, and Friday, and to be fast the rest of the week.

A sentence from the Book began to buzz in my head concerning Variation: "Ships have been piled on the rocks, and planes have crashed into the sides of mountains or have been completely lost, because of misapplication of this item."

I sat still for a while longer, mustering all the fortitude I had. Then I caved in. I suddenly knew my navigation had been all wrong. *Lost!*

My textbook had described the mental processes of pilots on such occasion, such things as wanting to keep more to the right; thinking that one's compass has gone crazy; zig-zagging erratically; wanting to get down; and making hasty passes at hayfields that are too small. It also described the pilot's attitude in such a case as "anxiety," and it advised: "do not let anxiety lead you to extremes."

But this was none of that soldierly anxiety. It was downright panic, a fierce, rattling sort of fear. Flying low and fast across that country, I was still in this world; I saw houses and roads and automobiles all the time, and even the faces of people—and yet I was already half gone over. Nobody could come up and help me, and I couldn't get down. The ship was a roaring demon, carrying me away. It was enough to make a grown-up man want to cry out for his mother.

At this point, I happened to see myself; on the instrument board, in the large black glass-covered dial of the altimeter I was mirrored back at myself. The fellow whom I saw there might be all a scared little boy inside; but he didn't show it; with helmet on and goggles down on the eyes, a man is pretty well depersonalized. He was without any doubt a pilot, staring at me with a mouth that was stony firmness itself; the wind and the vibration do that—in open-cockpit ships they make you press your lips together. I was not nearly as far gone as I had felt. Thus, by my own bootstraps as it were, I recovered my nerve.

I fetched up the book to check my navigation all over again. I must never tell anybody about this, I thought, half ashamed; this is just like me, flying with a textbook. I held the book on my lap, propped it up against the stick, and started turning the pages, with quick glances in between at the compass and at the country below, where pools of rainwater on the fields began to mirror up the gray sky. I remembered the main data of my map. I found the formulas and the diagrams and the jingles: "Can-Dead-Men-Vote-Twice? Compass Course; Deviation; Magnetic Course; Variation; True Course." Variation west, magnetic best; Variation east, magnetic least. And so forth. . . .

It seemed to be all right. I went on, 58 degrees by compass now.

The clouds began to blow faster; it was actually my own speed, now more visible against the clouds because they were coming down, torn shreds of cloud that kept blowing across my vision. But they looked as if it were storming. I felt that trouble was crowding me rather hard. I throttled back and went down to five hundred feet, which is none too high, even over the plains, and is the legal minimum height except in emergencies. It slowed up the clouds and gave me more vision; the tempo of the land below was now stepped up. I droned on, 56 degrees by compass; hewing to my magic line, though by now I began again to doubt that it would work. Once I broke out of the rain; it was like entering a wide room, but the view was still the same plain, devoid of landmarks. In the distance shone clearly the smoke trails of two trains, running toward each other; a railroad probably, a double-track one; but without a map from which to identify it, what good could the best double-track railroad do me? There was nothing to do; I must sit still and fly. I stuck to my compass, and bored ahead into the next curtain of rain.

It was a low squall, with strong wind and cold air in it. I had to come down to three hundred feet to keep clear of the scuds of cloud and the wind veered around. It was now from the left, and I had to kick her around and allow almost fifteen degrees for drift angle on the other side, crabbing towards my right, sidewise across the corn-fields, like a boat crossing a river.

I was alone, and very cold. Below me an occasional farmhouse went by, with smoke coming out of the chimney; the broad roof of a barn huddling in the rain. The only person I saw for minutes was the driver of a car that went splashing along a road between the fields; we were on crossing courses, but we met and I passed over him almost at speaking distance—except for my noise. He looked up; he was a white-haired old man. We parted company again immediately, he moving along his road, and I along my course—like two ships at sea.

I came out of the squall as suddenly as I had gone in. The wind let up and the rain lightened and visibility improved. But there was still nothing to see but farms.

I looked at my watch, and with a cold shock I realized that according to my dead reckoning there were only about twenty minutes to go. In twenty minutes or so I ought to have landed. But as yet, there was not even a sign of the Airport or of the familiar country surrounding it in which I had flown so much, or of the whole big city behind it. How could it be that a whole city could be hidden on a perfectly flat plain? And I now had only an hour's gasoline left.

I began to cave in again, and had to hold on hard. I'll crack up, I thought, on my first cross-country. Perhaps I'll go to jail. Why didn't I fly by landmarks?

I was only a green pilot; I shouldn't have been so tense; as I see it now, it wouldn't really have been a bad emergency to be lost, with all that flat country in which to find a landing place. But so much depended on this flight.

As I have said before, when you mix America, and the air, and an airplane, you get a mixture that makes an ordinary person talk about it for a long time afterwards. Here is such a mixture to talk about: how the country below me yielded and turned good. How I began to get home.

It began this way: every time when one of the big cities of the Middle West emerges for you from the country, it begins in the same way: there was that road where the old man had driven. It was suddenly there again: out of the checkerboard gridwork of roads, that one pattern had traced itself out a bit stronger: it was a highway now. It was running along with me but where I cut across lots, diagonally across the square farm fields, it went in the style Mid-western roads go: it jogged around the farm lots, going east for a while and turning north, going north for a while and then taking another jag east. But it kept going my way. And on my left, there still seemed to be that railroad; I could see in the distance the familiar white trails of smoke of the trains, three of them spaced out at intervals, shining white through the rain.

I thought of an old guide book at home, and its advice on how to find St. Peter's when in Rome: "Simply follow the stream of travelers." I looked at the highway with that in mind: could one follow it? And while I was still inspecting it doubtfully, it suddenly stepped itself up and cut diagonally across a section of farmland, going my way directly; there must be an important destination that way.

When running east and west it was still keeping obediently between the farms; but on its northward jags, it now cut diagonally across the fields again and again.

I wanted to follow it, but I still couldn't be sure; it might still only lead to some small town without an airport. I held on to my compass course; it was still the surest thing I had.

From the left now, a railroad track edged into my circle of vision, edged gradually over to the right, edged out of sight into the haze on my right—it was no good. Five minutes later it came back, and stayed under me from there on, running my way. It was good.

At that point the highway suddenly speeded up, picked up some roads, and began to run straight, like a dog who has picked up a scent, with no further regard at all for the farms, straight across lots.

It made me warm inside.

I still held on to the compass course. It had served me well enough so far. And the book said never to change without need.

A little later I came over a block of buildings with a high chimney and curiously compact. It looked like a factory, but when you looked into the factory yard you saw a baseball diamond, which was odd. It was a prison. I didn't know it then, but those are usually the first outposts of big cities: prisons and asylums.

I went on, riding the highway, riding my glistening wings, flying home. I was headed right all right; the city was coming out under me like a photograph in the developing bath. Another highway fell into mine, they did some swooping underneath one another and around one another, and then they merged. On the railroad tracks a yellow caterpillar was crawling without smoke—the suburban electric train. I had been on it. It looked comfortable. I was wet and I was stiff from sitting still, and my head droned; what a fool I was to be sitting up here in the rain, but how happy.

The suburbs: expensive ones and cheaper ones and ghost ones; the expensive ones with winding streets and the cheaper ones with straight streets and square blocks; and in between, still-vacant building lots with the street lamp posts and the electric poles and the sidewalks all laid out, the corn still growing in the meantime.

And then, suddenly out of the murk, like a giant out of the forest, there appeared my friend, the outermost of the big gas towers. For the first time the silence of four hours was broken, someone was speaking to me: there was an inscription on its top, an actual sign-post for pilots, in chrome yellow lettering: "Met. 5 m.," and an arrow. I knew where to go; I swerved off the highway, and saw it run like a canyon into the built-up area of the city, lined with red neon signs, luminous in the darkening afternoon. Two minutes later I was

in my familiar few cubic miles of air. I saw the Airport break out of
the rain, with the runways waiting and no traffic, and I brought her
in. George was standing in front of his hangar waving me in as I
taxied. He grinned all over and with that little voice that people have
after you have listened to your motor for hours, he said several
times, "Here comes Red with the mail."

I felt as if I had taken enormous punishment, but I was proud. I
was enormously proud.

Back I went into the library, among the book stacks, under the
electric lamp; and no way out again into the region called cross-
country. The best I would be able to do now for a long time was to
shoot a couple of approaches every week; it was also the least I had
to do if I wanted to keep my hand and my eyes in. I had my white
elephant by the tail again.

Outside, the summer was progressing. From the top of those
short practice flights, when I looked out toward the horizon now, I
could see the plains turning yellow with ripening wheat. But before
I could go out again, I must pay back the debts of my first flight, and
must save up enough for a whole block of flying time, at least another five hours. I must do that against the drain of my practice
flying and against the drag of knowing how foolish it was by all
ordinary standards. It looked as if I were stuck again until fall.

In the meantime, there was the airport. If I can't have the sea, I
take the harbor. I hung about the airport during all my free hours, an
aerial sort of beachcomber, watching, waiting, hoping for another
break.

4. A Living in the Air

At this point I must stop to report some things that had happened before all this, and also to explain the inner workings of the Airport (for an airport is not a closely knit business enterprise, but something on the order of Wall Street or Hollywood, a place of many firms and free lances and hangers-on)—and also, to pay my respects to my aeronautical godfather: the man who taught me to fly.

There is in practical flying such a thing as a pilot's conscience. It has to do with taking chances and with forgetting your personal limits and with letting your flying become sloppy; and in the long run, your safety depends on it more than on anything else. My own conscience will always be that first instructor of mine, saying through the rubber tube, "Come on, Red, you know better than that." In moments of stress, people revert to their earliest training in language, in manners, and also in flying technique. And it may well be that one day my passengers, my ship, and myself will come back whole from some adventure because of my first instructor.

I had found him by the merest chance. When I first made up my mind to fly, all I had, besides a ten-dollar bill, was a card which I had once picked up at the Airport on a previous visit. It said:

THE ORIOLE AIR SERVICE

GEORGE ADAMS, President and Chief Pilot

CHARTER FLIGHTS   FLIGHT INSTRUCTION

SIGHT-SEEING FLIGHTS

HANGAR 5   METROPOLITAN AIRPORT

I went to investigate.

Hangar 5 was cool inside, and a chaos of airplanes. I asked a mechanic where the office of the Oriole Air Service was. He said, "Right here. Want to take some Time?" I said I might. He called into the jungle of wings and tails and propellers, "Hey, George, here's a fellow wants to take some Time." George Adams popped up from under some wing, ducked down again and rose beside me, the man who was to teach me to fly: a long thin fellow with yellow hair and a khaki shirt, and no eyes but dark green sun glasses. Time? Sure, he'd fix me up. Just a sample lesson? You bet.

He took me out into the sun again. His training ship was sitting on the Line. He made me climb on it and lower myself into the pilot's cockpit, the rear one. That, I found out later, was his sales technique; let the airplane fan play with the controls, and he becomes a customer. The cockpit was strangely deep; if it had been a bathtub, the water would have stood at my mouth. Below, when you looked over the side, were the wings, and below them, the airport grass; but it was easy to imagine, instead, forests and fields and cities.

I took possession of the controls; there were two pedals for steering, and there was the stick, that almost legendary stick, the thing that fliers fly with: it came up between my knees and it was really simply a wooden stick, looking much like the tiller of a boat; but on that occasion with the airplane on the ground, it was leaning in the corner like an old broomstick, and when you moved it, it felt disconnected and useless.

It went on casually enough. He stood outside beside me and we talked. This was not Europe. Flying here was entirely the flier's private affair. The Government neither helped nor hindered; it didn't help financially, but neither did you need its permission, except for a medical examination; instruction was straight commercial merchandise, on sale to all comers, and the rate was fifteen dollars an hour.

"Well, now," I said, "if I should decide to take it up, how long before one could solo?" "Usually about eight hours," he said. Some people did it in five hours, but—looking me over—in my case it would probably take ten.

What if I ran out of money? (I knew all too well I would. I always did.) He said it wouldn't do any harm. In the beginning it was better anyway to take flying slowly, half hours at a time, with whole off-days in between. If you took it too fast you went stale.

But what if I damaged the airplane? That risk was included in the price. I wouldn't have to pay one cent. Then would I have to put up a bond at least before going up solo? No, the risks of solo flying, too, were included in the rate.

"All right," I said. "When do you want me to come?"

"Why not go up right now? The engine is still warm." That was the other item of sales technique, I later found out. Get the customer up, let him feel the controls in flight, and he is sold.

"As a matter of fact," I confessed, "I don't even have fifteen dollars on me now." ("On me now" was a nice way of putting it.) That, he said, was all right too. Just as long as I had seven-fifty on me, we could start. Did I have seven-fifty?

There was a pause and a perceptible stiffening.

"Sure," I said.

"All right," he said, "let's get going."

"Wait a minute," I said. "How about the medical examination?" Lots of time for that; you were permitted to take two hours without it.

But if I failed the test finally? Glasses? They wouldn't cause trouble, as long as I didn't want to fly commercially. The main thing was to start. The air was nice and smooth this afternoon, and the horizon sharp as a knife. Just right for instruction. "All right," I said, "let's go to the office."

"Why to the office?"

"Well, to sign the papers," I said.

"What papers?"

"Well, aren't there all sorts of papers to fill out? I mean, something to certify that we won't hold one another responsible—a contract that I am going to take lessons from you?"

No, he said, there were no such papers. Pay as you fly, was his system.

"All right, but don't you need my name?" (And my family's address, I thought, just in case.) He said he would take down my name and telephone number after we'd come down; no need to climb out of the ship now.

He showed me where helmet and goggles were hanging ready for use in the cockpit, attached to a rubber hose. That was the speaking tube. Through it, he would talk to me in flight. And with that he also climbed in and let himself down into the front well and jammed on a helmet. I noticed that no rubber hose was leading to his ears.

"And how do I talk to you?" I asked. With the thinnest of smiles he gave me the standard crack of the occasion: "You don't talk back to me." Somebody came and turned the propeller, and things got noisy and shaky. It was like being in the barbershop, when you have drawn a beginner-barber and he isn't cutting your hair right and you haven't the heart to protest: this shirt-sleeved, oil-spattered fellow, was he really a bona fide pilot or had I perhaps drawn some over-ambitious mechanic? "Fasten your safety belt," came the voice.

We were already rolling across the field.

He told me to put my hands and feet on my set of controls and follow him through. "But what if I freeze them?" I yelled, thinking of all the newspaper stories you read of student fliers who get nervous and hang onto the controls too hard and crash.

"Don't worry," he said, and he held up a fire extinguisher over his shoulder. "I'll knock you out." That, too, I learned later, was standard airport ceremonial.

We had turned around now and come to a stop, and he was watching the tower of the administration building, waiting for the green light.

"Wait a minute," I yelled, "what about the theory? Don't I need some theory first?"

The green light flashed. He said: "That? I'll explain that to you upstairs."

And upstairs we went.

I had been up in airplanes before, but this was the first time in earnest. And it was the first time I had ever had a chance to see what I saw then: how a flier flies.

His face was reflected back to me by his rear-vision mirror. His behavior seemed all wrong, he didn't act the way a man should act who keeps himself up and alive by his own wits. He didn't seem wide awake and ready for any emergency. He sat up here in the blue, looking nowhere in particular with a far-away expression, listening into himself, his shoulders slumped, with a mouth half sad, half bored, deep in thought.

The pedals made no motion that I could feel, and neither did the stick. Before us, the long nose and the motor stood out, forward pointing like the hood of a super racing car, but pointing only into emptiness. With all our vibration, we seemed to hang motionless in space. The blue-green sea of farm, far below, was drifting slowly. All around was emptiness, wind, and roar.

My altimeter showed two thousand feet when his voice came through: "She's all yours." He held up both his hands. Now. I was going to fly. I quickly once more thought over the working of the controls, all I had found out about it since I had been an awestruck boy reading about what fliers do. I took new hold of the stick and waited for excitement to break out. For an airplane surely would not stand for a man from the street, unlicensed, bespectacled, a $7.50 flier, at its controls: it would now buck or skid or slip or rear up or capsize or stall or tailspin or nose dive or whatever else airplanes did.

But it did not. It barged straight ahead, unconcerned, fool-tolerant. I made a few tentative moves with the stick, and the wings wiggled obediently.

And this fact produced a considerable emotional kickback. It usually does, in first-flight students. Merely because the ship actually responds to stick and pedals the way the kid's books had said it would, you think you are a natural-born flier, gifted with knack. Merely because you fill all the land below with important noise, you feel that you are quite a proud specimen of mankind. There is nothing to hit, whichever way you swoop or swerve, no harm can result; and that produces a sensation of freedom, sudden, like an injection of some drug.

But those first-flight impressions are mostly illusions. And the first-flight emotions have long since blown away. Now, in retrospect, I think that the great discovery of one's first flight is not an emotion, but a bodily feel—one of the great ones that will forever fascinate men, like the feel of a saddle and horse under you, or of a mast and sail over you, or of a rod and reel at the electric moment when the fish strikes: the feel of an airplane in the hand of the pilot.

In flight, the stick no longer felt disconnected and dead. It stood up, and there was life in it. When you moved it, it nudged back against your hand. I moved it more, and came against an elastic resistance. There was a will in it, soft, elastic, but unmistakably a will.

"Are you holding it?" I yelled forward. My voice was drowned out, blown away. Yet he noticed it. He was observing me in his rear-vision mirror as one would an ape, with the same thin smile. His voice came through the rubber hose: "Go ahead and fly." I now saw his hands resting on the cowling. It was not his will I was feeling. It was the ship's own.

I relaxed my hand to feel for this will. My flying career had begun.

Feeling my way, I pulled the stick back toward me against the ship's resistance, exploring what might lie that way. She nosed up willingly enough. I held on; the nose became heavy in my hand, and to hold it up, had to come back farther and farther. The ship protested with a steady pull. The instructor also protested. Some quick hard knocks came in the stick. They sided with the ship, away from me; and the voice said: "Don't freeze on the stick." I allowed her to come down from the cloud, and she became obedient again and light to the touch.

I pushed forward into the ship's resistance, wondering what I would stir up in that direction. Distant farmland rose up before us, then a small town that lay in the middle distance, then a nearby green field. I held her pointing at that field. The engine roared, and the stick became stiff and fought back roughly. "What are you diving her for?" said the voice. I let the stick snap loose, and she came up like a roller coaster. I became conscious of my stomach. So did the instructor of his. "Steady," said the voice. But it wasn't so easy; once disturbed she danced around and I was working all three controls, always a half a beat out of her rhythm.

The stick wrenched itself out of my hand with a circular jerk; he had taken over. With a few slams he put her nose and wings where they belonged. It was much the way a Bavarian waitress slams your beer in front of you: "Take it."

I tried to keep her there. In this position, she was willing again, almost too obedient, too sensitive. You had to guide her with two fingers and small motions, as if writing.

She kept jittering. I was too heavy-handed. He told me to take my hands off the stick entirely, and hold them up, and he did the same thing himself, and we spent the last few minutes that way. It looked silly; or rather, it would have looked silly had there been anyone up there to see us: two fellows barging through the sky with hands uplifted, like a couple of ancient Greeks in prayer, riding a sun wagon that vibrated and smelled of exhaust. But I could see the ship do its own flying, the nose hunting slowly for its own level, and finding it, the wings steadying down; and in my hands, I could feel the solid force of the airstream which held us up.

Afterwards I paid up as if it had been a taxi ride. He dived head first into his cockpit and came up with a disk of wax paper on which the ship's vibration had recorded itself in a jagged red line: thirty-five minutes, twenty-five cents a minute—$8.75.

He produced a new pilot's log book out of his pocket, and we entered the flight. Type of aircraft: "Travelair." Type of Engine: "Wright Whirlwind 175 HP." Flying time: "o *h.* 35 *m.*" Remarks: "Dual, Airwork." He told me to put my name into a blank space marked "Pilot." The whole entry took one line on one page, and there were a hundred pages still blank. A lot of experience still to come.

There was remarkably little to discuss. I wanted to know how I was doing, but he said it was too early to tell, and that I needed more Time and I had better get my medical permit soon. He wanted to know when I would come out again. That I would come again was somehow understood.

If there is one thing that clinches the 20th century's conquest of the air, it is this fact: that a man with an airplane can make a living in the air.

Even though he was a "Chief Pilot," George Adams was not the sportsman type, and even though he was "President" of something "Inc.," he was certainly not what you would call the executive type. He was just a fellow, a young man who worked with his hands; all the way up to the elbow, in fact, he dirtied himself all the time with grease and airport dust and oil.

His mind was on his engines, not on contracts, prices, goodwill, and promotion schemes. "Operations minded" the aeronautical magazines called that, and deplored it. And I used to think myself that he would never get anywhere until he put more pep into his public relations, and more greetership into his smile, and also more zip into his office equipment.

He didn't even have an office, unless you want to call the rumble seat of his car an office: there it was that he kept his log books, and a copy of the air regulations, and a few back numbers of the *Aero Digest;* also a file of aeronautical charts, and rulers and protractor and pencils for laying off a course to a destination; also a map of North America, on which he had drawn concentric circles, 120 miles apart, around Chicago as center. That was his basis for quoting prices on charter flights cross-country; 120 miles was what he could do in an hour.

He didn't even own a typewriter and a letterhead. He quietly refused to advertise, except through his business cards. If the customer was ready to fly, the customer would come to the airport. If he was not ready to fly, he would be ready later. He didn't even have a letterhead. His day phone was merely the general phone of the hangar in which he was one of many tenants.

His place of business was the open field. You could never talk to him except out on the Line, while he worked away under the fierce Midwestern sun, screwing spark plugs or checking valve clearances. Or at best in the hangar, while he washed the mud off his ship, mud that perhaps he had picked up during a take-off run the night before a thousand miles away in Texas. (For one of the odd things about his work was that in a certain sense his place of business was North America, and all the airports thereon.) But if it was business you wanted to talk to him about—well, you couldn't. Business didn't need to be talked about. Either a man had the cash and wanted to fly, and in that case he would fly; or he didn't really have the money, or he didn't really want to fly, and in that case, what was the use of talking? Most of the fellows who pestered him didn't really have the money.

He was probably right. Anyway, his method worked. The big money, with its own peculiar way of doing things, had been frustrated again and again in trying to make actual flying pay a profit. But little fellows, such as George, running this type of small enterprise known as a "Flying Service" had been riding up with their new business all through the Great Depression, all over the country, hundreds of them. George used to be a garage foreman; United Flying Service, better known as Al, used to be a bus driver. Other operators at that airport had been aircraft mechanics, circus strongmen, electricians, farmers, filling-station operators, automobile salesmen; there was also a kid who had dropped out of college, and an ex-army man, himself fairly broke. Almost all of them have used the same success pattern: no executive allures, no salesmanship, and dirty hands.

George Adams's capital consisted of two ships.

Number one was his trainer: a biplane, powerful, noisy, with an open cockpit in front, seating either an instructor or—after the dual set of controls had been taken out—two pay passengers; and a pilot's cockpit also open in the rear. It was one of the best airplanes ever built, although (or because) by present-day standards it was both overpowered and overwinged. It had been designed especially for barnstorming, and was able to pick heavy payloads out of farmers' small fields. Built without regard to cost, it was then six years old; four years later, with a new engine installed, I saw it still earning money.

If a responsible, well-run corporation had wanted to own a ship of similar performance, they might have had to spend five thousand dollars, for they would have chosen a new, up-to-date model. Thereafter, their ship would have had to earn at least a thousand dollars a year to appease such superstitions of the executive mind as depreciation, amortization, and interest. George had paid five hundred dollars for his ship. He had bought it as a crack-up, from a barnstorming pilot who didn't have the money to repair it; barnstorming as a way for fliers to eat had been failing around that time, and barnstorming pilots were going broke the country over.

In a truck borrowed over the week end, George had carted the ship home from the Iowa cornfield in which it lay. Then he had repaired it, with his own hands, working in the evenings for six months, after working all day in the garage.

With only a couple of years in high school, George was not an educated man at all; but he had a whole department to his mind into which I could never follow him. He was so completely at home with metal and metal working tools; he soldered and riveted and welded with the calmness with which your grandmother used to sew and embroider; he used calipers and feeler gauges and sawed, filed, and drilled hard steel to clearances of a hundredth of an inch—and he did so without even screwing up his face, with a natural grace that one could have found almost only in an American. For it wasn't a matter of systematic training or apprenticeship, but a matter almost of breeding, of a babyhood spent in the backyards of garages.

This ship's license placard, in the front cockpit, named as owner a Mrs. Somebody. Once I asked him about that. He said that she was his mother-in-law. He said you sometimes had to do that sort of thing to keep one's ship safe from possible creditors. "You see, no bank would even touch me with a pole."

Airplane number two was a fourseater cabin ship, fast and not so old. This he used for hopping sightseers, and for special charter flights with passengers. It cost thirty dollars an hour.

For a ship of this type (only, of course, a shade shinier) a clean-cut corporation would have had to pay about twelve thousand dollars. What George paid for her will never be known, for he had traded her in, and trading airplanes was an almost cashless procedure, veiled in mystery. It was the modern equivalent of horse trading, a shrewd, shifty game that went on at all the airports, with drawings-aside and whisperings and endless rumors. It also went on in the aeronautical magazines, and it can be best explained by the advertisements.

You started in, for instance, with your automobile and perhaps a little cash. Or many an old-timer started in at the end of the war, putting his discharge bonus into a surplus stock army plane—you may have heard of Curtiss Jennies. Or—my kingdom for a horse— you started in with the ancestral homestead:

> Trade for ship: all or part, 160 acres land, Southern Mississippi, good farm.

Thus you could get a ship, and thereafter, you traded on and on, and up if you could.

Or you made it a collector's game. A whole airplane is worth more than the sum of its parts. You bought crack-ups and salvaged the parts and the instruments, and then you traded duplicates with other collectors just as one might trade postage stamps; such an item as a Curtiss Fledgling, Lower Left Wing Panel, had a well-established market value and was always in demand. There were even brokers and dealers in crack-ups:

> If it flies we have it: airplanes, $25 up; Repairables, Flyables. . . .

There was Eddie's Wing Exchange, somewhere in Ohio, which advertised regularly: "We buy crack-ups." Thus you collected your airplane, offering, perhaps,

> Dance Pavilion for Airplane Engine, Aircooled, 125 horsepower.

or perhaps:

Beautiful 3-carat diamond ring for Directional Gyro.

or perhaps:

Eighty acres of wheatland for Artificial Horizon

until you had it all assembled and had it licensed, and then, likely as not, you used it again for further trading.

Or, cleverer still, you started in with things you didn't even own; things you got as advance payment for flying instruction from fellows who wanted their flying cheap. It might be cash; but in those hard times, with a lot of fellows crazy to get into flying, it was just as likely to be anything else, as witness this ad:

I want the best airplane I can get in exchange for any or all of the following items: New Zeiss binoculars, suburban houses, lots, white oak lumber, outboard motors, rowboats, second-hand libraries, standard steel shapes, office equipment, or tractors.

Those must have been the methods by which George had eventually gotten hold of his cabin ship.

So, you see, all those airplanes at the Metropolitan Airport were a funny sort of capital.

George lived near the Airport, on the hot West Side; went to bed at nine and got up in the dark; was never tired, never drunk, never preoccupied with the ordinary affairs of life; always shaved; had his ships' tanks always refueled, points adjusted, spark plugs cleaned, valve clearances checked—and his map of North America ready.

And, once a month or so, the big turmoil downtown cast up a big payload for him. Someone would appear at the Airport and want to charter a plane; want to pursue a certain bit of happiness by air; or pull a fast one in business by air; or want to get away—by air—with murder.

There was always some fellow whose mother was dying somewhere in Arkansas:

Five hours' night flying, at night rate, thirty dollars an	
hour	$150
Five hours' return flight, twenty-five dollars an hour	125
	$275

And there were always the news-reel people, the press photographers, and the reporters.

Spring floods (100 known dead, 300 missing)	$467
Hotel fire in Michigan (7 burned to death)	85
Bridge opening	35

Those were the stand-bys. But there are plenty of other payloads:

Banker to inspect oil lease during lunchtime	$75
Oxygen tent to mining camp, small field, using the old	
biplane	150
Corpse to Los Angeles	600
Alumnus and friends, flown to Homecoming Day, with	
landing on campus stipulated, two days' layover	280
Three observers searching lake for body of drowned	
child	75
G-Men to Kentucky, on man hunt	145
Three college boys to house party	155

A certain then-living underworld character once had George fly
him to a small prairie town about three hours out and then wait
there for him for three days at his layover rate of $50 a day and then
fly him home again—to no more sinister purpose than to get drunk
without fear of his enemies.

And more than once there had come a deaf man, shell-shocked
during the war, and had ordered a power dive from ten thousand
feet. Some doctors feel that a power dive, with its noise and its

pressure change, will cure certain types of deafness, on a medical principle somewhat like rolling an alarm clock down the stairs to make it work. These diving jobs cost the customers plenty: $75 for a single dive; for often the valves had to be reground afterwards.

Of his adventures on these flights he never told. He must have had plenty—with so much of this flying at night or through bad weather, and all of it urgent. I was at the field once at daybreak, waiting for him to turn up in his old Ford. Instead he came out of the sky in the cabin ship, his red-and-green position lights still on, and taxied up to the administration building.

I ran to meet him and said: "Hi, George." "Hi, Red," he said. He had a passenger in with him, a fellow with a brief case. I could see his fuel tank gauges were almost empty. He must have come a long way. He climbed out, and you could almost see the darkness dripping from him as water drips from a swimmer.

"Where from?" I said. "Texas. See you at the café." That was to cut me short; the passenger must be treated in business-like fashion, and must, if possible, be spirited off the field before one's competitors can find out who he is and perhaps send him offers of a better rate. They went inside to get a taxi and to settle the bill.

When he joined me for breakfast, I saw that his eyes were red, and while he ate, I thought that the same eyes had picked their way across the plains all night long by the beacon lights—

"Any adventure?" I asked.

"Adventure, hell. Four hundred bucks."

I think that in a sober way George Adams liked the air; but he never flew except for pay. No matter what the provocation, he would not fly without a payload.

There is one dare that almost every pilot will take up. In airport speech it is called "landing short," and by that, I mean "real short." Coming in over the same telegraph wires, against the same wind, with the same ship, a pilot of real skill will use only a third of the field for his landing run, while a solo student may use almost all the field, or even "run out of field" and roll into the fence. In case of a forced landing in a small meadow, you will be glad if you know how to land "real short." We, George's students, would sometimes taunt him, pointing out the spot on the runway where Mike managed to touch down this morning, and once in a while he took it up and started up his motor; but at the last moment he would yell: "Hop in, Red," and then the time would finally appear in my log book as "dual time, four minutes: one dollar."

His steadiest source of revenue was student hopping—teaching people to fly. This he did, as do most of the commercial flying teachers in this country, by flying much and explaining little. I always wanted to talk flight, particularly just after a lesson. Most students do. There is a nervous craving to take hold in words of that which eludes you in flight. But he never did explain to me about the theory, as he had promised before that first hop. He knew his theory well enough; they drill that into them good and hard, with all the authority of Uncle Sam himself, before they give them a license. Thus, in his simple clear speech, there would once in a while come swimming along technical terms gorgeous as tropical fish; "dihedral," he would enunciate, in describing the shape of a wing; or "longitudinal, lateral, and directional stability," in describing the behavior of an airplane. But he considered theory not worth a damn. Much rather than explain dihedral, he would fold a piece of postcard into dihedral shape, flip it into the air, and make you watch the way it behaved while falling. And much rather still, he would explain nothing at all.

He made you feel like a child that pesters people by endless questions. Although there is no basis for it in anatomical fact, I now remember myself with him always this way: he, striding from the ship back to the hangar and his work bench; I, trotting beside him, with many small steps, shooting questions out of my bothersome little face at his big wise face, and always getting the same answer: what the Goddamned Airplane will or will not do is something you must feel in your hand and the seat of your pants; and if you don't, why, Red, it just shows you need a couple of hours more Time.

That doesn't mean he took things easy. Instruction flying means earning one's living the hard way. Most of it is done during the first few and the last few hours of daylight; the customers have time off from their jobs then, and the air is smoothest. It helped to throw his household routine all out of step with that of the businessmen. He had to get up in the dark, and to go to sleep soon after nine. He had to be at the field all day Sunday. From the field, one could see the downtown skyline in the distance—and at night, the glare of the white lights. But George hadn't even been to the neighborhood movie house for months, and not downtown in years. His universe was bounded by his hangar, the airport café, and his apartment, a few blocks away, on top of a bakery-shop. Except, of course, when he flew—then the whole city lay below him many times a day, and sometimes his universe exploded and took in Los Angeles, Tampico, New York, Winnipeg—or at least their airports.

If his wife wanted to see him, she had to come to the Airport. She would sit in his car—that being about the only place on the field to sit down. She had been his sweetheart since high school, a pretty girl—fliers have the edge there, other things being equal—and he kept her in pretty clothes and leisure. He had married her about the time he got the cabin ship. Their wedding trip had been made in the ship—and in his spare time, George had taken up a lot of Wisconsin farm boys at a dollar a head. They had come back from their honeymoon with a small profit.

But he hadn't taught her to fly. He didn't approve of flying for women. "It makes them tough."

"Does it ever worry you," I asked her once, "having him go up with all us fool students?"

"Oh, no," she said, "he's on his toes. He may not show it, but believe me, he is."

"Red likes to *experiment*," George interposed with a grin. "He always wants to try out what the ship will do if he does this, and what the ship will do if he does that."

"But not with George in it," she said quickly, "please, Red, not with George in it," with a note of entreaty ringing in her voice that made me wonder.

Of the fifteen dollars George got per hour of Flying Time, at least half was profit if—and this if was important—if no student had a crack-up. Perhaps that accounts for his attitude toward his student. We might be his customers to be handled with care, and we might be his pupils to be given his best, but underneath all that I think we were to him a bunch of dangerous neurotics who hadn't any business to fly in the first place.

I asked him once why it was that people took up flying; he had the answer ready with a snap that showed he had thought about that one before.

"Ninety-nine out of a hundred," he said, "take up flying because they want to talk about it." Certainly we were far from the clear-eyed youth type of aviator of the magazine covers. There were two or three boys who wanted to get into the Flying Service business themselves; they ran filling stations or worked in garages and knew all about engines. They probably got a certain kick out of handling an airplane, but other than that they had no funny ideas; they simply wanted to get into a rising industry.

But the rest of us! Holy Freud!

We did of course in no sense belong together. We only met by chance, while standing around on the Line waiting for the wind to die down or for the ship to come in. But we did have this in common, that we were not flying, as they do in Europe, because a commission of experts had adjudged us particularly fit—on grounds of stable personality, good physique, good family, good education. We were not even flying because we were wealthy enough to afford a new and glorious sport; we were flying for no better reason than that we needed flying for our souls—which probably shows that our souls were functioning none too well.

Here is a list of my fellow students, remembered at random:

A fellow of about thirty-five who worked in the advertising business. He said he was going to buy a ship of his own when he got the money, and he was going to get the money soon. Meanwhile, his flying was too erratic for George to let him do much solo flying.

A boy of about twenty-two who worked for a grain exchange house, and looked as if he needed a quick puffing up of his ego.

Some son of the messy rich, trying for thrills, hoping perhaps to stop drinking so much; he had been in trouble about motorcycles and fast driving. He thought an airplane, being twice as fast, would give him twice the thrill, and he was finding out that he was mistaken. Often he appeared for instruction with deep black shadows under his eyes.

An auburn-haired girl who usually came in a Cadillac driven by a dark, soft-looking man. He would always stay on the ground while she flew, and his melancholy eyes would follow her through her maneuvers. It was said that he was in the clothing business, and that he paid for her Time.

A Chinese college student. He was hard to talk to and hard to teach according to George.

A girl about twenty-nine. She had just given up trying to get on the stage.

A college boy who wore riding breeches and high-laced boots and wore helmet and goggles even on the ground. He always found something to do that would take him all the way over to the administration building where there were spectators and airline passengers and passengerettes.

Then there was Ellen. About her, more will have to be reported later.

About myself, I don't know. Throughout this book, I try to make it appear that I am a reasonable citizen with regular ambitions and a regular career; and that I am flying only by way of recreation, the way another man might play golf. But don't you believe it; for actually, from that time on to the moment of writing, the air has been for me life itself. It got then, as it is getting now, every cent I can spare and practically all my thoughts, and I have sacrificed a couple of incipient careers to it. In short, my soul, too, was sort of strange.

There were also a few pilots who had licenses and experience, and who were allowed to take George's ships out cross-country alone. In airport speech, they also were nevertheless rated as students; they way a woman's children remain her children even when they are grown up.

They were important; out of one hundred students who started in with a few hours of dual instruction, they were the ten or twenty who came through, past the first solo and past the factor X and past the first "strange field landing," and past the license test and past the first cross-country—and really became pilots. And they were important also in another way—one might almost say politically; for the way they flew was the way in which the vast majority of American fliers managed their flying—and still manage today: renting their airplanes by the hour from a Flying Service operator such as George. For private ownership along automobile lines, airplanes were too expensive to buy and maintain at that time, and still are, for most of us, at an age when we want them most badly; and there was no system—as there was in England—of government subsidized clubs; thus the Flying Service operator and his students were the mainstays of the American airports, and more than anything else you could see at the airports, they represented the American way of flying.

Student-hopping was completely systematized. One took off, circled counter-clockwise around the field, turned-in again for a landing, took off again, went around and landed again, usually just barely touching the ground and immediately gunning her through into the next take-off. A circuit of the field every four, five minutes or so; you seldom climbed even as high as the highest gas towers and the radio masts. You flew grasshopper-like rather than bird-like, hop after hop.

You did that same short flight over and over for a total of five hours or eight hours or twelve or whatever time it took to make it completely smooth and sure; three perfect circuits in a row, and you were ready to do it solo.

For the instructor, it was much monotonous hard work. The hardest thing about it, George told me once, was sitting so close behind those exhaust stacks all morning: that was because students, with their rough handling of the throttle, produced a lot of backfiring, much like rifle shots; and to be so cramped into the front seat so long and have to refrain from interfering while the student makes a fool of himself.

More than once at the end of the lesson he asked me to pay him while we were still in the air; he had recognized the next student's car parked by the hangar or knew the next customer was waiting. Then I would dig past the safety belt into my pockets and while the ground was coming up I would hand forward my ten-dollar bill; while the telegraph wires seemed to scrape our bottom he would hand me back my change; then we would pay strict attention out forward for a moment, and we would hit and roll up to the hangar; another student would take my seat and grab stick and throttle and poor patient George would be carried away again in his little cockpit, once more to be blasted, jerked, and jittered through the sky.

There was little talking during flight. Once in a while he would say, "Look at your knuckles; all white." It was a blind guess on his part, but correct. My knuckles were all white for I was handling the stick with a cramp-like tenseness. "You are using too much rudder," he would say, and again and again he would repeat patiently: "You are using too much rudder. You keep making your banks too steep." In the glide, when talking was easier, he might casually mention "What are you diving her for?" (Diving, in airport speech, doesn't mean anything spectacular. Like all the finer points in flying it means a difference so slight that an unskilled eye doesn't even notice it; just holding the ship's nose a few inches too low and picking up a half dozen miles per hour of unwanted speed.) And then just before the landing he usually reminded me: "Now don't forget to put that tail down." If I did manage to put the tail down and hit all three points, tailskid and wheels, he would turn around and grin like a boy and say, "Attaboy," and I would feel happy.

It was much like dog training: you knew the tricks you had to do after the first two hours or so, but you couldn't get yourself to execute them. It is so hard to keep your mind on the essentials when to your groundling mind the non-essentials are so much more exciting. The essentials are so mild: certain very small differences in the route you choose over the surrounding fields while making your new approach to the airport will mess up your landing, or a matter of inches that you may hold your nose too high or too low during the glide will make all the difference. But the non-essentials—that it roars, and that it blows, and that in the curves the ship seems to stand on its wing tips, and that once in a while it hits a gust and jumps—the non-essentials are what thrills the newcomer. They do to a student flier what strange people and interesting smells and fearful noises do to a puppy dog: they keep his mind off the job.

Again and again all the teaching George had to do was to snap: "Come on, Red, you know better than that," which is exactly what one would say to one's dog. After the first few hours, the smallest gestures were enough to remind me: a poke of the thumb, a shake of the head; at most a few light, quick slaps against his controls, which I could feel in mine and distinguish from the soft, steady pull of the airplane itself.

During all our dual flying, I remember only few occasions when he actually took over the controls himself. He did that with a quick, circular jerk of the stick which wrenched it out of my hands, and when he did, it was usually high time. It was mostly during landings when I had let her touch down before her flying speed was gone and she had bounced off again and was going to sit down a second time twice as hard; on the top of such a bounce, he would sometimes take over, and, with a blast of throttle and some wiggling of the stick, would ease her down lightly.

I remember one case especially, a few seconds that built him up. It happened because I had insisted on trying to fly the ship from the front cockpit, just from curiosity. The farther forward you sit in a ship, the harder it is to judge its exact altitude, and thus it was that in a take-off run I held her nose somewhat too low, and on the rough stretch of runway she bounced in the fashion which is technically known as galloping. The bounces disturbed the flow of fuel, and while rolling at sixty m.p.h., the engine began to stutter; when I finally got her off, there was no room left. A fence was before me, a row of trees, some houses too near and too high to climb out over; it was a trap. Nothing to do, I thought, but to cut the ignition, land, roll straight ahead into the fences, and crash. I cut the throttle and reached for the switch, feeling cold and sad.

He pushed the throttle forward again and it was then that he took over the controls with his quick circular jerk. I could not turn around to see him; my eyes were busy measuring the height of the trees above us and the rate at which we approached them. But I could feel him; he held her level, to let her pick up all the speed she could, rushing her forward at the trees; my whole attention was wrapped up in it: in the fact that he was there behind me and had taken charge, and that he was going to lift us out over that wall. He didn't pull her nose up a bit: he charged directly against the trees. I could see every leaf on every twig before me, and I thought the propeller must now begin to hew into them, and for a split second I thought that now, after all, we were crashing. But then I did feel myself lifted up, and saw the twigs get out of the way and saw us come clear over the top. There was a surge of pride, not about being out of the trap, but for the man. There is no use beating around the bush—that moment I felt for him the way I imagine a woman in love would feel for a man; and it was a long time wearing off.

As my Time piled up, though, he tried to vanish from the picture and let me do my stuff alone. He would bury his head in his hands; he would with a great show of concentration polish the windshield; he would whistle to himself and look the other way. But he never quite succeeded; for like dog and master, I knew him too well. Even in dual flying, the student must, of course, deal with the factor X of the air and must make a somewhat well-judged approach. From the low altitude of the dual hop, and from the familiar flightpath, it is not a major difficulty, but still, the student must himself choose the moment when the throttle is to be cut and the glide begun. But I was anxious to solo, and I figured I would get down somehow, and so I cheated. On the last leg of each hop, I simply watched his ears. He could play the unconcerned passenger very well, but when the moment came to cut the throttle, I could always tell: his ears seemed somehow to stiffen with expectation. When they stiffened, I cut my throttle and began my glide. And every time I came down just right.

He wasn't even quite out of the picture when I finally soloed. It took me—let it be confessed out loud—twelve hours of dual time to solo. I had been eager to solo earlier, and had felt competent enough; but like most students at the point when they finally do get turned loose, I thought at the time, I was far from ready.

I had just made a rough landing. He said: "I want to look at the tail skid," and climbed out. Then he said: "Let me see the stabilizer," and, leaning in, adjusted the stabilizer so that the ship would balance with only one occupant—but I still didn't catch on. He said, "O.K." and fussed with the safety belt on the front seat. He was actually tying it into a knot so that the front controls couldn't get caught in it, but I thought he was merely preparing to get in again. He said, "O.K., Red, take her around," and there was absolutely no time to debate. With a cold shock all through me, I pushed the throttle open and kited away.

With all that load off, the ship climbed madly. I was alone, sure enough. I had long looked forward to doing this. And like a true student flier, I had looked forward perhaps even more, to telling about it. "Oh, boy," I had planned to tell 'em, "that vacant seat in front of me looked like a Hole in the Universe." But now it turned out differently. I banked around for my first turn and then throttled back to stop the climbing, and when I took my eyes off the tachometer I saw him standing deep below in the green, a miserable figure in a white shirt and dark pants, looking up at me. From there on, I forgot about the vacant seat. It was practically dual flying again. I could tell what he felt, even at that distance. He was worried whether I would get rattled, and what I would do to the ship. I turned again and flew past the field at six hundred feet, and my main thought was to set him at ease. I wanted to reach out and wave to him, but then I decided no, he would not like that, he would want me to keep my mind on his ship. And so I did, craning my neck right and left, looking out for other ships, checking the instruments: a picture of a man Exercising Good Judgment. The ship was still climbing, seven hundred feet now, even though throttled back. I knew he wanted me to level off, I knew he feared I would *screw up my approach* if I tried it from too high an altitude. But I, myself, felt quite confident. The poor fellow down there was turning slowly as I circled, following me. Now I understand why in airport speech, an instructor never says, "He went solo," but instead: "*I soloed him.*" I was being soloed right enough.

There was no trouble with approach and landing. George came up, and we shook hands. He thought he was shaking mine, but really I shook his.

5. Knapsack of Salvation

One day that summer, the Airport grapevine had news for me. A fellow named Barnes was making certain inquiries around the field. He was an operator and did a small business in sight-seeing hops on Sundays at some small flying field in the Sunday motoring country. It seemed that he wanted to have a parachute jump every Sunday. He hoped a parachute jump would help to attract a crowd to which his barker could then sell rides. As payment he was offering the jumper a block of Time on one of his ships.

"I wonder if it would open?" I thought.

Remember, this was several years ago. Mass parachute jumps were still in the future. It didn't seem likely that things would come to an end, but it seemed possible.

I went to George. George said no, he wouldn't touch the thing; in an emergency, perhaps; but he thought even then he would probably prefer to ride his ship down and take his chances. He guessed that it would open all right; what worried him, he said, was the landing. You might come down into a river or a high tension wire and even if you didn't you were as likely as not to break a leg or a hip bone. A proposition for circus men, he said, but altogether too risky for a pilot. He was in no way advising me to do it.

I cornered Barnes. Barnes kept his ships in Hangar 3. He had the usual equipment, a biplane trainer and a cabin ship; the latter was a

six-seater. He turned out to be the fellow who always wore a get-up
halfway between a yachtsman and an airline pilot; blue pants and
jacket and a cap. His cabin ship bore a large inscription: "Barnes
Airways, Los Angeles—Chicago—New York," which was meaning-
less except that it allowed back country yokels to think they were
riding in a Giant Airliner.

Barnes proved amenable enough.

At that time, parachute jumps were no longer worth much. In
cash they were worth perhaps fifteen dollars a jump, with perhaps a
ten-dollar bonus for landing exactly in front of the spectators. Usually, in fact, they were worth whatever the jumper could afterwards
collect in his hat. But Barnes, just like everybody around the Airport,
was short of cash; I believe he was a little shorter of it than most of
us. The only thing he had plenty of was Time.

As I have already explained, the flying rates we students paid
included a large share of clear profit and/or reserve against accidents. Beyond that, when you looked into airport economics, you
found that a big part of the costs of operating an airplane fell due
only after several hundred hours of flight, at the time when ship and
engine must be "majored," i.e., more or less completely rebuilt. The
actual, immediate cash expenses of taking a fifteen-dollar-an-hour
ship into the air were only about three dollars an hour.

Thus, I made a good agreement: three hours of ship Time per
jump, and two hours extra if I landed in front of the spectators. But
there was one condition. Barnes had recently been in trouble with
the Government inspectors for overloading his ship with passengers.
He was afraid he might get into trouble again in case something went
wrong with one of my jumps. I was to make a practice jump in some
other way first, so that I could technically be rated as experienced.

He who says A, must also say B. If I wanted to do cross-country
flying, the thing to do was to learn how to handle a parachute.

Parachutes are special stuff—in a class with sharks, snakes, poisons,
drugs.

Miller and Johnson, Parachute Service, lived inconspicuously in the rear of Hangar 3 in a small workshop. When one wanted to practice tail spins or acrobatics, air law prescribed that 'chutes must be worn and one rented a 'chute from Miller and Johnson at a dollar an hour. It was understood that in case one should actually use it, one would owe them ten dollars additional for inspection, repairs, and repacking. Air law also prescribed that a parachute must have been opened, inspected, and repacked by a licensed rigger within at least sixty days "prior to being worn in flight"—which provided them with a steady stream of jobs of repacking such 'chutes as were privately owned.

Their advertising notices were posted in every hangar:

If given the proper care, parachutes will last for many years, but it has been our experience that many parachutes have been ruined through neglect, due to being stored in damp places, not being aired out at regular intervals, or allowed to remain in pack over sixty days. If they are neglected, the silk as well as harness will deteriorate rapidly and as your life may depend on the complete functioning of your parachute as regards both material and packing, surely you cannot afford to take a chance on a parachute failure due to your negligence.

And it warned of certain highly technical faults possible in parachute packing, known as "twisted lines" or "thrown lines," which would prevent the 'chute from properly opening even after the pack had been ripped open and the silk was stringing out behind the jumper; an event which, according to Miller and Johnson's restrained language, created embarrassment for the user.

One of the peculiar things about parachutes was that whether one bought them or rented them, one always had to buy a pig in a poke. The working depended entirely upon their having been properly packed, but if you had opened them to look, you would have undone the whole job and would have had to pay three dollars for repacking, and then, unless you had opened them again, you would again not have been quite sure. That is why in American airport lore there was the story of a pilot who bought a parachute secondhand

and sat on it during many hours and trusted it, and then after sixty days opened it and found that its inside was not a silk canopy, but a batch of old newspapers.

But not Miller and Johnson's parachutes. Miller and Johnson were reputed to be good honest people. I went to talk to them, in confidence.

At their workshop, only their old assistant was in. Miller and Johnson themselves were out in the country on a jump, whatever that meant. He took down my request and promised not to talk about it at the Airport, for I had to think of my reputation as a steady and reasonable pilot of good judgment. He said they would write me an offer, and the next morning in my mail, it came.

It was a glimpse into a side of flying which I had not known existed at all, let alone at our modernistic Metropolitan Airport; only two hangars away from George, cold-blooded, reasonable George Adams: the world of the air circus.

The letter was three-quarters advertising. At the top and on both margins was crowded the following copy:

MILLER & JOHNSON PARACHUTE CO.

Balloons, parachutes, harness, safety belts, rope ladders, aerial apparatus for performers.

Special parachutes for the landing of freight, express, mail.	Experimental work, drop testing.

Reliable service men and performers from the far north to the tropics, from coast to coast.

Parachute leaps furnished from airplanes and balloons.

Fair Secretaries, Park Managers, Airport Operators, Carnivals, Celebration Committees, Lodges, and Campaign Managers consult us for prices on this 100% Crowd-Pulling Feature. A real treat to Young America. Operating in compliance with Air Commerce Laws of the U.S.A.

The letter itself said:

Dear Sir:

Replying to your enquiry, advise that we frequently break in new men on parachute jumping, and if you are physically fit, will give you your first jump for $30 and $20 per jump thereafter, at the local airport here, Dept. of Commerce approved type parachute for the pilot, his service, airplane, and our service truck with licensed rigger in charge.

Two or three days' notice is necessary and the jump would be held in private, just before sundown, as we do not commercialize on jumps of this nature.

Awaiting your further reaction, and hoping you will get in touch with us, remain

Yours truly
Miller & Johnson.

P.S. This proposition is subject to cancellation after we look you over, but from the information given to our rigger, believe we can O.K. your case.

Then a final burst of advertising:

SUPER SPECIAL. DIAVOLO: *braving death in its most horrible form;* allows himself to be ejected from a roaring cannon suspended from an especially constructed monster balloon—returning to earth with a parachute—leaving the spectators breathless at the sight of his recklessness. DIAVOLO also leaps from airplanes at dizzy heights, using bat wings and two parachutes.

Death in its most horrible form, I thought; you mean if it doesn't open, you pancake. Or rather, you burst. People are supposed to turn out practically liquid; except the skull. But you needn't be so outspoken about it. You are saying the right thing to the wrong party. I am not the looking kind of customer, but the jumping kind. You ought to have two different letterheads.

My further reaction? I got in touch.

Miller and Johnson turned out to be two grizzled men in their fifties. There was nothing in their appearance to connect them with the circus, or with airmanship, for that matter; it was more like being measured for a new suit at the tailor's. We fixed the third day from then for the jump, weather permitting, and they went to work immediately selecting the 'chute and fitting the shoulder straps and leg straps and chest straps of the harness. The 'chute itself was not the usual seat pack type, but was worn knapsackwise; that was to make it easier for the jumper to climb out of the ship deliberately without doing damage. Carried that way, it was heavy, and that was reassuring; it made you feel that at least you wouldn't have to jump off there defenseless.

"Now, when you pull the ripcord," began Miller, "don't be gentle about it."

"Give it all you've got," said Johnson. "Yank the ———— right out."

"You bet I will," said I.

The ripcord ring was painted red; it looked much like the emergency brake in continental railroad cars and, under the circumstances, that carried a pleasant suggestion.

When your inner man complains and wants to put his trust in something, there is nothing quite as suitable as a gadget. The gadget will presumably work, while the same thing cannot always be said of one's intelligence or of one's own nerve, or of the grace of God.

Then came the second 'chute. Air law says two 'chutes must be worn on "intentional jumps." The second one was only a small one, eighteen feet in diameter. If I should have to use it, Johnson said, it would bring me down "awful fast." It was worn on the stomach, buckled onto the harness of the first one. When it hung, it acted as a counterweight to the first one, and made you feel like a pack horse.

But all to the good; as far as I was concerned, the more gadgets, the better.

"Now when you take off—" said Miller (what an elegant circumlocution, I thought, for letting yourself fall from an airplane) "now when you take off, the main thing to remember is not to pull too soon. It is as much as your life is worth." And he explained how the 'chute might get fouled in the ship's tail and throw the ship out of control; the pilot, he said, was going to wear a 'chute himself, that being another legal requirement and would jump. But I would get killed.

Johnson had a story to reinforce that. Some years ago, some dizzy heiress had tried a jump and had caught in the ship's tail. By the grace of God, her 'chute had caught in such a manner that the ship was not thrown out of control, and it had plenty of fuel; but she had dangled there under the ship's tail for two hours. One had heard her from the ground, crying out pitifully above the ship's noise. Men had tried to reach her by rope ladder from another airplane and to let a knife down to her by rope, but to no avail. The pilot had tried to shake her loose by stunting, but with her weight and resistance on the tail, he hadn't been able to shake the ship much. They had considered landing the ship on water, but decided that it wouldn't improve her chances. And when it finally seemed that she must surely be killed as soon as the ship ran out of fuel, her 'chute had by pure chance come loose, and she had come down O.K.

Miller said I was to take off in a shallow dive, away from the ship—"the way you dive into a swimming pool." That way, he said, I would fall face downward, and would pull the cord in that position, and the canopy would be free to string out nicely behind me. That was a new one. Wouldn't a parachute open in any position? Johnson said yes, absolutely in any position, but smoothest that way. But he thought if I pulled in any other position, it would be just as well to keep my legs together and pulled up against the body in a crouching position, so the 'chute wouldn't get caught between them. Miller started to emphasize again how important it was to wait and clear the tail of the ship. "Don't worry, though," said Johnson, "the pilot has done this job many times; he will kick the tail out of your way."

I asked how long I should count before pulling. Miller said not to count at all. "A man can count so goddam fast." He said it was better to use my own judgment and to wait until I had fallen clear.

"After all," said Johnson, "you are a pilot, you are used to the air; you won't be nervous."

"Not much!" I thought.

Johnson advised me to have my hand on the ripcord before I even jumped. Miller had some parachute lore to cover that point. Some fellows got excited and couldn't find the ripcord, and went clutching for it all over themselves in a panic before they could find it. "Like this," said Johnson and started emitting guttural sounds of horror and clutching at the air, with a facial expression that was most convincing. Both of them laughed heartily.

Johnson had a companion story of a case where a newspaper writer had tried a jump. He hadn't trusted himself to keep his wits about him, and so his rigger had tied a long string to the ripcord, and had gone up with him in the ship to do the pulling himself after the writer would have fallen deep enough—which was, said Miller, more or less the system of parachute that had been in use before 1919 and the invention of the self-pulled ripcord: a line connecting the jumper and the aircraft and jerking out the 'chute. But it had often failed to work. Instead, the man had got tangled up in the string, and jerked it out of the rigger's hand, and being entangled, had then been unable to pull the cord himself; he had fallen straight down like a stone.

Between them they discussed an expedient sometimes used for breaking-in new jumpers: tie one corner of a handkerchief around the ripcord, tie the other corner into a knot, and have the jumper hold the knot with his teeth. A man always knows where his mouth is, said Miller. But it sometimes happened, said Johnson, that the jumper in his excitement pulled out all his front teeth before he pulled out his ripcord.

"Now when you land," said Johnson, "just go limp. Never mind if it rolls you over a few times. Just go limp."

Miller said, "Now don't worry about the landing. If you come down on the field we will be under you anyway."

It had been decided that I should jump into an abandoned flying field, near the state fair grounds, five miles from the Metropolitan Airport.

"But, of course, it is hard to judge," said Johnson. This year they had bad luck—their last man had fallen into a canal, and the man before him had landed on the roof of the grandstand and had broken a leg.

The three days before the jump were like the last days of a school vacation when one's forward perspective in time used to be completely shut off. The third day was fine; there was no storm; there was no high wind. At five I went to the Airport.

Miller and Johnson were waiting. First of all there was a little thing to sign, all typed out for me. I, my heirs, executors, administrators, and assigns would make no fuss, whatever happened.

Then there was a long pause while we waited for their pilot. Miller sat on the workbench, and Johnson just stood around, watching the sun come down. I looked over the ships in this hangar. I didn't feel like talking. If the thing worked, there would be lots of time to talk afterwards; if it didn't, talking would be pointless.

The pilot came, looked me over in passing but said nothing. He grabbed a 'chute from the shelf, went out and started his engine. And they began to dress me up, goggles and 'chutes.

We filed out of the hangar, Miller ahead, Johnson behind me, not unlike a condemned man's walk to the chair.

At this moment, my whole past life flashed through my mind—it really did. This way: was there any evidence of mental disorder? There was the time when I wanted to quit school; there was the matter of the forgotten address; there was the fact that at parties I get moody and contrary; but all that wasn't convincing. Had it perhaps broken out suddenly? Rapidly, I ran through uncles and aunts; no insanity in the family.

I seemed to be sane.

"Just a moment," Johnson said, and took me aside. "Want to pay us now?" I couldn't get at my pocket past all the harness. We went in again. He unbuckled me, and we settled. He buckled me up again, and we went out. Miller and the old assistant started up the truck to drive to the fair grounds and be under me when I landed.

Johnson thought of another thing: "Now that ripcord, you better hold onto it; don't throw it away in your excitement. It costs five dollars."

I said, "I'll do my best." He said: "You pay for it if you don't."

I climbed into the ship and climbed out again on the wing, by way of rehearsal. What, I said to myself, if when we get upstairs all I do is shiver and finally shake my head and climb back into the ship and sit down. I could picture quite clearly their polite smiles as we came down again and they helped me out of the ship; certainly, they would say, you're damn right, it is really not worth the risk.

Was I sure that wouldn't happen? I was not.

I climbed in again.

He took off.

We rose across the familiar fields, swung around and climbed over the open country. A phrase went through my head: "I earnestly hope."

At a thousand feet, the silliness of the enterprise had faded: now in the air, it was simply an aeronautical job to be done, and to be done with the usual aeronautical attitude—judgment, deliberation, control. At two thousand feet, that attitude had taken full possession of me; so much so that now if anything had seemed wrong, I would no longer have minded even calling the whole thing off and return-ing to the Airport, the way a good flier sometimes will.

But nothing did seem wrong.

At three thousand feet, we crossed over the state fair grounds, headed into the wind. The pilot poked me in the back and throttled back, to slacken the propeller blast and make it easier for me to climb out. I was glad I had rehearsed the job. It went smoothly, and I had attention to spare for easing my two 'chutes past all sorts of hazards without having the ripcords catch and rip open.

He put on the power again, and I had to hold on tightly, for the wind was pushing me heavily from behind and threatened to throw me off.

I looked down; half a mile down . . .

I should like now to report hair-raising sensations. But actually I was cool—or perhaps the better word is dead. While I stood out there and looked down, my heart stopped pounding. It was the factor X again, coming in handy; I could feel no animalic fear of falling, because I could get no animal sense of the depth. Looking back into the front cockpit, I could see the altimeter registering 2500 feet; we had lost altitude while I had climbed out. But the position of a needle on a dial was evidence too thin and intellectual to give you a good scare. It was different when I looked at the pilot. He was tense and worried, thinking probably about the job ahead and the chance that something might miscarry and he might have to jump. I preferred not to watch him; for fear can be induced the sympathetic way from man to man.

He throttled back again and nodded. I felt no reluctance. I let go of my hold, took hold of the ripcord ring over my heart, and with one long step walked out into the farms below.

The fall was violent. I fell and fell. I fell face downward, my left hand clawing at a cornfield, right hand on my heart, holding the ripcord. I fell so hard that I couldn't even be afraid; I was all filled out by one feeling, a feeling which, translated into colloquial language, was: "Oh, boy, oh, boy, here I go."

Falling is falling, from old habit, whether you do it in an optic vacuum or not. No factor X deadened that sensation. I held my breath, or rather my nerves did; they expected me presently to hit with terrific force, and to get hurt; because they had never known me to fall and then not hit and get hurt. I remember hearing myself gasp, which shows that I must have fallen quite deep below the airplane and its noise. I waited as long as I could. Then it seemed horribly urgent to find out whether or not the contraption would work.

Then I pulled the handle.

I gave it all I'd got. It came out with hardly any resistance, and went slack in my hand. I pulled it all the way out and stretched out my arm and held it far away from me, and grasped it hard; I must not lose it: point of aeronautical honor. Even while falling, I held it stretched out with my right, the way Marshal Bluecher holds his saber, in the pictures, riding an attack; even while falling, I thought that was funny. And I waited with some impatience to be caught up.

Nothing happened.

Then there was a vision of laundry fluttering on a line. That was the silk, stringing out behind me. A gentle force seemed to lift me by the shoulders and pull me upright, much as one might pick up a child who had fallen, and I had just time to think, "Is that all?"

Then the canopy opened. The harness grabbed me around the thighs, jerking my legs apart. A bolt of energy struck down on my head, traveled down along my spine, my legs, and my feet, just as a crack travels along a whip, until I thought my feet were going to snap off. Something jerked me upward with a huge lift—a fish would feel that way when he is hooked. And I remember hearing myself groan—against that peculiar stillness. Then the forces subsided, and I was afloat.

Of all the sensations of air-faring, that is the most dreamlike—floating under a parachute. It begins with a wave of triumphal emotion which is standard accompaniment of everyone's first parachute jump and is unlike any other experience—there is in it the sudden deliverance from danger, also release from perhaps the most concentrated bit of waiting there is, and also exultation of being high up in the air, flying for once in silence, for once almost without a machine.

I looked up at my 'chute; the simplest of all aircraft. It quivered, high above me, the merest handkerchief in size; it seemed incredible that so small a bit of silk should have so much holding power. In the stillness it gave out a thin sound, like a peanut whistle. That was the air, escaping through its center vent hole. It was a warning, though I didn't understand it: an indication of the speed with which I was actually coming down.

For the time being, I was well afloat with my magic carpet. The harness was holding up my weight so evenly that I was hardly conscious of it. It is like flying in dreams, flying simply because you are light. My feet were limp under me hanging into a cornfield. The view was the usual one from an airplane, the green plain, the distant horizon. But there was no wind; when I moved my hand, the air felt thin.

I experimented with steering the 'chute by pulling the lines so as to set the canopy askew; it let me slide off sidewise obediently enough. But it also set me to swinging, pendulum fashion, and I had to stabilize myself by throwing my weight about the way a child stops its own oscillations on a swing. When I looked down again, I found myself bearing down on the race course. There was the landing to think of now.

My descent had become more noticeable. I watched for a while, with an eye practiced by so many approaches, and it seemed to me that I was undershooting the intended.

The race track seemed the probable point of contact and within the race track, the corner where the stables were and that grandstand. If so, I should get hurt. Beyond it, there was the abandoned flying field. I grabbed the two forward ones of the lines and hung onto them. It helped a lot; the wind combined with the 'chute to carry me forward beautifully. I flew across the roof of the grandstand, across the race track itself, sliding along weightless, without footing, like a ghost.

But again the maneuver threw me into violent swinging. I worked hurriedly to stop it. The grass was beginning to dilate under me as if pulled up by a magnifying glass. Only one hazard was now still before me: the fence of the fair area. Beyond it was the clear field. There was little time left. The wind was drifting me toward the fence, but not fast enough. And I was too low now to do any more maneuvering. I had to take whatever was coming, and it began to look like a 50-50 shot. I could already distinguish the individual strands of barbed wire.

I was floating down steeply now, the sinking much more visible than the forward drift. I saw that I was going to light exactly on the fence, but in my innocence, I was not much worried. I decided I would simply step lightly on the top wire, kick myself off from it, and step down, still borne by the 'chute, still weightless, from the fence into the grass, on the airport side. As it was coming up against me, I stretched my right foot down to meet it; and I missed. The wind had carried me forward by about two feet or so, and I was across. Then the grass took a lunge. There was just time to go limp.

It came up through my legs and my whole body as if they had been unsubstantive as a ghost's, went right at my chin, and swatted the living daylights out of me. And that was only the beginning. For a long time thereafter, though I thought I was down, legs and arms kept falling all around me and kept me wondering where it all came from. Then the bombardment subsided and it was quiet.

I looked up. The 'chute was standing upright in the grass, tugging at me with the force of a sail. I pulled in one of the lines and made it collapse and unbuckled my harness, working with a breathless haste for which there was no other reason than that my whole system was still timed for fast airwork. From the distance, people were running across the field, old Johnson doing his best to keep up with them. And the ship was coming in for a landing. I looked at my hand, and my ripcord was gone. Just before everybody arrived, I found it lying in the grass: a piece of wire rope, one yard long, attached to the ring. I also found a deep hollow scooped out of the soft ground, of the kind which in skiing is called a bathtub. That was the place where I had hit. My shirt was torn, and my trouser legs were torn. My cheek was bleeding; despite the goggles, my spectacles were bent.

There was a great deal of excited talk. I had been lucky. The fence was nine feet high, with steel posts and very tight wires, not an ordinary farm fence at all, but more like a burglar-proof factory fence. If I had landed on it, on this fence, with that force—I would have been cut in two. We stood around the 'chute. It lay there flat and dead on the grass. I felt as if I had landed some monster fish.

6. First Time in Earnest

Miller and Johnson made me out a certificate that I had

. . . made a parachute jump near the local airport at 7 P.M. this evening. This jump was cleverly executed in a plane piloted by Bill Stewart, and we are pleased to recommend this man's performance to anyone in need of the parachute jump attraction.

I took it and went immediately to look for Barnes. I was now an experienced parachute jumper, and would jump for him every Sunday, and would get a lot of cross-country Time in return. At the café, no one had seen Barnes. At his hangar, the mechanic said he had flown to Kansas City two days ago.

I kept calling up, and three days later he was back. I went to the field early. I found him at the café, with a lot of fellows. He was embarrassed to see me; the deal was off. He was sick and tired of being an independent operator, and had got himself a job as co-pilot on an airline.

What about our agreement? He said it was too bad; he had forgotten all about it. I said it really was too bad. He thought maybe he could fix it up with me. The new owner of the ship was to arrive the next morning to take possession. In the meantime, if I wanted to take it out today, it would be all right; provided I paid for my own fuel and oil, and provided I didn't crack up. The ship was not insured; if I cracked it up, he would sue me for damages. I said I had no money with which to pay for a crack-up. "Never mind," he said, "I'll sue hell out of you," and on that basis I decided to go out cross-country once more.

I mustn't lose any time. If I want to build up my cross-country Time substantially in a single day, I must save every possible daylight minute for actual flying. It was then eight o'clock. I asked him to come up right away, check me out dual fashion; for I had never flown that type of ship.

We pulled out the ship and went up to do a series of landings and some airwork. The ship was lovely to fly. It was a Fleet, so called after its designer; although its basic design was of the twenties, the Fleet is probably the loveliest to fly that has ever been built in America. Flying it gave you a feel similar to that which dancing gives you with the girl, not often found, who is really light on her feet—so light that there is almost nothing there. Compared with it the Travelair felt like a truck. The Fleet was built for maneuvering, and it was almost a pity to fly such a ship cross-country, straight and level for hours.

I had no trouble handling the ship though the engine gave me some trouble. After the third landing, Barnes had me taxi back to the Line, and climbed out: "Well, now, remember about that insurance," he said, and went back to the café and his farewell celebrations.

I called up the university and made excuses. I grabbed a few maps, borrowed a watch, some money, a pencil and paper, a protractor, and sat down on the hangar floor and calculated my course. And then, I don't know what small impressions made me think of it, it occurred to me to hunt up Barnes's mechanic and have a heart-to-heart talk with him.

The mechanic (who worked for Barnes in return for flying Time rather than cash) admitted that the engine was not in satisfactory maintenance condition. He said it was badly in need of a major. Barnes had been running down his equipment, all right. The job had come just in time, he hinted, with a grimace. Hell, the ship was hardly his own any more, he owed so much money on it. He showed me the ship's license card, posted in the front cockpit. There was a fresh notation: "This aircraft subject to lien."

"Is she going to quit on me, you think?" He thought it over slowly, and decided, "I don't believe she will."

I thought of my instructor: "Come on, Red, you know better than that." I knew better than to fly behind an engine of which I had doubts; but I knew that if I wanted to fly cross-country at all, I mustn't be choosey.

"All right," I said, and climbed in. "Turn her over for me, will you?"

"Contact."

I took off at nine o'clock of a fine August morning. The weather was fine, the wind light, the whole day still before me, and the great region called cross-country again below me. Thirty minutes later I had settled on my course and was happily at fifteen hundred feet over the farm country, listening to my engine and day-dreaming. The last thing I had leisure to think was something like: "Pretty country."

Quite suddenly and swiftly the country was not pretty any more, nor was I dreaming. Something had shocked me awake: for one quarter-second the engine had cut out. At least, I thought it had; it was running evenly again. I listened.

A seven-cylinder engine, running at 1800 revolutions per minute, makes 105 distinct impulses of power and as many beats of noise each second. You can't listen that fast. I listened as hard as I could. There it was again, a missing beat: or rather, there it had been again; it was past by ten or twenty beats by the time I had finished hearing it. I listened again. There was an awful crack, consisting of silence: for a quarter-second, the whole engine had cut out. Damn that mechanic, I thought, here we go and no insurance. My eyes pounced upon the landscape below with a new and urgent interest. Quick now, a place to sit down: forced landing, at last in earnest.

The engine had taken hold again but small roughnesses were occurring so fast now that its whole tone had changed; she would presently cut out again. In the meantime, without ever thinking about it, I had turned back.

There it actually is now, I thought. Engines do quit, and if they quit, you do have to pick your landing spot; and having picked your spot, you do have to hit it on the first approach. For the first time, I looked at the country below the way the older pilots were always telling us young ones to look: always looking for a possible landing place, all the way cross-country, picking this cow pasture, that hay field, that broad highway, much as a man might walk across a stream and pick his stepping stones.

By pilots' standards, and for purposes of shooting a one-eighty, the country below me was beautiful—beautifully flat. The Middle West is all one big flying field—but one on which some underhanded inspector had laid out an assortment of ground hazards to mess up one's approaches. There were various types of fences, clusters of houses, barriers of trees; there was plenty of that abomination of airmen, electric pole lines. The lay-out below might still on occasion sort out those who deserved their licenses and those who didn't. And that occasion was now.

If a forced landing goes wrong, you know that by your instruments. The instrument board comes back and staves your face in. If you are lucky, you wake up in some hospital with a case of aviator's nose. If you are less lucky, you don't wake up.

Better play safe, I thought, better go upstairs.

More throttle, and a finger hooked around the stick to hold the nose up. There was more rough noise, and more vibration, and the hands of the instruments were shaking on the dials. The rate of climb showed three hundred feet per minute, and the altimeter needle creeping up towards two thousand. Already the ground had sunk away a bit, slowed down, flattened out. Nothing like a little altitude to take the squeeze off a flier's system. Every thousand feet of altitude gives you almost two miles more gliding range, and a choice of about one hundred additional farm fields to sit down on, and almost two minutes more time in which to collect your wits.

I couldn't help thinking of the nice old lady who had advised me at tea not to fly so high—for the higher you fly, the harder you fall, don't you?

No, ma'am, a flier likes to have plenty of air between himself and his country. . . .

I now hoped I might get back to the field before she would quit. I was half sorry that I would miss the experience, and half relieved.

Then it did come: there was silence except for the humming of the wind on the wires. The propeller was windmilling so slowly that each blade was visible as it flicked around. I was without power; she had quit.

Keep your wits now, I thought. For just a few minutes keep your wits, or nothing else will ever matter. Meanwhile she had dropped her nose by her own volition, as ships will, and gone into a fairly steep glide. The wires were singing up the scale as she was picking up speed. I took her with two fingers, and began to slow her up, pulling her nose up into a shallow glide; being new to her I didn't have her feel very well. But I must take care to establish a good slow speed right away, for further down, I knew, I would be busy with other things, and excess speed is hard to get rid of in an airplane. As to my field, I had already decided; I would use a hayfield, surrounded by cornfields. It wasn't large; if I overshot, I would go into a fence; but it was well away from the road and the electric pole lines, and it had clear approaches.

I banked around and began to spiral down. It was the very thing I had practiced for so many hours; a great occasion, my First Forced Landing. It was like the time when after dancing with your sisters you danced for the first time with a real girl; there was the same fear and trembling to suppress, and there was the same relief when you found that it was working in earnest exactly the way it had worked in practice. For instance, during the spiral, while banked steeply, I could look down over the side and make sure that the field had no ditches just as George had told me I would want to make sure. At one thousand feet, I blended the spiral into a regular one-eighty with its triangular one-two-three: one away from the field and 'round so as to put the field on my left side, slightly forward; two, gliding past the field until its perspective seems right; three, turn-in and shoot for it.

The whole maneuver seemed to slide down along a familiar groove. At two hundred feet or so (my altimeter was so near zero that it was useless) I was floating low over the corn, looking down, thinking how nice and right everything looked; I must have been guided largely by the appearance of the cornstalks. It was depth perception method number 7b: the apparent size of a familiar object. They appeared so nice and tall: I must be nice and low.

It's in the bag, I thought.

I was making a mistake, though. One should never try to judge one's height by looking straight down; it is misleading in many ways. When I looked up again and around, it seemed to me that on the contrary, I was coming out much too high, and would overshoot. I wanted to kill height, and I stuck my left wing down at the cornfield to do a sideslip; but looking down at the ground again along the down-pointed wing, I saw the cornstalks so close to the wing tip that I recovered in a hurry: I was, if anything, too low. I looked around again, and again I was too high. Something was horribly wrong with my judgment. On my very first forced landing the factor X was getting me.

I had a sickening feeling of getting into trouble and being unable to take action. It isn't true what some people think, that you need split-second decision; but just then, I could not afford to sit para-lyzed while a whole string of seconds went to waste.

At that point I saw a small boy who stood in the corn below me cultivating a row; a small boy with a large straw hat. He must have heard the swishing of my wings, for he presently turned his head up to look at me. Then I saw the face under the hat, a full-grown man's face. The next moment, things snapped back into scale for me: he was a full-grown man. The corn was about twice as tall as I had thought it was.

Since I had last been flying cross-country, weeks had passed. The familiar object had grown. If the corn was so much taller, I was not as low as it had appeared to me. If I was not as low, I was going to overshoot. If I overshot, I would go into the fence and wreck the ship. While these deductions reeled themselves off in my mind I had already stood the ship on its ear and was sliding off my height side-wise as violently as a fully kicked rudder and a hardover stick would do it. I must have smiled for the airstream, now blowing crosswise past my face, caught inside my mouth and pulled it askew and made my cheek flutter.

I made it easily. She touched down as smoothly as if it had been an airport, and rolled to a stop.

7. Flying Team

I spent the rest of the morning phoning the Airport and waiting for the mechanic to drive to the location, and the afternoon I spent sitting on a farm fence while he fixed the engine. Just before sundown, I flew the ship out, and arrived at Metropolitan with a total of one hour and ten minutes added to my cross-country experience.

I was discouraged. It seemed to prove that there were no breaks in flying for a man who couldn't fly commercially and who wasn't rich. I stayed away from the field for two weeks, half thinking of giving it up. Then I went back to George Adams to fly his ship meekly around the Airport again, half-hours at a time.

George, being a careful man, insisted on checking me out; he went up with me dual, and made me do some airwork and some approaches. It was meant mostly as a disciplinarian measure; he disapproved of my jumping a parachute, and he disapproved of my flying that ship with the badly kept engine, and he wanted to show it.

But when we came down afterwards and climbed out in front of the hangar, he actually had found a fault. Something had gone wrong with my technique of making turns, which is really beginner's stuff. "You are slipping your left turns," he declared, "and you are skidding your right turns. What's the matter with you now?" I said I didn't know. I was discouraged. It seemed that I was sliding backwards from lack of practice, and that I might as well give up. He said:

"Don't you know how to judge your bank?" I said, sure I knew: "By the seat of my pants."

Behind me a woman's voice spoke up: "The professor's seat of his pants is no good." It was Ellen, the big blond girl flier, who was always hanging around at the field.

"What do you mean, no good?" said George.

"The professor is out of whack," she said.

She said I wasn't holding myself straight. And it was true; from all that work in the library, draped over a desk, resting my head on my hand, I had begun to hold myself crooked, one shoulder high, and one shoulder low, and of course I was out of whack. It might indeed be the trouble.

I got George to go up with me for ten more minutes and to check me again. I held myself straight, and sure enough, the turns were smooth, and on my instrument board, the little steel ball of the bank indicator remained centered in its glass rollway.

The discipline of the air.

When I came down, she was still in the hangar, talking to a couple of mechanics. She wore yellow pajamas at the field, and used to keep one hand in her pants pocket just like a man.

"Did it work, professor?" she asked.

"It worked all right," I said.

I was grateful. That may sound a bit overdone, but remember, it cost us a quarter a minute. Ironing out some flaw in your flying technique might cost you months of your life; and a flawless flying technique was—besides one's log book—the only thing one had after years of sacrifice.

I was grateful, and for the first time, we fell to talking.

Her manner and speech were not quite free of the airport flavor which comes from a predominance of mechanics. Her yellow pajamas were unfortunate. But with all that she had more of a gentleman's slant on flying than any of the people I had then met at airports or have met since. She wanted to fly airplanes the way a gentleman rides horses or sails boats—not for business, not for show, but for some deeper reason.

She had never been out cross-country, she didn't like the 'rithmetics involved, but she wanted to go.

We went to the airport café for a chocolate malted milk to talk it over.

She had forty-five dollars saved up, and I had a similar amount. She thought she could get more from some aunt, and I thought I could get more somehow. She knew of a ship, soon to come to the Airport, a new design that would rent for ten dollars an hour; by compounding our plans and our resources, we might be able to get a lot of Time.

But two inexperienced pilots in one ship—before you do that you look twice. By way of mutual baring our souls, we showed one another our log books. Hers showed more than a hundred and fifty hours of solo time, twice as much as mine did, and you know how among flying students rank is reckoned by hours and minutes. Aeronautically, she was my aunt.

I had thought that I had done well, building up my Flying Time the way I had; Ellen made only eighteen dollars a week, typing in some real estate office, and out of that she paid her parents seven dollars a week for board, and bought her own few poor dresses; she had built up her Time on the remainder.

The entries in her log book, for all their cold and conventionalized language, carried considerate overtones of pride.

For instance, she had soloed George Adams's big six-seat Bellanca. Later on I rode around the field with her a few times while she did approaches and landings on that ship, my function being that of ballast to weigh down the tail. If you had seen her at the airport café beside some pilot's girl, she would have seemed rather far on the robust side in a Dutch way. But when you watched her handling that big brute of a ship, holding the wheel with her bare arms, her blonde hair fluttering in the gusts of slip stream that came in by the window, she seemed almost too girlish for comfort.

She had an L.C., a Limited Commercial License, which permitted her to carry pay passengers within ten miles of the Airport.

There was an entry indicating two passengers carried over the city on a sight-seeing hop. In the remarks column, there was a note, "for hire," indicating that those had been pay passengers. And around those two words was drawn a heart of the kind that you might find drawn around someone's initials. For like most of the airport crowd, including myself, she departed from the amateur spirit in this respect. Flying with pay loads was a better sort of flying than flying for fun. The professional air taxi driver was to us much more glamorous a being than the amateur; we all, even the amateur pilots, even the owners of private pleasure ships, tried to act as much as possible like commercials. We would rather have been taken for a penniless, debt-ridden operator than for a wealthy gentleman pilot.

There was another entry that set this typist far apart from us ordinary students. It had, she said, required tactful statement: "Spin in: major damage to aircraft, no injury." Which meant that she had come down once in a tailspin and should by rights have been dead. She had lost twelve pounds during the next few days, and she was slightly ashamed of the fact—as if she should have been tougher.

Her log book was almost a diary. Lying between its pages were pictures of airplanes including one of the old biplanes that had spun her in, and including one of a military ship, a two-place combat. This girl, who was quite pretty and beneath all her airport manner quite feminine, had cut that out and kept it, not because one of the two men whose heads were barely visible in the cockpit was anything to her, but because she wanted the ship. She wanted it as another woman might have wanted a fur coat, she wanted to be in it and feel it and be seen in it, and meanwhile in her diary she did a sort of window-shopping. Or perhaps she even had that picture the way another woman might have the picture of a man. I thought that some of her capacity for loving had been deflected onto airplanes, and I could very well understand how that could be.

We decided to team up.

"I can navigate you into any position you want," I said.

"I can land you in any hayfield anyone can land in," she said.

By solemn agreement we split up the responsibilities and also the way in which we would book the Time in our log books. Outward bound, she would have the controls; homeward bound, I would have the controls. Navigation was to be my final responsibility, though, on all flights; maneuvering was hers. Thus, in case of engine failure, or of some other emergency landing, I was to give the controls up to her, even if it occurred during my spell of piloting; in case of crises concerning weather, navigation, altitude, or our flight plans, I had the say.

We were an efficient crew, and we had no fights.

In the course of that fall, before our team was broken up, we managed to cover the whole Middle West, in weekend flights along routes determined by a geography of convention: we had to pick overnight stops where the girl had suitable aunts.

Our ship had a long narrow cabin, broad enough only for one's shoulders; we sat in tandem, the pilot in front, the navigator in the rear though both were provided with a set of controls.

I admit that on one recurrent occasion the arrangement grated a bit on my sense of he-manhood—those times on Saturday afternoons, when we taxied out to the take-off, past the administration building fence which at that time was crowded with spectators. The girl sat proudly high up in the nose, craning her neck right and left out of the windows (the way a careful pilot will while taxiing), while the man sat meekly and useless deep down in the back, leafing through his maps and tables, and feeling like a nephew being taken for a ride.

But in the air, there was nothing wrong with the arrangement. Having a woman in the ship did not spoil the flying. It might have been different had we been climbing mountains. There, you use your own strength, and sometimes, to some extent, you risk your own life, and being tied up with a lady usually tones things down. But in flying, you are not allowed to risk your ship. It is an axiom, at least in civilian flying, that no mission can possibly be important enough to risk a ship; a pilot's first duty is to his ship, just as a sea captain's. And a ship must be treated like a lady, only more so.

Thus when we sat out the long hours high above the country, we were both happy.

It was the first time I had ever flown a cabin ship; the first time I had ever flown in ordinary clothes without helmet and goggles. Contrary to what one might think, a cabin ship gives you more air and more vision than an open cockpit one, where you are sitting surrounded by metal cowling up to your ears, and when often the smells from the engine are sucked in to bother you.

We sat under the wing, and, as I have said before, in tandem; that is perhaps the best arrangement for vision in a small or medium airplane. In turns, when you banked, the inner wing comes down and blots out your vision of the very sector of space into which you are flying; but on a cross-country trip, you make no turns, and thus we sat over the country like on an ordinary chair standing on a carpet.

On outbound flights Ellen sat before me, beautifully relaxed, steering the course and the altitude which I figured for her, watching the ship and the country with a motherly sort of delight.

Years later, I found in the pocket of an old coat a batch of the slips of paper on which we wrote messages back and forth, and there is a note from her hand saying "Pretty country." That one was for the Indian summer in Wisconsin, which was turning the ground more colorful every week. There is another note saying "Pretty country." That one was for the fields of South Dakota: they were flat and large and many of them harvested; you could see the characteristic diagonal patterns and parts and cowlicks that the harvesting machines leave on the stubbles—and any field which is flat and hard and large enough for harvesting machines is good for landings.

There is another note: "When you lean forward I can feel the C.G. shifting. Do it again."

The "C.G." means the ship's center of gravity; whenever it shifts, even by inches, the ship noses up or down a bit and seeks a new balance; it was a simple physical action but she was as delighted with the feel of the ship, its balance, its stability as a mother might be in her baby's first talking. When the ship wallowed through a bump, she would turn around and smilingly imitate its wallow with a motion of her flat hand.

Meanwhile I watched over her and over our flight. "Don't worry," says one of my notes; and another one says in her writing, "This stuff going to make trouble?"

That was at three thousand feet on the way back from Detroit when a layer of clouds slid in between us and the earth like a stage curtain, cutting off our view of the ground, except for holes; it slid away again ten minutes later.

"Don't think so. But if so, emergency field Coldwater now bearing 73°, distance 12 minutes, located on E shore small lake. Stay on top for time being."

I liked that experience of doing navigation without having to bother with the controls. It allowed to come out pure and unhampered that part of flying which goes on in a pilot's brain (or which ought to go on there, anyway) while his nervous reflexes steer the ship. What that part is like I should like to explain this way: it is like watching a cageful of lions, all of whom you must stare down, none of whom you must ever let sneak up within pouncing distance, let alone pounce.

The weather for instance, not only where you are, but also at your destination; and then also at the spots to which you might have to run if it should turn bad at your destination. And your engine, both of its ignition systems, its temperature—to catch the first signs of trouble early. You watch the ground, quite apart from all navigation, you keep in mind that you might have to land. Then there is the wind, your drift, and the effects of your wind via speed, or gasoline range; and your gasoline; your speed, and your range. You don't want to run out of gasoline in the air—not even if your destination fogs in and you have to beat back to some other airport against the wind. Your navigation again: if there should be a mistake in it, if at the proper time your destination should not turn up, what are you going to do? Have you the fuel on which to do it?

In this game, which most of the time is pure hypothesis, the trick lies in never letting one lion gang up with any other lion. For that is how the dangers of the air actually work: when you are low on fuel and then the wind shifts; when your destination fogs in—and then your alternate landing field happens to be flooded by a river; when

the weather turns bad and forces you to fly low—and then your
navigation has been off and you can't find the airport; when your
engine starts skipping—and then you don't know which way the
nearest airport bears.

On homeward-bound flights, Ellen sat behind me, doing navigation. As I had bossed her in navigation, she now bossed me in piloting. "You keep carrying the ball on the left side." That referred to
the bank indicator; I was holding the left wing a shade low. Most of
the time, though, she didn't work through slips of paper, because
there was no time, but through auntly slaps of the fingers, admin-
istered via the dual controls.

On almost every take-off, I could feel in my pedals the impatient
taps of her right foot. That was for my tendency to give the ship its
head immediately after take-off, and if you do that, the full-power
pull of the propeller puts it into a left turn, and you climb away along
a crooked line. There is nothing dangerous about it, but it is not
considered good style—and on a much later occasion it was too
important to me. . . .

And when we would once more be back in familiar territory—
where navigation was not important because we simply knew our
way—she would sleep. The rear seat was windier than the front seat;
she would take an old blanket which served as seat-cushion and
wrap it around her head and shoulder, until she looked like a Dutch
peasant girl. I once sent her a note saying that this was a hell of a
way to treat Flying Time; but she wrote back that it was so wonderful
to wake up again and find you were in an airplane, and had I ever
done it?

You could duplicate a large part of our experience simply by sitting
down in a boiler factory, with a piece of paper on your knee, and
doing a series of geometry problems involving speeds and distances,
compass headings and variations, angles of drift and elapsed times—
and that item out of your physics classes which you may remember
as the "triangle of velocities." That was the part of our experience
which had to do with dead reckoning and with navigation as it
should be done.

That doesn't mean it was dull. Don't forget you can have a lot of fun working out puzzles with paper and pencil. One of my notes to her in flight said: "Stop ask qu. Mk. up mind steer 315° and I give you Minnap. 51 min."

That was when she had been so bold as to doubt my brainwork. And you can bet it was fun not even to look (except maybe on the sly, when I could be sure she wasn't watching me in her rear-vision mirror) and then fifty-one minutes later to look down and point at the Airport served to her right under her nose.

We worked out some of the more ambitious problems in navigation. "Where the h. are we?" writes Ellen.

"Don't know, don't want to know till 4.30," is in my writing. That was the time when we executed problem 51 of the navigation text-book: to lose yourself, and to find yourself again. You fly for a while on all sorts of compass headings without paying attention to land-marks, and then when you are thoroughly lost, you dead-reckon your position from all the courses you have steered since your last known position; and from that dead-reckoned position, you then set a new course to your destination. I had done that, and at 4.30 I handed word forward, "Steer 128° for 37 min: Madison, I'd like coffee."

The trouble with that one was that after steering 128° for 37 minutes Madison, Wisconsin, failed to turn up. Visibility was about twelve miles that day, light heat haze; I asked for five thousand feet altitude and after fifty minutes it was still not to be seen nor that constellation of lakes by which it can be located from afar, even through haze.

I was thoroughly lost. Ellen sat up forward keeping up her good work with the stick, but glumly waiting. One tank was dry, the other more than half dry; we could fly for one more hour at most, and below, the country was both rough and wooded, tough to have to land in. Something had to be done.

"Take off yr. hat," wrote Ellen, nastily.

That referred to a story which was being told at airport cafés about two Englishmen, one of them a pilot-instructor, the other a student-navigator, flying somewhere over England. They were doing this same problem of losing oneself on purpose and then dead-reckoning one's position. "All right, where are we?" asked the instructor, and the student went to work with pencil, paper, and protractor. After ten minutes, came the solution: "Take off your hat. We are in St. Paul's Cathedral."

Something had to be done in a hurry, but what?

There is usually some course which will get you out of such a predicament, and usually only one; to find it is a matter of pure reasoning. There was an airport café story about that, too. A pilot had flown to Florida above the clouds. When he came down, intending to land at Tampa, he could see nothing but waves: the Gulf of Mexico. He turned east in a hurry to pick up the shore and then follow it to Tampa. He flew east for a while over the waves when suddenly it occurred to him that this water could possibly be the Atlantic Ocean; if so, he was now flying away from land. That pilot used his head. He saw that his best chance was to fly north, which was the only course that would lead him to shore from either sea. He made his land fall on the Georgia coast: it had been the Atlantic.

That was the kind of reasoning I now did, involving a double-track railroad, the beaches of Lake Michigan, and my textbook's proposition that it is better to be *lost* over good country than to be *found* over bad. We came out at Lake Forest, Illinois, with our tank almost dry. The mechanic who refueled us marveled at the number of gallons she took.

"You planned that one right on the nose," he said.

"Yes, I rather go in for precision," I said airily, since Ellen was not around.

1. Langewiesche's Cub on the Great Salt Lake Desert in western Utah. While this broad lake bed is an easy place to land a balloon-tired aircraft, the pilot may find it difficult get the machine into the air again should the tires sink into the mud or the hand-propped engine fail to start. And from the center of this desert, it's simply too far to walk to safety without water.

2. I passed over the remains of a shipwreck. She was high and dry on the beach, a sailing vessel, her masts gone, her hatches open, but her black hull intact.
Near Cape Hatteras, North Carolina; note Cub tire at bottom of frame.

3. Then suddenly I had arrived. Ahead of me on the beach there was a light-house, marked as the charts had said Hatteras lighthouse would be marked, with a spiral ribbon of paint.

The Cape Hatteras lighthouse crew helps secure the Cub against Atlantic winds.

4. If from an airplane the world looks like a map, that doesn't speak against the airplane, it speaks for the mapmakers.
Sinuous bends and oxbow lakes of a slow river somewhere in the Midwest reflect the curved lines of nature.

5. *What was sliding by under me, with a rumble and a roar, was not spectacular; it was just ordinary Middle West. There was a fence line, and I slide across it, without a jar: straight across lots. A house, and its backyard, and a woman hanging up the wash.*

The straight lines and right angles of the Jeffersonian grid control some 69 percent of the U.S. landscape and are especially evident here in the Midwest.

6. *I took everything to the airport in a taxi, and stowed it into the front seat of the Cub, strapping it well down. Then I took off.*

A bedroll, extra fuel and oil, simple tools, minimal luggage, and an overcoat composed Langewiesche's meager travel outfit, limited by the weight considerations of the Cub and the high mountains in the West.

7. Langewiesche's Cub climbs toward a snowcapped high ridge in the distance somewhere out West. The altimeter appears to read 5,300 feet.

8. A newly engineered and recently paved highway (today it's Nevada 341) conforms to the landscape just north of Virginia City, Nevada.

9. From above and at certain sun angles, forests like this one near Lake Tahoe seem no longer to be made of individual trees, even losing the shape of trees to become a study in texture.

10. "SL–O–8" identifies emergency field number eight on the old transcontinental airway segment between Salt Lake City and Omaha. Reliable aircraft, improved poor weather navigation, and high-altitude flight long ago rendered such fields obsolete. There is no airfield here today at this place known as Leroy, Wyoming, just off Interstate 80 between Fort Bridger and Evanston.

11. Wild horses in the Nevada desert bolt as Langewiesche slips down for a closer look.

12. *So, deep in the twentieth century, air age and all, you personally met this continent: its mountains, plains, rivers.*
Location unknown

13. Virginia City, Nevada, post-mining boom, pre-tourist boom

14. A grand estate somewhere in the West

15. Above Norden, California, just west of Donner Pass: U.S. 40 (*center*); the snowsheds of the Southern Pacific Railroad (*left*). This is a route of the California Trail, the route of the first transcontinental railroad and the Lincoln Highway.

16. Wolfgang Langewiesche and the Cub, circa 1939

8. Pilot's-eye View

Another part of our experience you could not duplicate in any way except by flying. But to understand what that was about, you might take a real estate man to a pretty lake, or an infantry officer to some mountain village, and let them explain what they would do in a professional way with that particular bit of country. What those thirty hours of experience gave us was the pilot's peculiar slant on the country: seeing it as an expanse which lies between point A and point B, and across which you must pick your way; a landscape whose purpose it is to provide emergency landing fields and landmarks by which to steer.

For our flying was seldom purely dead reckoning. Navigation in the air is not like that on the sea. At sea, the currents are known and charted, and by plotting the courses he has steered and the drift he has suffered from the currents, a navigator can reckon his position with great precision. In air navigation, the winds are the currents; but the winds are forever shifting, and thus one must take a look at the ground to check one's drift. One can, of course, get a fairly accurate picture of the winds for that particular part of that particular day; at the weather bureau they keep track of air conditions all over the country, and with reports from airliners in flight and from special weather patrol flights and from special balloons they know all the different air masses that keep stalking around over America and getting into dogfights with each other. They have them named and labeled and keep track of every one of them.

Thus, before one took off from the Metropolitan Airport, one could drop in at the weather bureau and get the latest "Winds Aloft."

One got them over the counter like pullman tickets. The weather bureau's interior arrangement was like that of a travel agency. One went in and said, "Good morning, Charlie, how about a tail wind to Saint Louis this morning?" And Charlie would lay out his Winds Aloft maps on the counter before you and point with his pencil: "Well, Red, we've got a twenty-mile-an-hour quartering tail wind at eight thousand feet." "That's a little high. I would waste more time through a climb than I could save through the tail wind. Haven't you got anything around two or three thousand feet?" "At three thousand feet, there is a cross wind, ten miles an hour. But, if you want to wait for it, I could let you have one right on your tail late this afternoon, I think," he would say, leafing through the sheaf of Six Hour and Twelve Hour Forecasts. "She is bound to shift around five o'clock." "Oh, she will, will she?" "Yes, sir, you are going to run into a cold front somewhere along the way. It was at Des Moines, Iowa, at eight this morning and will be here at five." And so forth. You came away with a slip of paper listing all the winds at all altitudes, both for the present and for the next few hours. But an element of uncertainty still remained.

If you fly for three hours in a cross wind which is only five m.p.h. faster than you think, you are going to be fifteen miles off-course and out of sight of your objective.

Therefore, in flights, one still needed a check on one's dead reckoning. The big fellows got theirs by radio; but the small ships at that time couldn't carry radio sets so easily from a weight standpoint and also from a financial standpoint. The small fellow kept his map on his knee and every once in a while he compared landmarks.

Thus, on all those flights, you could never look at the country with the mild benevolence of a tourist; you looked at it the way a golfer looks at a golf course. You looked at it first of all as a possible landing ground—all the time, without even consciously thinking about it, you were picking out flat open spaces. And secondly, you looked at it for landmarks.

One trouble with landmarks is that half the time you can't see them because of haze or mist or smoke. A day with visibility of three miles is still considered all right to fly, but three miles takes even a slow ship only two minutes, and the pilot on such a day therefore has less of a view ahead than a pedestrian on a foggy day.

A visibility of ten miles is fine, and anything over twenty is unusual; yet at an altitude of five thousand feet, your horizon, the ultimate limit of possible vision, is actually eighty miles away. Therefore, a pilot can seldom "raise" his landmark, i.e., see it come up over the horizon the way lighthouses do for ships. You may be flying within the city limits of Chicago or New York and see no skyscrapers; then suddenly they will stand before you full-sized, like ghosts materialized out of nothing, and give you a scare. On a day with little wind, even a small mill town will throw up so much smoke that you have to cross over it on instruments because you can't see anything beyond your wing tip. Sometimes parts of your own ship cover up the landmark you need. One January afternoon, I was flying through rain at two thousand feet, looking down over the left side, watching for a certain town that was to give me a fix from which to steer for an airport. Elapsed time showed it must be near, but it didn't come. I showed it to my passenger on the map, and drew a question mark. She promptly pointed down at the right and there it lay, right under us, a whole not-so-small town, neon signs already lighted, main street crowded with automobiles; so much warm and comfortable life, and yet almost lost in the misty gloom.

Another trouble with landmarks is that the ones that count most on the ground count least from the air.

Hills are no good; they flatten out under you. Once I took off from some airport, climbed to one thousand feet, and shoved off on my course. I sailed peacefully through the blue, my eyes on the compass, my mind who knows where. When I looked out again, there was a farmer with a team of horses right below my wing, plowing his field at an altitude of eight hundred feet. That is how hills can sneak up under you.

Culture is no good. Culture is what cartographers call the works of man, particularly his roads and his settlements. Roads are useless because there are too many of them, cities and towns are no good because they are too much alike. They are worst in the Middle West. There, every town has its high school, usually the biggest building in sight; every county seat has its capitol-like court house. It shows a spectacular belief in self-government and in human betterment through education, but if you drop out of some clouds and want to know where you are, it is merely annoying.

Remember, there are no cops to ask and there are no signs. What that means the terrestrian can hardly imagine; most of us don't even notice any more how much our landscape consists of inscriptions, signposts, signals, pointers, arrows, etc. Ellen herself, surprisingly enough, discovered and formulated that for me. After twenty hours of flying cross-country it stood out for her as the main difference between flying and other modes of travel. No inscriptions; nobody explaining to you what's what and what to buy and where to go next. No billboard to tell you that this is the Wisconsin Switzerland, or the Ohio Côte d'Azur. Just stark blunt country with no talky-talk.

Once I thought I saw an exception. It was on our first landing at North Beach Airport, New York City. It was my turn to do the piloting, and I always circle distrustfully a few times around a strange field, just like a cat around strange food, to look it over. I noticed a line of big red letters flat on the ground. I had to spell it out upside down but it said unmistakably: "Clear heads. . . ." And it was unmistakably meant to be read from up here.

Fine new idea, I thought, giving visiting pilots landing instructions that way. But: "heads"? North Beach is surrounded on three sides by the water of Long Island Sound. What they must mean, I figured, was to circle outside of certain heads of land projecting pierlike into the water. Obediently I went around once more in a wide circle, clearing everything. This time I saw, now right side up, "Clear Heads Demand MacIntosh Whisky." An advertisement! And right on the landing area! I closed the throttle and cut right across the field, which is very bad airport manners. Have we come to that, I thought, ads to confuse you just when you need your head for making your approach? And liquor at that! Then I had to mind my landing. When I looked again, I saw my ad now being dragged through the sky by an autogiro. They had merely been laying out their banner on the ground, a couple of poor fellow flyers trying to make a living off the air.

Another exception is airmarking. More and more Chambers of Commerce or American Legion posts paint their town's name in standard yellow on some prominent roof. But these signs are just like cops. I've never seen one when I needed one.

That leaves as the most helpful landmarks in U.S. culture some odd little things so small they cannot be drawn on the maps and so varied they cannot be represented by symbols but have to be described by small-print legends. Aeronautical maps are sprinkled with them. If you ever see someone circling over your neighborhood in thick weather, you can bet that he is looking frantically for some such thing as "large silver ball," "traffic circle," "seven smokestacks," "stand pipe, 100 ft.," "promnt. bldg.," "race track," "lumber mill," "abandoned derrick," "dam & power sta.," or "slag piles."

In the landscape and on the map, there are four things that one can really fly by: railroads, rivers, high tension lines, and section lines. Each has a personality of its own.

A railroad track is never obtrusive. It is dark and narrow, and you can see it only when you are right above it, never sideways from a distance. On a clear day, hopping from city to city you can kid yourself that you are proceeding entirely by dead reckoning as an ambitious navigator should; and yet be subtly reassured by a railroad track that trots along, now under your right wing tip, now under your left one—much like a stray poodle, nice to have around but not important. But in thick weather no one is ashamed to come down low and follow the track around every curve and bend. Riding the railroad, or the Iron Compass, pilots call that. Of course you must hope that you are following the right track, and you usually are; there are not so many railroad lines as to be confusing. Unlike rivers, or high tension lines, all railroads finally lead to a big town and the big town may have an airport. Besides, they have stations with names written on them, and if worst comes to worst and you are lost,

you can circle low and read the name. At least you can try; it probably won't help but it will make you feel better than just barging
around all tightened up with worry.

Rivers are different. They shine from far away. Water reflects the
light, and you can see bodies of water through haze or darkness that
swallows up everything else. Rivers have characteristic bends and
shapes and are easily identified. They usually lead from rough country into smoother country and that may be helpful if you are lost and
low on fuel. Finally, over rough country there is sometimes the
thought that you could always set her down in the river with no
injury to your passengers and little damage to your ship—better at
any rate than on top of a forest.

A high tension line is not quite comfortable to ride. It is likely to
run straighter than a railroad but that means it goes across mountains and forests regardless of your comfort in case of a forced landing. And it is harder to keep track of. Through forests it shows up as a
long cleared strip, but over open country you have to pick out the
steel masts themselves and they are more like marching ghosts, only
half visible, half transparent skeletons; also, like ghosts, they are
likely to lead you somewhere into the hills and there to disappear,
leaving you puzzled.

Section lines you find all over the United States, except along the
Eastern seaboard. Yet the terrestrial public hardly knows of them,
except perhaps in the shape of long straight country roads that run
exactly north-south or east-west and of straight neat fence lines. To a
flyer they are the most visible feature of the landscape. From the
Alleghenies to the Pacific, they divide up the country into blocks one
square mile each; and each line is an avenue that runs straight from
horizon to horizon.

These lines don't lead anywhere; but they do keep you straightened out better than the steadiest compass. They have no variation,
no deviation, no northerly turning error, no overswing, no oscillations. They point out true north, east, south, and west all the time.
Also, they convert the land below you into a paper graph that makes
your navigation very exact. You can time your shadow with the second hand of a watch as it crosses line after line, and calculate your

ground speed. You can calculate that your compass course of 315°
will take you one section west for every section north.

Just a line, and it is hard to say what it consists of. Originally, of
course, it was a pencil line drawn on the map of a government desk
in Washington back in the early nineteenth century. The surveyors
went out and marked them on the ground to divide up the new land
for settlers who were yet to come. And now? Once I swung off my
course, went low, and followed a section line straight South through
Middle Western farm country just to find out.

First it was a dirt road, narrow between two hedges, with a car
crawling along it dragging a tail of dust. Then the road turned off,
but the line went straight ahead, now as a barbed wire fence through
a large pasture, with a thin footpath trod out on each side by each
neighbor as he went, week after week, year after year, to inspect his
fence. Then the fence stopped, but now there was corn on one side
of the line and something green on the other. Next it was a narrow
dirt road again with farms on either side, and then suddenly, a broad
highway came curving in, followed the line for a mile, and curved
away again. For a short stretch it didn't consist of anything, but the
grass, for some reason, was a little greener on one side and a little
more yellow on the other. Was it because one owner was in the grace
and the other was not? Again it was a hedge until it broadened and
became a road, dignified itself and became for a few blocks the main
street of a small town, filled with parked cars; people stepped out of
stores to look up at me. Then it thinned out again. When I climbed
away and resumed my course, I left it as a fence which had cows on
one side and no cows on the other. That's a section line.

Rivers, railroads, high tension lines, and section lines—such
things are company in a way, but even they are tricky company. You
can't ever leave your wits on the ground, not even if you plan to ride
a railroad: the tracks are likely to split in two under you. Then, if you
are perhaps trustingly sitting on your map, and have to get it out and
unfold it with one hand while flying with the other, you will be far
along on the wrong track before you can help it. Or it may happen in
thick weather that your selected track suddenly disappears in a little
black hole in the earth and leaves you up in the air, if you are lucky; if

you are not, it leaves you pancaked on a mountainside. And rivers: one day I followed one out of New England trying to get home through the hills under very low ceilings. The air was thick with rain and mist. I could see bridges far enough ahead, and so I felt safe; it stands to reason that you can't run into hills or radio towers or factory chimneys while you hang over the water. I came out at Long Island Sound, and followed the shore line home. In the hangar I showed one of the old timers proudly on my map how I had done it and come through. He answered nothing, but he tapped with his finger on the margin of the map, and I read:

"Caution: when flying during low visibility, airmen are cautioned as to the existence of high tension wires crossing many rivers shown on this chart."

So you see—

Once we came home from a week's cross-country flight and Ellen's aunt was at the Airport with a car and asked, "Was it beautiful?" I thought of all the land I have flown over, whole kingdoms every few hours, kingdoms glimpsed through clouds, kingdoms flat in the sun—I thought of all that, and found that the best one could say for it is, "Well, we negotiated it successfully."

As far as I was aware, Ellen had no beau all this time. She probably scared them off. A fellow would have had to be quite a fellow before he could go around with an L.C. and not feel bothered in his ego.

One day she told me that a new pilot had come to the field. There was a peculiar ring in her voice, but that it was an attack of love, I never understood until long afterwards. What she told me was merely that there was a new man now, and that he had the most marvelous— Well, you know what one might expect to hear in such a case; but what she said was that he had the most marvelous inverted fuel system. His engine kept running even while the ship was upside down—when ordinary engines quit after a second or two.

The new man was a professional stunt pilot. He performed acrobatics at airshows, and between shows he also picked up money as an itinerant teacher of acrobatics, at twenty dollars an hour, staying a few weeks at one airport.

He was a man and a half, with a huge body and huge face and a bearing that made a man want to address him as Major.

Ellen went in for his art full out. She had begged some more money from an aunt, and she went up with him dual several times a week, at a special rate, I suppose.

"You know I love to take a ship up and kick it around," she said to me. "Not rough like, you know, but nice." She added, *"precision-ally,"* and she made a gesture with hands and hips that only a pilot could understand—half of it was a pilot kicking a ship around, and half of it was meant to be the ship itself, rolling over.

The stunt-man kept his ship in hangar 5. Once after one of their flights together, while Ellen was lugging back her rented parachute to Miller and Johnson, I asked him what he thought of our girl flier. He seemed rather eager to talk about her, and especially about her hair: blond hair, bobbed medium long. He liked her hair, he said, and he was thinking of teaming up with her. He might teach her upside-down flying and might have her fly upside-down at county fairs, a few feet above the ground past the grandstand, with that blond hair streaming out behind her in the wind. He thought the customers would eat that up.

One evening when I came to the hangar, George was standing there and looking up; almost everybody else was looking up. Word had gone 'round that Ellen was up solo in the stunt ship, and she was going to do an inverted spin: a tailspin done while the ship is upside down and the pilot is hanging against the safety belt.

So I stood with him and watched. She started at about five thousand feet, high up in the evening sun. She went up into the first half of a loop, and straightened out on her back, wheels pointed at the sky and the yellow topsides of the wings shining down. The ship was a special paint job: black bottom sides, yellow top sides, so that the pay customer could readily follow its rolls and loops. She shut her power off and pulled her nose up to stall the ship; and one could see her kick the tail around, to give it that twist which starts the spinning. She capsized over and started coming down, whipping around as she went, the nose pointing down at forty-five degrees or so.

Everybody counted the turns:

One—

Two—

A tailspin is not a simple fall; it is slower. She was approaching the ground at the rate of perhaps ninety m.p.h., twisting down in a corkscrew pattern.

Three—it was about time she came out of it.

It is bad policy, even in stunt flying, even in show flying, to have no margin of safety, some excess height, or some excess speed, or both. The only way to get out of a spin is to dive the ship, and that dive uses up a lot of height.

One could hear her give small bursts of power; but whether that was to keep the ship in the spin or to get it out I couldn't tell. She was doing a twist about every six seconds. She was losing about seven hundred and fifty feet a twist, but from below, looking up, one couldn't see that; one could only see the spinning of the ship, and its glistening in the sun every few seconds, and how it gradually became larger.

Four—

My heart began pounding. She was shaving it so closely; she should have come out after three turns or so. But she didn't. She must be getting confused from all that turning. She was doing number five. I could see now her head in the dark hole of the cockpit; she was not wearing her usual flying helmet, which was chocolate-colored and grease-spattered, but a white one that looked pretty. She went right on twisting after my heart began to pound, still headed down at forty-five degrees.

I didn't know what it was I was seeing—a stenographer coming to grief in a hired airplane, or a flier, trying as all fliers must, a thing that was beyond her personal limits, or a woman doing a dance to please a man.

Six—

When she went into the sixth turn everybody stopped counting. Someone said, "Come on now, jump." I felt exceedingly angry. I thought that I knew by that time how her mind worked. To recover from an inverted tailspin, like all upside-down flying, is a task much like writing with your left hand, or like writing mirror-script with your right hand, or like crossing a street in a country where traffic keeps to the left—you have to do the right thing the wrong way. To throw the airplane into the recovery dive she must handle the stick in opposite sense to right-side-up flight, not pushing it forward but pulling it back, which in right-side-up flight would have been the one sure way to lock the airplane into the spin for good. It was easy enough to think all this out on the ground; but thinking is slow in the air, and I knew that this type of reasoning came hard to her, just as navigational reasoning did.

Half a turn later, horribly late, she began to recover. She succeeded in stopping the turn and went into a straight dive, first nosing down at about seventy degrees, then vertically. As if coming out of a loop, she was beginning to pull out right side up, but still pointing almost straight down, when she hit the ground.

The front of the ship crumpled, and the wings cracked and folded backwards, and thus the ship stood on its head, for a moment quite like an arrow that has been shot into a tree and quivers. It was a quarter mile beyond the airport fence. Everybody started running, but there was a bit of smoke, and a slight sound saying "P!" Out of that broke a high yellow flame which kept burning for almost half an hour while the sirens howled.

9. Neurosis in Miniature

Soon after that, I contracted aero-neurosis. Aero-neurosis is a form of "industrial fatigue," the special form that gets airmen. Sometimes one hears of a pilot who has had to stop flying, not because he has grown too old and slow, or because his physical condition is no longer good enough, but because he is somehow "used up." Aero-neurosis is the way he has broken.

It is a type of nervous trouble, brought on by that constant preoccupation with possible emergencies which makes a pilot safe. A pilot must maintain in his mind the proper attitude in regard to the dangers of the air—neither forget them, nor let them scare him. When a pilot does too much flying, or flying which is more risky than suits him, or if he flies ships which are too hot for his piloting ability, something in him tires and he can no longer look at all the possible dangers in a cool and hypothetical fashion. Instead, he starts looking the other way; in that case he is bound to run into a whole string of troubles: mishaps, scares, crack-ups; he also is likely to talk a lot about luck without actually quite trusting it; and to drink a lot; for he knows the air is not to be fooled with. Or else he begins really to *mean* it, as it were. Instead of merely keeping in mind that the engine might quit, he thinks it really will; instead of merely keeping a couple of navigational emergency exits open in case his intended airport should fog in, he thinks it probably is fogged in already. Then in order to keep on flying, he tries to suppress his fears; and after a while, his nerves revolt.

My own case was mild—as all my flying has been mild; I am, as I have said before, no big-time flier, but just an ordinary person who likes to take an airplane up once in a while. I wouldn't even have noticed it if I hadn't been so interested in all sides of flying, even the nervous one, and I wouldn't report it if I didn't think it interesting as a miniature sketch of the real thing.

What brought on my case, was that I found a very old ship that was in bad maintenance but very cheap to rent. I had come out of our cross-country flying with some debts; and so I took it up. I decided to practice tailspins and recovery from tailspins on it, but it would not straighten out when given the usual control helps, but only through a frantic, more-than-vertical dive, in which only the safety belt kept me from being catapulted out into space. That was because it was in such bad condition that its wings had actually lost their shape. But I did not know that. I flew it first because it was cheap; and then I persisted in flying it and spinning it again and again because I thought its sluggish recovery was my own fault. It was finally grounded by the inspectors, along with other ships of its make and year, even while I was flying it: I taxied back to the hangar one morning, and the owner walked up to show me the letter from Washington.

By that time, I had my little aero-neurosis, and here are the symptoms.

My timing was bad and hasty and my work on the controls had become jerky and unrhythmical, especially my foot action. The only way in which I could fly nicely was to sing while maneuvering; "Parlez-Moi d'Amour" was the most effective.

One day, flying George's Travelair again, I found my attention suddenly fixed on the struts and wires that hold the wings; how flimsy they really were and how it would be if they came off, and the bottom dropped out from under me—which was unreasonable, for wings simply do not come off.

I lost confidence in the power of flowing air which is what holds

an airplane up. In dreams, I often had the feeling that I was stalling—that unmistakable feeling that you get when you slow up an
airplane beyond the critical point. When the wings lose their grip on
the air and begin to feel like legs that have gone to sleep, numb and
useless, and then they buckle—not actually, but it feels as if they did,
and the ship falls off forward and unless there is altitude below you,
it falls onto the ground.

Another dream involved the code in which weather reports come
in over the teletype. In this dream I was returning from a cross-
country flight but was unable to land because of:

Light rain—moderate rain—heavy rain—light snow—moderate
snow—heavy snow—light freezing rain—moderate freezing rain—
sprinkling—light mist—heavy mist—light fog—moderate fog—dense
fog—light ground fog—moderate ground fog—dense ground fog—
hazy—thick haze—smoky—thick smoke—dusty—thick dust—blowing snow—thick blowing snow—blowing dust—thick blowing dust—
blowing sand—thick blowing sand—light ice fog—moderate ice
fog—dense ice fog—light freezing mist—heavy freezing mist—light
sleet—moderate sleet—heavy sleet—light hail—moderate hail—
heavy hail—mild thunderstorm—moderate thunderstorm—severe
thunderstorm—hurricane.

In automobiles I had a sense of relief, and sometimes I actually
thought the way to travel might be on wheels, after all. In a car,
control seemed so steel hard and positive, and you could slow down
with never any fear that she might drop out from under you.

I felt unreasonable annoyance at the smell of motor exhaust, even
if it was only an automobile's; or the sound of airplanes, even if they
were only airliners which didn't concern me.

The same with heights. Heights made me feel listless and sad,
even quite modest ones. I remember walking in the park with some
girl and all of a sudden turning gloomy, merely—I discovered afterwards, upon thinking about it—because she chose to take a path
which crossed a stream on a high-slung Japanese garden bridge.

But the oddest thing was that it made me uncomfortable to see
any object fall; even a ball. Walking across the campus, I once saw a
fellow throw a raincoat out of a fourth floor dormitory window, down

to another fellow on the lawn. That seemed to me an act of utmost barbaric crudeness and a personal threat; for the arms of the coat were flapping and it looked altogether too much like a human body coming down.

I decided to do something about it.

First, following one set of advisers, I took a couple of weeks' rest from flying and the Airport. Then, following the other set of advisers, I took a delayed-opening parachute jump.

My old friends, Miller and Johnson, prepared the parachutes. But of my intention to delay the pulling of the ripcord, I did not dare tell them. I was a bit awed by it myself.

Though this was to be my second jump, it came harder than the first one; curiosity was gone, but all the worries were still left. Would I get clear the ship, or lose my nerve and pull right away, and catch in the tail surfaces? Would the 'chute, in opening after a long delay, tangle with my feet? Or would the harness tear under the opening shock? I now had much respect for the landing itself; I thought of all the places where I might land; pointed and sharp ones, or perhaps live wires, or the river. Least reasonable worry and yet uppermost: Would the 'chute open properly? And if it didn't, how much time would there be to think, and what would I think?

When I reported on the appointed day, Johnson was out. Miller had my equipment still on the workbench, where he was checking it for the last time.

His assistant was frying hamburgers for lunch. The heat was good, and so was the smell. Outside, it was late autumn. The ceiling was four thousand feet, a solid overcast; the wind was N.E. 12, and it was chilly. Not an inviting day to go falling through the sky.

Was I asking for trouble?

Miller himself had given up jumping years ago. He now spent his life firmly on the ground, servicing other people's parachutes, trading in parachutes, patching and cleaning and folding parachutes; a tailor instead of an airman. Was that his final judgment on parachutes?

"How often, would you guess, can a man jump before it will get him?"

To that type of question most flying men have two answers. One answer is that everything is now under full control, that we have now achieved real mastery of the air. That is the answer you give to cash customers. The other you give to yourself sometimes, and always to the girl you want to impress:

"It is all a chance. When she is ready to hit, she will hit."

But the rigger, wise old bird, had a different point of view. Even parachute jumping, he said, was all right and reasonably safe nowadays, provided you kept your wits about you, and used only good 'chutes packed by reputable riggers like himself—after all he charged only three dollars for a repacking job—and as long as you observed the law that two 'chutes must be worn on intentional jumps. But the trouble with the parachute-jumping public, as he put it, was that they got used to it and became careless and sloppy. "Then," he added, "it is sure to kill fast."

He snapped and tested one after another the rubber cords that were to tear open the canvas bag and spill out the silk, once the latch was ripped out.

"And don't fool yourself," he said, "that you are an exception and will remain careful; because you won't."

He was right about that in a way. Instead of a straight baling-out, I wanted to make this a delayed-opening jump. The idea is to let yourself fall, hand on ripcord ring, for a thousand feet or so, and only then to rip. It wouldn't have taken much to discourage me, on this cool, gray morning, but I didn't want to be discouraged. So I put it to him gently. I said I had arranged this time to be dumped from a little higher up, because I wanted to hold it a little longer, and that might be easier to do with a little more altitude below.

"All right," he said, somewhat to my surprise. As a matter of fact, and quite frankly, last time I had pulled too damned soon, and it might be wise to learn to hold it a little longer. From below it had looked as if my 'chute had just barely cleared the ship's tail.

I knew that. Last time I had ripped not when it seemed best but when my nerves had ripped—at the exact moment when the fear of tangling in the tail had been overpowered by the horror and confusion of the bottomless drop. This time, I must try for absolute nerve control.

The rigger put the finishing touch to his job. With indelible ink he signed his name and the date on a white cloth label sewn to the pack. This is a licensed rigger's guarantee that a parachute has been opened, inspected, refolded, and repacked within sixty days preceding flight, as the law demands; that it will work. Then he handed it to me for my inspection. I handed it back, and he cracked the standard joke of the occasion:

"If it doesn't work, bring it back and we'll refund your money."

Miller phoned to town for the pilot to come out: this guy was here now and wanted to jump. The mechanics still had considerable fixing to do on the old biplane and its World War engine before it would fly. Meanwhile, there was nothing for me to do but to stand around on the field and wait.

Hard on the nerves, because it gives you time to think, and you can't help calculating your chances. The speed of a man falling through the air is one hundred and twenty miles per hour; faster than that he won't fall, because of air resistance, but that is fast enough. It would give me three seconds for every five hundred feet. It would take keen timing not to pancake.

I didn't feel like talking, but a reporter came and questioned me: why jump parachutes? Someone had told him that the Army and Navy don't allow their men to do intentionals and that many civilian pilots don't even wear parachutes against emergencies, but prefer to take their chances sticking to their ships. What about that?

I told him what I had told myself so many times: that parachutes are required for certain maneuvers, and that therefore one might just as well know how to use them; that collision in the air is becoming the biggest and least calculable danger in aviation, and that after a collision only a 'chute will save you. I talked of fire in the air, structural failure, engine failure over rough country.

But then why make delayed jumps?

Again I could give him good enough reasons. How in war you might want to get down and out of shooting range in a hurry; how after a collision the wreckage sometimes falls almost as fast as the pilot, necessitating long delays in order to clear it. How pilots have bailed out because of an uncontrollable tailspin, and have then been chased by their ships almost down to the ground before they could rip. How in jumping from very fast ships you have so much speed that you might tear your canopy, or your harness, or your intestines, if you ripped right away; whereas if you delay you actually slow down to mere falling speed. And how anyway, if you use life-saving equipment, you might as well be wholly familiar with it and learn to use it coolly.

The real reason, of course, he would not understand, nor would his readers; least of all would the farmer understand it into whose field, in case of mishap, the final mess would burst. The real reason was that a man likes to test his nerve and to get closer and closer and still a little closer to the edge of life.

They were now wheeling the ship out of the hangar. Time to get ready. Word had somehow spread, and cars had come in from the highway. A small crowd was collecting, truck drivers, salesmen, store clerks off for lunch, hoping for a thrill.

The reporter wanted to know if I was married, and whether my mother knew about the jump.

Around and around in my head went a song I had once heard somewhere about "A Little Home in Flatbush." That was what I wanted just then, a little house and a complacent wife and never again any nerve testing. I had had enough of that.

The worst moment of a parachute jump comes when they dress you up and strap the 'chutes on you.

Moriturus: one who is about to die. That was my role as far as the crowd was concerned. They stood and gaped only because they thought that they might see me die. And I felt a little solemn myself. I might die; yet I probably would not die; as a matter of fact I had a date in town for that afternoon. But just now my plans for more than a quarter hour ahead were somehow tentative and strangely uninteresting.

The field manager came to supervise the preparations, and must have seen me shiver in the cool wind. He took off his leather jacket and put it on me. He made me feel better. It kept the wind out, and it also showed that he did not expect to get it back all messed up with dead Langewiesche. The good old Swede.

The rigger and his assistant brought out the 'chutes. They had adjusted the harness. This time it gripped me tight around the legs and around the chest and over the shoulders. It almost hurt, but the feel was good; it pulled you together.

On top of that hung the heavy back pack. Then the chest pack, for emergencies, buckled on in front. Heavy armor. It set you apart from the crowd, and marked you for a strange man off on a strange adventure.

It struck me that nobody wanted to talk to me. The men just stood around, watching. Beyond them, the ship was now noisily warming up its engine.

Again I could feel—by what little signs I could not tell—how some of the crowd were pulling for me but most of them against me. The field manager and the pilots and the flying students were for me, not because they liked me, not because they didn't think I was a fool, doing this without getting paid for it, but because they liked to think that parachutes always work. The rest were against me because they wanted a thrill; the reporter particularly was smelling blood.

The rigger alone was unexcited and workmanlike. He said, putting still another belt around me: "Now don't get mixed up, else you will be down before you know it."

Only the gray-haired little assistant—he who had been with the circuses for forty years—liked me. He reached down and rearranged the leg straps, to make sure I wouldn't be emasculated when the opening jerk hit. He spoke some German and he said: *"Mach's gut,"* calling me thou. He was pulling for me all right.

They put the flying helmet on me and fastened the chin strap, damping out the voices, shutting me off still further from the crowd. Then the goggles.

Only a few more minutes now. The pilot was climbing into the ship.

One girl was standing there among the men around me, the

airport typist, or something like that. She alone now came through to me sharply, body and soul. For a moment I had an experience not given to many men in times of peace, thinking that she might be the last woman I should ever see. She was blond and good-looking. She was talking to a man while looking at me. But I could not make out whether she was pulling for me or against me.

The ship was ready. There was nothing more to discuss, nothing more to wait for, and I might as well go. It was clumsy walking with all that weight on me, and the rigger had to help me lower myself and my chest pack and my back pack into the front cockpit. Then he said, "O.K.," and stood back. We took off.

At three thousand five hundred feet, ready to take the jump, I stood outboard, on the root of the wing, on the trailing edge, facing the tail. It had been difficult to climb out with all that bulk strapped to me, and now I had to hold on with both hands to the fuselage, not to be blown off.

With the pilot I was almost face to face as he sat in his cockpit, looking forward, and I stood beside it, looking rearward. Close enough, but I felt alone. He was busy, scowling at his instruments, at the horizon, at the ground. He was trying to maneuver into a position that would land me—maybe—on the flying field. He didn't look at me, he didn't smile. There was no comradeship with him, merely the feeling of a job to be done. The job was to get away from each other smoothly. He hoped I would take a determined jump away from the ship, and that I would not pull prematurely and be blown into the tail and kill both of us. I hoped that he would give a well-timed kick on the rudder, the moment of jumping, to swing the tail out of my way. After that, we would worry each man for himself.

Around me was the empty world of the flier, the gray sky, the sad horizon. From the field, they were now probably watching breathlessly, but the field was small and far away; it was hard to distinguish among the farms. The town was small and far away, too. Word was spread and people were probably watching in the streets, but I was up here alone, shivering in the propeller wash, and all that didn't help me.

Below me was the depth.

Looking down along my fluttering trouser legs I saw the tips of my shoes—good solid shoes for good solid sidewalks—stick out over the void. Far below them, creeping slowly, the farms, a highway, a factory chimney.

There was plenty of time to look down and to face it. Now, I would crash through the roof into a farm wife's soup; now, I would be impaled on a telegraph pole; now, a little wood, much more inviting—the tree tops looked soft and bouncy.

Nervously, I went over the top. I wanted to jump. Not much fear was left. My nerves themselves at last remembered again the experience of the first jump; the big fall that had not ended in a catastrophic hit, but in that wide, joyous rip across my chest; the opening shock that had jerked me all over heaven; and, after that, the comfortable sensation as I floated down. Some animal fear of falling might indeed spring up again the moment of actually stepping off, but the thing to do against that was to concentrate on the first few moments of falling, to control myself, and not to pull the ripcord.

The pilot throttled back the engine and went into a glide. He nodded.

It was up to me.

I let go with my hands. Immediately the air stream bowled me over. A cold shock; my right hand gripped frantically all over my left shoulder and chest for the ripcord and couldn't grab it. Balance was already gone, there was no stopping. A quick look, and I found it. Then I kicked myself off, away from the ship.

Down I went in a violent, breathless, silent tumble. The bottom dropped out from under me, from under my brains, my intestines. I couldn't see, I couldn't hear. I only felt I was going to smash.

Now was the time to hold it.

My hand was on the ring, but I must stand this until I could stand it absolutely no longer.

I must hold it still a little longer.

My head cleared, my breath came again, and I saw the ground. It was only a brief glimpse, but it was enough. I had won over the first confusion. I had not ripped, and now the ground was still far away, and there was still plenty of time.

I was falling face downward.

The ground was steady. It was not rushing up to meet me, as water rushes up when you dive off a spring board. It didn't move at all. At this rate, I could keep falling forever.

The fall rolled me over on my side, and then on my back. Between my feet, I could now see the horizon, and against the horizon, the ship. It was flying away from me, and doing a curve. Watching it, watching the familiar rhythm of an airplane in flight, gave me back my sense of timing. I got a good long look at it, marveling all the while that there was so much time, jumping down from the sky. I could see how I was losing height fast; for although the ship's nose was down and it was gliding, it seemed to float upwards rapidly.

A new twist, and I lost sight of it.

I was picking up more speed every instant, and I could feel it in my innards. It was the law of gravitation, at work on a falling body, and felt from the inside out. One moment it felt as if I had been merely loafing around. A moment later I seemed to be dropping away like a stone.

Yet, there was still no hurry. I could see the horizon and by it could tell that I was still 'way up.

It may have been three or four seconds after jumping, but it felt more like six or seven, when I first became conscious of the thickness of the air. There was a new sensation. I was no longer dropping through a void.

A bottom was back under things, a soft but firm bottom of air rushing up against me from underneath. I could feel my back lying on it, the calves of my legs, and my arm and hand. It took all the fright out of falling. It was the same thing that holds you up in flying, and that fliers get a feeling for and learn to trust: air plus motion.

The tumbling began again. My head was heavier than the rest of me, and sank faster. I felt myself sliding off my air mattress backwards, headfirst. A glimpse of my own legs, flailing against the clouds. Overhead, which was now below, a flash of green ground. Then the legs fell over in a nasty backwards somersault. It didn't feel safe at all. I almost let her rip.

Somehow I got stabilized again, falling face downward, lying flat on the air stream, lying comfortably, with face, chest, belly, legs, arm, fingers, on a solid transparent nothing; and looking down through it, too. I fell steadily now, not speeding up any more. I had reached terminal velocity, one hundred and twenty miles per hour or thereabouts, and it felt fine. I had worried about it, and about the sharp timing that would be required. But now it wasn't like falling at all, more like flying, and I was quite relaxed. The ground was coming up, but only slowly. I saw a highway, white through the green grass land. I saw the farm I was falling into getting steadily bigger, as if being pulled up by a magnifying lens.

This was comfortable. It took three seconds perhaps, but it seemed longer.

Then the air stream gave me a new twist. I began to roll over sideways, and my head sank away again. I began to wonder if I hadn't better pull now, while the 'chute could still string out away from my body. I might be all the way down before I would be again in a favorable position. I was still wondering when the farm suddenly took a lunge, blew up, and exploded in my face.

I was THERE.

I managed to pull the ripcord quite slowly, deliberately, with no particular force. So much had the feel of the air stream taken the catastrophe out of falling. I could feel the latch pins snap open; the ripcord, a little farther out, was getting stuck; for safety's sake I gave it another easy pull and got it all the way out.

There was again that ugly split second when you have a piece of slack wire rope in your hand. You can do no more with it, and nothing happens.

Then the big jerk—vicious, quite unelastic. I might as well have lassoed a locomotive. It hurt plenty, but it was all over in a moment. I hung.

I heard excited shouts of children from somewhere. I found I was very low; I hadn't pulled any too soon. There was no time to enjoy the floating down. I was drifting onto a telephone line—or was it high tension? I grabbed two of the shrouds above me and pulled on them, sideslipping the 'chute into an open field. It was dark bare earth, with yesterday's rains still on it in pools. The slip made me swing viciously, pendulum fashion. I was worried about the landing, but there was no time left to steady myself. I was falling through fast. I went limp, and hit.

This time I hit very lightly; it must have been because of the cool, heavy air. I sat down, but only because I was limp. I could have taken it standing. The canopy was still open and tugged in the wind. I pulled on one shroud until it collapsed. I got up and looked around for someone to come and greet me and help me. I had landed far from the flying field. I was alone except for some cows. The ship was gone from the sky.

I unbuckled the harness and rolled up the silk. Still nobody was in sight, and I loaded my seventy pounds of parachute on my shoulders and started walking, ankle deep in black soft soil.

10. The Poor Man's Airplane

Soon after that I moved to the New York area. I had a job as instructor at a college, and I had a salary. It was only a college instructor's salary, but I stayed on a student's standard of living, and spent the rest on airplane rent. I had made the grade, or so I thought.

On the very day when I cashed my first salary check, I started going out to the airports to pick myself a ship to fly. No trainer this time, I thought, but a real airplane; something big and fast, something slippery and hot; something that would take a real pilot to fly. I was fully recovered from my neurosis.

That was my idea of painting the town red: to have a little money in my pocket, and to walk down the line at some airport, looking over the sky buggies, poking through the hangars, picking out a ship to fly.

People sometimes won't believe that one can get an airplane to fly at almost any airport in America by simply walking in cold and asking for it. Yet that is so. More and more, that is what American airports are turning into: Fly URself agencies, as it were. When you look down the Line at Roosevelt, at Floyd Bennett, at Flushing, in fact at almost any airport in America except the airline terminals, there are two or three ships for rent for every one that is truly privately owned and privately flown.

You pick your ship, and then you go and find the owner or his mechanic, and ask:

"You give Time on this ship?"

"Sure."

Then comes that airport ceremonial known as the "check-out." The owner or his pilot goes up with you, watches your flying, and gets to know you.

Airmanship is remarkable in that respect. There is something about it that shows almost immediately in the way a man behaves with airplanes; even in the way he merely talks about them at dinner. It shows in magazine stories; you often feel you can guess the exact number of hours the author has had, if any.

It certainly shows to the full on a check-out flight. A good pilot can guess what kind of pilot you are from the moment when you walk out with him to take the ship up. He gets a line on you from the manner in which you climb into the ship and look over the instruments and controls; and he has you pretty well sized up by the time he has watched your manner of taxiing the ship. By the time you have flown the first circuit of the field and shot your first landing, a good check-pilot can often guess the make of ship you have been flying last, or the make of ship you were originally trained on, and after the third landing or so, he can tell whether you are or are not a pilot with the same certainty with which you can tell whether a lady is or is not a lady.

If you are a pilot, you can afford plenty of faux pas. In fact, the check-pilot wants you to commit them. He wants to make sure that your judgment doesn't go to pieces in times of trouble; he wants to have seen you make corrections for a misjudged approach or for a bounced landing. And you can afford to ask plenty of questions. I have been checked out in ships where the controls were differently disposed around the pilot's seat, and where at the proper moment I didn't find the stabilizer, the flap control, the lever that lets down the landing gear, or some other important control. Turning an imaginary crank at the proper moment would serve to ask the check pilot for it, and he would simply show it to me, and that was all. It was perhaps half hidden under my own seat, perhaps even in full view, but the point lay in which gesture you made at which time. I remember one case where the ship so overawed me, and the pilot so flustered me, that both my hands and my feet were visibly jittering; but he simply stepped out after the third landing and said: "You'll do much better alone."

That was the side of flying that took hold of me now: the fascination of handling a highly bred ship merely for the sake of handling it, working my gadgets and my radio and my instruments and my brains. I no longer cared what I saw below me. I actually spent much time and money on learning to fly blind, with the pilot seat tightly hooded by canvas curtains, steering by instruments and navigating by radio, while a safety man sat outside the hood and watched out for other ships. I came to consider flying with outside vision somewhat slack. Finally it became unnecessary even to go up. For the same money for which I could have flown a small ship once across the continent, I sat in a back room of the hangar, inside a dark wiggly box that had imitation airplane controls and an imitation instrument panel, and flew imitation approaches by imitation radio beams to imitation airports.

And I am not sorry. The whole story of that type of flying would be well worth telling, for the advanced methods of piloting an airplane, the turn indicator, the directional gyroscope and artificial horizon and the radio beam and the radio direction finder, make the most fascinating of games. But that story doesn't belong in this book. For that kind of flying is related to the kind that the average man can do in his spare time and on his spare dollars the way the handling of an ocean liner is related to small boat cruising.

As I found out.

For when the time finally came when I wanted to fly cross-country again and apply my new techniques—hoping it would be cloudy all the way and that I would not be able to see a darned thing outside—I found that I could not afford to rent any of those high-priced ships for more than an hour at a time. In fact I had been spending money so hard that I could hardly afford to buy a worth-while block of Time on an ordinary training ship: I was back where I had started.

In the meantime, something big had been happening in the American air. You might almost say something big in American life; it may well keep future sociologists busy explaining its repercussions on (a) the family, (b) housing, (c) city planning, and so forth. It had kept happening for years, right under my nose, at all the airports. But in common with most of the airport crowd I had failed to recognize it. It was the advent of the people's airplane; the flivver, as it were, of the air.

I remember when I saw one for the first time. That was actually way in the beginning of my flying career, back at the Metropolitan Airport, before I had even soloed. I found it one morning in hangar 5, sitting under George's big Bellanca, an airplane calf under an airplane cow, very small, very low, but an almost exact replica of the big airplane. With its overgrown wing and big soft feet and spindly body, it was appealing in a personal way. "Not a bad airplane," I remarked to the hangar mechanic. But he replied rather sharply: "That ain't no airplane, that's a powered kite." Hell, it cruised at only sixty miles an hour. A man might as well travel by train.

The pilot who had bought it, though, was soon doing a lot of business—more business, counted in flying hours, than any other operator at the field. At all times of the day, the little ship could be seen cluttering up the air around the airport, making silly little noises like a motorcycle.

George Adams thought it was sheer waste of money, but I flew the ship myself a few times. I was curious, and it was cheap; it cost only six dollars an hour. Against a good breeze, it took off almost from the spot, which was nice enough; but thereafter I sat up there forever and watched the cars go by below. It was a strange ship to handle in the air. Felt through its controls the very air was different: not like air at all, but thick, more like mashed potatoes. That was because its wings were so big in proportion to its weight: they carried only five pounds per square foot of wing surface. When you stalled it in flight, it merely dropped its nose a bit and took hold again almost without losing altitude. And when you wanted to come down, it settled down, against a good breeze almost at walking speed, said "rrrumps" once as the tailskid struck the asphalt runway, and stood still.

All of which should have been attractive enough, except possibly its slow cruising speed. But with my judgment primed by a lot of old-timers, I decided that I didn't like the ship.

It seemed obvious to me that a big-winged kite like that could never teach you proper flying. And for purposes other than training it seemed even less attractive. As far as cross-country flying was concerned, why, it carried fuel only for three hours, and it didn't even have a compass.

Still the little ship had become more popular as time went on. The fellow had soon bought a second one, and by the time I had begun to fly cross-country, you could find one at almost every air-port, busily earning money by lugging around heavy loads of ham-fisted beginners, for the new low flying rates were building up some sort of distaff side of aviation: flying for women and children and fools who wanted to fly without taking it on the chin, who wanted the title of pilot without the substance.

Or so it seemed to us.

Thus the "light stuff" was called all kinds of names: pop bottles, puddle jumpers, playthings, round-the-airport ships, and not with-out venom; for the bare truth was that they were undermining the most precious thing around the airports: the secretness of the art; the insiderdom of the insiders.

Pilots are nothing if not conservative. In America, they were cast in the dreary role of financially not very responsible business men, but in their hearts they were nevertheless more like armored knights; their inner worth was based entirely on their command of a dangerous and exclusive art, for which they had trained their nerves and their bodies in a long and tough apprenticeship.

They were, of course, wholeheartedly for the progress of aviation and all that sort of thing. But at heart they still liked ships that were dangerous and hard to fly. Such comment as that she was a man-killer, or that she was too goddamned hot, or that she was awful blind, were actually signs of affection and respect; of some airplanes it was

said lovingly that they had to be *flown* every minute; and such airplanes—unstable, tricky, abrupt-stalling ones, nasty spinning ones—
gave their pilots artistocractic status; while the stamp of ultimate
vulgarity in aircraft was the judgment: "It flies itself." And when you
stood around at the hangar gates and watched the flying and the new
ships, you were sorry deep down in your heart every time that flying
was made a degree more fool proof or more easy to afford.

Still, when a new fellow came out from town and began to poke
around the hangars and talk of taking up flying himself, it became
more and more difficult to uphold these standards of aeronautical
decency. It required more and more talking to make such a new
customer see that there were real airplanes and airplanes not so real,
and that he wouldn't get the real thing unless he spent at least twelve
dollars an hour, preferably fifteen. By 1935 it had got so that at any
one moment at an airport, the chances were for the real airplanes to
stand on the Line waiting for customers while one or two of the
small ships were doing all the actual flying.

But even then, such flying was all 'round the airport. The only
cross-country flights one ever heard of were the delivery trips from
the ship's factory to its new home airport; and one never heard of
them without some remark about the fellow's patience; yes, sir, one
needed plenty of patience in them light fellers; and for that matter,
many ships went cross-country on trucks or in box cars. There was
the story of a wealthy California kid who took just enough instruction to solo, and then came East with his instructor, bought one of
the little ships, and flew it back to the coast. And by the time he got
home, by golly, he had built up enough Time for a license!

Up to that time, every ship at an airport had a personality of its
own, or at least a paint job of its own. One came to know almost
every ship within a hundred miles or so, and could recognize it in the
air, knew who owned it, and could guess who was probably flying it,
and from the manner of flying it, one could tell whether he had a girl
with him and was showing off, or not. But now, there were sometimes three or four lightplanes of the same make at one airport, mass
produced and looking so shockingly alike that one could not tell
them apart.

Of this mass production, one heard amazing stories: one factory was turning out those ships at the rate of one a day for several months! For civil flying that was spectacular; one was accustomed to factories that turned out a ship a month, and where each purchaser kept up cordial personal relations with the manufacturer.

They began to be sold much in automobile fashion. There were networks of distributors and dealers; there were prices doped out for popular appeal, such as $1,498.50; there were "easy-payment" offers, one third down, the balance in twelve installments, lights and accessories extra, prices f.a.f. ("flyaway at factory"), delivery charges extra; there even were advertising campaigns for them—something that had not happened to airplanes since the great airport blight of 1930. "It looks like a real airplane," said one of the manufacturers. "Yea, but what is it?" said the airport old timers.

Sprinkled among those advertisements that offered the cracked-up airplanes and the fancy deals, there now appeared a new type with a peculiarly folksy flavor. "Learn to fly for $2.50 a week," they said. They were all put in by one small airport operator named Bennett in New Jersey. But I thought: fleecing the suckers. "We start you out in aviation with a brand new airplane; little or no capital necessary," they said; but I thought: so you do, do you? And "Fly; it's easy," but I thought: the hell you say.

Now, when my flying had again come to a dead end and I wanted again to travel cross-country, I did some independent thinking. I decided it would be cheap, small planes for me, or no airplanes at all. I went to Roosevelt Field to try to hire one for a cross-country trip from one of the air service operators who had recently given in to the trend and bought one. "How about letting me fly this thing up to Boston and back?" I had said.

The owner had been embarrassed, as if I had said something indecent. "Why, it would take you all day," and that had been a clear refusal. Being an old timer, he didn't ask himself what was wrong with taking all day for the round trip, seeing that a car took almost all day for the one-way trip.

I went to Floyd Bennett Field, to a man whose ships I had flown;

he didn't believe in lightplanes for cross-country—not safe, he said; the least bit of a headwind, and you ran out of fuel. I went to Flushing: ships were insured only for airport flying. And on Long Island, I went to still another outfit: Cross-country? They didn't even have a compass in the ship.

Finally, I decided to see the man behind the folksy ads. I found him, way out in the New Jersey countryside near Princeton, on his field; it was apparently just an ordinary cow pasture with one small hangar on it of corrugated tin, a wooden shack for an office, a few gasoline cans lying around, and a dozen of the small bigwinged fellows sitting in the grass.

Could this sort of ship be flown cross-country at all? I asked him.

Of course, they could. Why not? Seventy miles an hour was seventy miles.

"Minus headwinds," I said thoughtfully.

". . . plus tailwinds," he answered, bristling for his ships. If you got up early and flew till sundown, you still could cover a lot of country. Why, where did I want to go?

Actually my dream was to fly the whole Atlantic Coast, down to Key West and up to Bar Harbor. But it seemed a bit wild.

I said, "I had thought maybe of Washington."

"Sure," said Al Bennett, "I often send my students to Washington."

"How about Richmond?" I said, feeling my way.

"Let me see your log book," said Al Bennett, and leafed through it for a while. "Sure," he decided.

"As a matter of fact," I said, "I have sometimes thought of Charleston." He seemed to become more interested rather than less.

"Why not?" he said; "that is the kind of thing people ought to do."

"How about Miami?" I asked. He thought that sounded like a lot of fun. "You ought to fly out and see Key West," he said.

"A lot of water there between the Islands," I said, to show him how conservative I was.

"That's all right, you aren't proposing to walk across, are you?" he said.

"What happens if the engine quits?"

"That engine quit?" he said, and gave a grunt of disdain.

We went up together to check me out, and from then on, that New Jersey meadow with the one hangar was my homefield. The small light airplane became my kind of ship, and a very different style of flying it was.

In the conventional sense, that cow pasture was perhaps the least interesting spot between New York and Philadelphia. There seldom were spectators; no newsreel man had even thought of catching any of the activities. There were no sleek airliners, no modernistic buildings, no flavor of long-distance travel; there wasn't any of that sense of a future in the process of coming to pass that you sometimes get.

In all those senses, it was like no airport at all, but mild; more like some concession on the park lagoon where one can rent a rowboat by the hour. Why, it was almost like a grocery store—when you got through flying, they rang up your bill on a cash register.

The only thing about the field that was in the grand old style of flying was Al Bennett himself, the man who owned and ran it: tall, of military bearing, and with a twirled mustache, he might have been a test pilot of the kind you see in the movies. And for himself, he was as proud and cocky a man as you will find, a skillful pilot and a daring one; once in a while he would go up in an old powerful biplane he kept just for that purpose, and roll himself over upside down, for old memories' sake. But that was strictly private. As a business man, he promoted quite a different idea of flying.

It was the usual flying field idea in reverse. Instead of keeping prices up and guarding the prestige of his art, he made his living by democratizing. He believed that the air age was at hand and his vision of it was in the best American tradition; the Good Thing, brought Within the Reach of All. He had jumped off the deep end. He must make the public accept piloting and the small personal airplane as it had accepted the automobile, or else lose money. When you looked at his field you had to know all that; you had to understand the intention. If you did, you could see there a most remarkable sight: the people flying; thirty years after Kitty Hawk, the common man taking to the air.

Al Bennett would take on all-comers, and undertake to solo them
for fifty dollars. Someone might think he couldn't do it; he might say
he was not cut out to be a flier. Al Bennett would answer: "Have you
got two dollars? Hop in. I'll show you." He had soloed his mail man
and his grocer, and when I first saw him, he was working on his pants
presser. They were gliding in together for a landing, and one could
hear Bennett's voice sing out his instructions all over the quiet farming country: "Back," he was commanding, "pull it back now"—
meaning the stick.

He delighted in making people fly who had never flown before,
were not thinking of flying, and were actually afraid to fly. Once I
watched him administer the aerial baptism to an elderly lady who
had been dragged there by her young nephew. Bennett noticed her
sitting in a car at the edge of the field, viciously uninterested in
airplanes.

He asked her courteously to take a short flight with him. His
manner inspired confidence and was at the same time gay; he was
amazingly effective at describing the beauties of the air, the houses
like toys, the soft, clean, fleecy clouds. He made her do it.

Once installed in the rear seat of the little ship, she found out that
she must take hold of a funny-looking stick and put her feet on two
pedals, and I think she knew so little about it that she probably
thought one always had to do that in an airplane. He got into the
front seat. I gave him a twist on the propeller, and off they went
together. When they came back at three hundred feet, they seemed
a bit wobbly, but his hands were sticking out of either side window
for us on the ground to see. When they taxied up again a little later,
she had made a complete student-circuit of the field, take-off, turns,
glide, and even the landing, all with her own hands, guided merely
by his gestures and his conversation from the front seat.

Bennett figured that such educational flights, thrown at random
into the population, would do more than a lot of publicity to dispel
fear of flying; but I suspect it was actually largely exuberance with
him, a happy conviction that the small airplane deserved not much
more awe than a rowboat.

With all this, though, his field was definitely a business enterprise, designed to make money and making money, and it should be reported as such.

His main business was, as usual with airports in recent years, student instruction. It was done mostly after five in the afternoon, when the factories and the offices let out, and on Sundays. His customers were very much the common man; he had some two hundred of them; quite a few women among them. They came from the machine shops, from the filling stations, from the offices of New York and Trenton and Philadelphia, from the farms. And they were most of them strictly amateurs. They came trickling along, singly or in pairs, "Can you let me have a ship for a couple hours, Al? I gotta go to Philadelphia." "Sure thing, Mac,—get in. I'll pull your prop." Then Al gave a twist to the propeller to start the engine, and Mac flew off, chug-chugging into the distance.

On a balmy Sunday afternoon, sometimes, all his ships were up in the air at the same time, and the customers were lying around on the grass, waiting their turn: a batch of fliers, some of them only passengers, some of them extremely competent pilots who looked like what they were: farmers and mechanics and housewives, and salesmen, and not a helmet, a pair of goggles, or a bit of the old pilot swagger in sight.

On such a day, Al would bring the table and the cash register out into the grass and do the business end outdoors. His wife, at the table, would do the timekeeping, and he would stand beside her as a man might stand in his garden on a summer afternoon and watch his bees, pleased, watching them buzz and gather honey, bit by bit.

In aviation circles, he was sometimes attacked. No one, it was said, could possibly learn to fly decently for $2.50 a week. Why not? answered Bennett, weren't they flying and flying year after year without accidents? He had high school kids flying under his supervision; he delighted—you may try to talk about him as a business man, but you always come out talking about his various delights in matters of the air—he delighted in getting licenses, or at least solo permits, for people who at first had been refused by the official examiners. He had trained a man of sixty-eight and sold him an airplane; he had soloed a boy both of whose legs were lame; for him he had rigged up a special arrangement through which the rudder could be worked by hand. And with all his nonchalance, he kept watching his customers' technique sharply, not only his students' but also the more experienced pilots'. "Remind me to tell that fellow in number six not to glide so damn slowly," he would say, and when the fellow came to pay his bill, he got his lecture.

There was another angle to that New Jersey cow pasture: Al Bennett was one of the people who sold the new, mass-produced lightplanes. And he was reputed to sell more civilian airplanes per year than any other man in the world; which at that time meant that he had sold a new airplane on the average every two weeks, and any number of secondhand ones.

He did not sell them the way some men might have sold expensive cars or motorboats. Only about one out of ten went to a private owner for private flying. I remember a young married couple, he a Cornell man, she a Wellesley graduate, who bought a secondhand one for eight hundred dollars instead of buying a boat, learned to solo it within a week, and were gaily flying every weekend all summer, and by Christmas, negotiated the trip to Miami. There was another couple who, after more training and on a sixteen-hundred-dollar ship, flew across the continent with their six-month-old daughter (protected by earmuffs), using the luggage compartment as a crib.

That was nice. But more interesting was the way in which many of the other ships were sold. Later on, when there was so much talk about training large pilot reserves for national defense, I often thought of the fashion in which he had managed all along to get the people into the air without government help, without subsidies; training indirectly a lot of pilots who became pilots not because someone else paid for it, or because it was good to be on the band wagon, but for the simplest and most powerful reason there could be: they wanted to fly.

He had doped out the patent solution of the whole problem of how people can fly; i.e., can fly now and here without waiting for airplanes to become cheaper. The way it worked was this: he trained some student until that student could in turn act as an instructor. Then he sent him to some small town, often the student's home town, and there he would drum together ten or twenty of the local boys into a special sort of organization, half club, half commercial flying service, along lines all worked out for him by Bennett, using advertising literature written by Bennett. Each member would pay in advance for a number of flying hours, perhaps fifty dollars, perhaps only twenty. The money thus collected would go to Bennett as down payment for a new airplane, and thus a new flying service operator was set up in business; a new local group of young pilots was started, and another cow pasture blossomed forth as a flying field.

Seen from the vantage point of that little unspectacular flying field, the air age was well under way.

11. You Must Beware of Hatteras

Thus, in a poor man's plane, I began air touring in earnest. The Atlantic Coast became my hunting ground for the next hundred and fifty hours of flight.

Sometimes in the New York subway, when it is dark and stuffy, I now find myself reciting in my mind a list of those capes the way a mountain climber might recite a list of his peaks, names which once were cold geography and which now are full of enchantment: Cape Anne, and Cape Cod, Montauk Point and Sandy Hook, Cape May and Cape Henlopen, Cape Charles and Cape Henry, Cape Hatteras, Cape Lookout, Cape Fear. As modern flying goes, I haven't been anywhere; but I did see this one big sight: that outermost fringe of America, the lonely barrier beaches and lighthouses, the uninhabited regions where ocean and continent are mixed in swamps and lagoons, the great Capes.

It is a sight at which few people have ever troubled to look.

Take Cape Hatteras, for instance. That was one of the first longer flights I did on the small ship—a trial trip on the ship before I made the longer flight to Key West—and it was almost like an expedition into unknown territory. In New York, no one seemed to know anything about the Cape. "Cape Hatteras? Boy, batten down your hatches." For people who had been South by ship, the Cape was something which made for rough seas and shipwreck, something to be given a wide berth. To automobile tourists it was something which lay behind the Dismal Swamp. Railroads and bus lines didn't go near it; no passengers came from there and no passengers wanted to go there. Coastwise shipping schedules didn't list it. Highway maps showed no highways at all. The Airport Directory listed no airports. In the New York mind, Cape Hatteras was a complete blank spot.

I had the Cub for five days between weekends in April; on Saturday and Sundays it was too busy making money with students. It had special oversized tires with less pressure on the ground than a baby's foot, which would be most important for landings on the beach. It had a new type propeller of shallow pitch that would pick me out of the smallest field or jerk me off the softest mud or sand. I swung its compass and tabulated the errors, and then I flew it South over the now familiar route, down the Eastern Shore of Maryland, into the Spring. I jumped across the mouth of the Chesapeake from Cape Charles to Cape Henry and sat down at Norfolk, Virginia, to spend the night and make local enquiries.

"Cape Hatteras?" said the locals. "Nothing there." The flying service people had never been further out to the Cape than half way, because they had never had a payload beyond Kitty Hawk. And since I had no business at the Cape either, they suggested, why fly to the Cape at all? Especially in this little putt-putt?

Next morning I went and fitted out; and the beauty of my kind of flying is that I could do my fitting out at the nearest hardware store. I would have to carry my own fuel supply with me. I couldn't be sure even of getting automobile or motor boat gasoline. I bought containers holding nine gallons, which was good for three hours' additional flying, even though I would still need a stretch of smooth, firm beach in order to land and pour the stuff into my tank. And as an airport I would have to use the bare beach, wherever I might be when my fuel gave out. Or I might be forced down by weather or darkness or engine trouble, and once on the ground, a light plane is defenseless. Any strong gust will pick it up and wreck it. So I bought lengths of rope, hammer and stakes, empty sacks, and a coal shovel to dig myself into the country. I took everything to the airport in a taxi, and stowed it into the front seat of the Cub, strapping it well down. Then I took off.

I hung myself over the beach. For a man who drives his own sky-buggy, there can't be a more pleasant morning drive than down a beach. All the usual worries are relieved. One can't possibly lose one's way while following a coast line, and if the weather should turn bad or the engine give trouble, there is always a perfect landing strip right underneath.

I would follow it all the way out to the Cape. There was a high overcast and a stiff southerly wind, which for me was a headwind. I settled down for a long sit.

I rolled the stabilizer forward so as to gain speed and slowly pay out altitude. I set my throttle and scribbled down my clock time as I passed the hotels of Virginia Beach. The wind might be stiff, but it was without flaws. The ship lay in my hand almost without motion, and I found I could clasp my hands behind my head and fly by feet alone.

I leaned back and took in the sights. I saw the Atlantic, the same old Atlantic, blue and vacant, that you have seen at Southampton or Atlantic City or Miami Beach. But you will never know how vacant the ocean is until you have seen it from the air. That day, I was to survey more of it than you can see from a steamer deck in three Atlantic crossings: but never a ship. A swell was running from East to West, and a new set of waves was running crosswise from South to North; between them, they made the sea look like a piece of blue woven fabric.

And I saw below me the barrier beach. Barrier beach is the characteristic Atlantic shore landscape, from Long Island all the way down to Miami Beach; beach that is separated from the mainland by lagoons. You don't pay any attention to that at shore resorts because it doesn't make any difference to you; if the resort is on a barrier beach, as is for instance Jones Beach or Atlantic City, then it is because somebody has built a trestle or a dam out there from the mainland, and in an automobile all you notice is a swampy smell. But you do pay attention to it when you fly: it is the one big thing you see.

The beach here was exactly the kind of beach you see at resorts, clean sands, a white ribbon of surf, everything festive and as if waiting for a Sunday crowd. But the real estate behind this one could not possibly have supported a resort. The hotels would just have sunk. It was too soft. As far as I could see landward, there wasn't anything solid, there were only salt marshes, bleak even in the sunlight, and lagoons with barbarous names: Currituck Sound, Pasquotank Sound. And beyond them, still farther inland, the Dismal Swamp.

I was alone with sea gulls and the wild geese, and I stayed alone for the next two hours.

The beach ran south, between the ocean and the lagoons, straight as a boulevard, and I purred down that boulevard at five hundred feet. The engine ticked over smoothly, drinking away its jiggerful of fuel every minute. As she lightened in the nose—where the fuel tank is—she wanted to climb again, and every twenty minutes or so the stabilizer required another twist to re-trim her for level flight. That was all the work I had to do; in fact, all the entertainment I had.

In all that time, the only landmark I saw was a tall lighthouse. It took me half an hour to reach it, and half an hour more to put it out of sight behind me—even though the airspeed indicator stood steadily at seventy miles per hour. I looked it up on the map, and took my clock time, and worked out my ground speed on the slide rule. It amounted to little more than forty miles an hour. That meant the headwind up here was nearly thirty miles per hour. No chance of making the Cape without a landing. Some chance of not making it even with all my fuel reserve. That is what a fast wind will do to a slow-plane pilot's plans. I began to worry, after all, about that beach landing. . . .

By the time my fuel gauge was bumping bottom I had raised the next landmark: the Three Dunes of Kitty Hawk. They were not high, but on this low coast they stood out. They are one of the oldest landmarks in all America; there are maps of North America so old that they do not yet give the continent its proper shape, but even these maps carry them prominently and call them the Three Sand Hills. In those days, they were the navigators' only help along the

Hatteras coast, and already in those days Cape Hatteras had a bad reputation: "If the Bermudas let you pass, you must beware of Hatteras." All of which would be neither here nor there in a flight report except for this fact—which is one of the things I like about air touring—that even for me that day they were not merely idle historic sights; to me in the airplane they still were landmarks by which to navigate.

They were also a historic sight to see. For they are the very place from which the Wright Brothers made their first glider flights, and the beach in front of them is the place where they made their first powered flights, the first powered flights in history. That is how isolated those barrier beaches are; the Wright Brothers had moved there from Ohio to keep what they valued as a million-dollar secret from the reporters, and they were so successful that they later had trouble convincing the world.

Today that particular spot is no longer so deserted. An ugly memorial stood among the dunes, and a macadam road came out from the mainland across the lagoons on a trestle, and there was a local infection there with twentieth-century roadside architecture, not beautiful but welcome to me just then. I saw a general store, and in front of it a red gasoline pump and a sign so big and red that I could read it from five hundred feet. It said "Esso." It meant I could replenish my reserve.

I circled the monument, and surveyed possible landing places, and then decided for the historic beach itself. As I cut the throttle, I was more than a bit worried: fourteen hundred dollars' worth of ship, a slanting beach, a soft spot in the sand, a ground loop, and a nose over—I think every pilot worries when he sets a ship down onto ground which is not certified to be smooth and hard by being an established airport. I swung out over the water and cut back across the surf in a regular 180° approach on the dark, wet sand next to the water's edge, because that is always the firmest. I picked my exact spot and cut in towards it. I put on considerable power, so as to touch lightly and to have a good propeller blast on the tail surfaces, and get positive and quick responses out of the controls. Should the touchdown feel wrong, I would blast her off again immediately. She touched down lightly. The tailskid dug into the sand right away and stopped her sharply. I cut my ignition switch with a grunt of relief, and the answer was a boom that made me jump in my seat: it was a big roller breaking over the beach a few yards from me, almost licking my wheels. I had forgotten that the sea makes sounds.

The rollers kept thundering while I worked. The wind was so stiff that she shook in the gust. The beach had more slant to it than I had guessed from the air, and the houses were out of my sight. No one came to help me, or even to stare. I got out my sand sacks, shoveled them full of sand, and tied the wings to it. I poured new gasoline into my tank. I panted across the deep sand to the general store and refilled my reserve containers. The pump was worked by the store-keeper, a woman, young but aging. She didn't ask me where I came from with my canisters nor where I was going, and I didn't tell her. I took one load to the ship and came back for another, and went into the store and had a cake 'n' coke from her, but she wouldn't talk. As to what her life might be like on this lonely shore, all the impression I got was her silence and the periodic thunder of the surf.

I took my last load down to the ship and stowed my things and took off.

Low in the lagoons I saw Roanoke Island, where the white man tried his first settlement along this coast. A road branched across there from the Wright monument, and there is an amphitheatre there where shows are given, and all sorts of other provisions for tourists. Then I came to a gap in the beach, where the sea has broken through the barrier and where the tide current was sweeping from the ocean into the lagoons. I jumped it, but the Kitty Hawk macadam stayed behind, as did the architecture and that whole cluster of civilization. I was alone again over the beach.

The Cape lay fifty-five miles further out, fifty-five miles against the stiff ocean wind. I didn't bother to climb very high, because with a headwind one makes better time lower down. Ordinarily it would have been against the regulations to fly below five hundred feet, but here it didn't matter, because if there was any no man's land left in this country, this was it. It loses its last ties with the mainland, and becomes the quintessence of a barrier beach, a beach for beach's sake, a narrow strip of sand that sweeps far out into the Atlantic, so far that the lagoon thus formed, Pamlico Sound, is as big as an inland sea, and that even up at three hundred feet I lost sight of the mainland: a seagoing bit of America.

It is absurd what sense of gay excitement some kinds of country can give to a man who is well mounted on a good airplane. This strip of country looked in reality exactly as it had looked on the maps, the land in the same shape, with but slight perspectivic distortion, the sea in that same Rand McNally blue. But that doesn't mean the view was dull; if from an airplane the world looks like a map, that doesn't speak against the airplane, it speaks for the mapmakers. Perhaps it was mostly my own smooth high gliding over it that I liked, the way my left wing seemed to stretch far out over the Atlantic and my right wing far out over the sound; the brisk manner in which mile after mile of long, thin island fed itself into my propeller.

There are a few fishing villages on the Islands, and there were automobile tracks on the beach—automobiles can be ferried across most of the gaps in the barrier. But for the next half-hour I saw no house, no car, and only one man.

He was exactly under me, and was riding a horse. He was going my way. He, too, kept on the dark damp sand next to the surf, and I duly noted that for my own purposes. He was jogging up and down in a trot, the horse stepping hastily and laying down a long straight line of hoofprints. A traveler in a hurry. But from where I was I could see the strip of beach stretch ahead of him all the way to my horizon, much farther than he could possibly look, and that made him and his horse look futile. In fact, they made me think of the business end of a sewing machine, rattling up and down and leaving a seam of many small stitches, but not getting anywhere. In a few minutes, he was left far behind, and there was no more to see now but sand and bits of driftwood and once the skeleton of a boat. And I thought that if one wanted to describe this coast, one would have to overwork one word: lonely.

Down the long beach.

I flew even lower now, at the hundred-foot level approximately, looking at the sands with a new respect. Sands and the stiff rushing air: those are the substance of that region. Between them, I discovered, they had produced a type of wilderness that is strangely twentieth-century, in that it is literally a streamlined wilderness. Under the chiseling of the wind, the soft shifting sand had arranged itself into shapes which belong essentially to the air age: standard streamlined bodies. On the lee side of every chunk of driftwood, on the lee side of every clump of beach grass, on the lee side of every obstruction whatever, the same familiar shape had built itself up, the shape which you know from the bodies of "airflow" automobiles, from the fuselages of airplanes, and from the rear ends of streamlined trains—that tapering tail which smoothes out the wake of a body moving through air. Behind some obstructions it was thin and shallow and so slightly marked that you could distinguish it only if you looked for it with the interest of an airman; behind others, it was so pronounced that it reminded me of an exhibit in the corridor of some school of aeronautics.

I passed over the remains of a shipwreck. She was high and dry on the beach, a sailing vessel, her masts gone, her hatches open, but her black hull intact.

I passed over a Coast Guard station. It did not even try to look like a permanent human habitation. On its barren sands it looked rather like some outpost of civilization, perhaps the camp of a polar expedition. On an air photograph, one could easily have mistaken the sand for snow. There was a lookout tower, and as I flew past, almost as low as the tower was high, I exchanged a wave of hands with the man on duty. I could see his face, which was a deep tan, and even his eyes, and I thought of all those men keeping a lookout day and night, summer and winter, all up and down the coast; a coast with eyes.

Then suddenly I had arrived. Ahead of me on the beach there was a lighthouse, marked as the charts had said Hatteras lighthouse would be marked, with a spiral ribbon of paint; and beyond it there was nothing but sea. The beach turned westward here at a right angle, sharp and precise as a city street-corner; that was the Cape. Again the view was a piece of pure geography; there was nothing in it that I hadn't already seen on the map, except that on the tip of the corner the sea was playing in a special pattern, with the surfs of the two sides overcutting one another; and that the clouds had broken up, and there was over everything a dash of live sunlight that you can't reproduce in maps.

I circled around and took in the human geography, for I was hungry and I wanted company. On the naked sand of the triangle there was a Coast Guard station. Farther back, in the dunes near the lighthouse, a C.C.C. Camp, with flag fluttering. Still farther back a radio station and a couple of houses, one of them a general store, and in front of it the one thing that, it seems, you will find anywhere, even in the middle of the Sahara: a red gasoline pump. It looked nice. Still farther back, hidden under trees and among dunes, was the little village.

I cut my gun, came in past the lighthouse, and set her down on the sand flats at the tip of the triangle. And before I had stowed away my maps, unbuckled my belt, and cut my switch, men were coming across the sand in a truck, and I found myself taken over by the people of the Cape.

It was an all-male population, almost military, all wearing some uniform of Uncle Sam's, Coast Guard, Navy, Lighthouse Service, C.C.C., all fighting against either the sand or the sea. The weather, they said, was going to hold out a little longer. I was tired, and decided to stay out there overnight. And before I got away again I had eaten their fish and slept in their bunks, and had seen their Cape through their eyes.

We rode across the hot sand flats to the Coast Guard station. Inside, it was cool and white painted and regulation shape, and a little barren, U.S. Government style. For a few minutes I made a stir among the men, or rather my ship did, and there were the usual questions, how many miles to the gallon, how many miles per hour; but then the station went back to its routine, the grandiose routine of a sentry post at the edge of the ocean.

They were just polishing their lifeboat, and the Captain showed it to me lovingly. After all that coast, a lifeboat seemed a sight of the greatest importance, and it seemed entirely fitting to have come out

here all the way from New York by airplane to inspect the Cape
Hatteras lifeboat.

It was a big brute of a boat. It was poised, ready for action, on its
special truck in the boat shed. It was self-righting and self-bailing,
and its engine had an attachment that outside the Coast Guard
Service is used only by stunt flyers; it would keep running even
though the boat might temporarily be upside down.

The gates of the boat shed were open toward the surf. That
afternoon, the surf was keeping up only the softest of murmurs. But
one man was shining up the breeches-buoy gun, a device that shoots
a line across the surf to a stranded ship to take the men off her; and
the Captain himself was fondling the explosive cartridges one by one
and looking them over. The station was keeping its powder dry all
night.

Looking slightly incongruous on the wall over the boat was a
bookshelf with a long series of leather-bound volumes. Those were
the log books of the station, reaching back to eighteen-hundred-
and-what-not. I sat in the shade for a while and studied the ledger of
Cape Hatteras, an account kept in terms of lives lost and lives res-
cued, but mostly of long, uneventful watches such as the one that
afternoon.

One of the men, a retired fishing captain, wanted to go for a
flight, and so we dumped my luggage on the sand, and filled up on
the Kitty Hawk automobile gasoline, and flew some more, following
the barrier still further on. It wasn't further out, Cape Hatteras
being the outermost point; in fact, the barrier was now curving back
toward the mainland again; but if anything, it was still more deserted. We flew at two hundred feet, and he showed me wild geese
and ducks, and when we came to another inlet, another gap in the
beach, he showed me something I would not have seen alone. The
tide was ebbing out now, and the water from Pamlico Sound came
shooting through the gap like a fast river, with waves like rapids, and
in the rapids there was a school of porpoises. They were playing with
those rapids the way they often play with the bow wave of ships,
jumping and breaking the surface with their shiny backs, swim-

ming against the current and yet remaining stationary. But we went them one better. We stood our ship on its ear and hung ourselves over them into a tight circle, and went round and round while we watched them play.

While I held my head half back to understand him, the captain pointed out to me how shallow it was. You could see bottom all the way across and also thick clouds of mud, stirred up by underwater whirlwinds. It had not always been so shallow, said the captain. The bottoms of all the gaps in the Hatteras barrier had been building up during his lifetime, and the result was that the big fish didn't get into Pamlico and Albemarle Sound any more the way they used to, and that the bigger ships couldn't get in and out any more, and so the fisheries were shot, and the coastal towns, some of them famous and very old, were being strangled. I had been told that story before, but it was a different story now while I sat up there with a sore old man and watched God's gristmill actually grinding.

We turned around and climbed, and in climbing saw the barrier beach re-join the mainland and then sweep out again toward Cape Lookout, and we saw the Cape itself as a white streak of surf through the afternoon haze.

At two thousand feet I leveled off and let the captain have a free hand at the dual controls. He marveled at the quick responsiveness of the ship, which made me smile because Cubs are rated among the most sluggish of airplanes; he was used to steering real ships. But, just like most men who have handled real ships, he found the feel of her immediately. There was something about her behavior that struck this seaman as laughable. Points of humor can't be explained, and I can't explain this one, although I thought I understood him. At any rate, he was grinning over his whole face as he steered her, and we arrived over the Cape in high spirits. My raincoat, my gasoline cans were lying deep below us on the beach, forlorn and tiny, and I took her over and shot a spot landing right beside them.

The sun was coming down by that time, and the C.C.C. fellows came out of the dunes, Carolina farm boys mostly, deeply tanned, extremely husky. You could feel the authority of Uncle Sam in the disciplined way in which they crowded around but refrained from touching the ship. They knew all about it, though: performance, price, terms of payment. The aeronautical magazines are read by young men the country over, and the light, cheap ships have taken their fancy. They knew about Al Bennett, too, and his ways of getting the people into the air. Among these fellows, he was famous as a sort of miracle doctor.

What had brought them out to the Cape was the shifting of the sands. The same shiftiness of the sands that had permitted this barrier to build itself up in the first place and that had produced all the streamlined shapes. The dunes were wandering and threatening to bury the village, and the waves were gnawing the beach away and threatening the lighthouse. The Camp's commandant, a Naval Reserve officer, offered me a bunk for the night. And I started up the big noise still once more and took him for a flight over the Cape to see his men's handiwork.

It was the kind of thing you see only from an airplane, and then only if you look for it. It consisted mostly of fence, short bits of it, enclosing nothing, low and flimsy, strong enough only to stop the blowing sand particles. The fences snaked all over the island in seemingly random convolutions, and looked very much like fancy-free pencil scratches on some piece of paper; and it was odd to see out here, on the edge of nowhere, such evidence of Washington central planning. But they did their job, as I found out on a small scale myself.

It had worried me all afternoon that overnight I might get too many sand grains into the Cub's carburetor or oil system; for out on the flats I had felt the ubiquitous sand even between my teeth. But from the air the Commandant pointed out another landing field to me, also a sandflat, but one where his men had stopped the drift and planted some hardy grass. It was near the Camp. I landed him on the sandflats I knew, and inspected the new spot on foot, and then flew it in and staked it down. And the spot was good. You could not call it dry because grains of sand are not drops of water; but it was as good as getting into a dry place from a drizzling rain.

That night, we drove in a truck through the sand hills to look in at the U.S. Navy radio station. They were busy listening in and sending, for their purpose is to take signals from ships at sea and then tell them which direction they bear from the station. To a terrestrian tourist it would hardly have been a sight, but merely some complicated gadget of which he would not have understood the human meaning; but to a pilot there is nothing so immediately appealing as any device by which a man who is lost can find out where he is; and thus for me it was quite a moving thing to see that all along this coast they keep listening for ships day and night over loop antennaes; a coast with ears.

And voices, too. They gave me a pair of earphones and twirled, and I got the calls of the light vessels and of the maritime radio beacons along the coast, each signaling in turn during its appointed minutes of the hour. Not pretty voices at all; in fact they sounded like a lot of chickens cackling at one another. But exciting voices once you knew that they were the Capes calling out to the Bays in the dark of night, and the Bays calling back to the Capes—and even if it hadn't been exciting it was simply the kind of thing Cape Hatteras has to offer by way of an evening's entertainment.

Conversation that evening was mostly about shipwreck. They were all seafaring men. There was some talk also about the weekly Thursday night dance in the village and about fishing, but when they talk shop on Cape Hatteras they talk of shipwreck. In a negative way, shipwreck was their job. Most of them were making a living out of the dangers of this coast.

It had been years since I had last talked to seafaring men, and perhaps you know how seafaring men talk to a land lubber—very much down. But now it struck me that I could talk to them about such things in navigation as cross bearings and running fixes and dead reckoning and the behavior of compasses very much as man to man, as skipper of my little ship to skippers.

I gathered, though, that the Cape's own reputation for disaster is undeserved. The real danger spot, the spot that they all were guarding with radios and lifeboats and lighthouses, was Diamond Shoals, a sandbank about seven miles off shore. The bottom of the sea there, they said, was strewn with sunken ships. On calm days with smooth water, Congressmen and other privileged characters sometimes had themselves taken out there in the lifeboat to have a look. Diamond Shoals was the real works, they said, and I had better fly out there and take a look myself. And the Coast Guard Captain lent me a life jacket and said he would keep an official eye on me.

And so the next morning I went.

It was not entirely comfortable to head out over open sea with nothing in my tanks but low-grade automobile fuel. It felt a bit like visiting a graveyard alone, at night—you knew it was going to be all right, yet you knew you never could tell. The ship's insurance, at any rate, would be automatically voided by flying out of gliding distance of land. But I trusted the Captain's official eye, and a strong offshore wind shouldered me out a little faster than I really wanted to go. I stayed down at only three hundred feet, and studied the surface of the sea with much dislike. It was a watery and shifty place. The wind was blowing me one way; the whitecaps, by some optical illusion known to every seaplane pilot, seemed to be blowing the other way. My ship was headed still another way, and there was also a tide current. If you looked straight down too long, you got confused and felt all adrift. A slow, light airplane simply hasn't the sovereign go of a fast airplane. I picked out tiny bubbles in the water as reference points by which to gauge my motion, and then I found I was making almost as much way sidewise as I was making forward.

I found the shoals. They appeared as a place in the ocean where the waves broke with considerable foam. But I could not see bottom. I went farther out and swung around to get the sun in my back, and sure enough, the water became transparent and opened up, and there lay a ship: a brownish zeppelin-shaped shadow underneath all the glimmering and shifting blue. Then I saw another one. It had a mast stump that came out of the shadowy depth almost to the surface, the topmost part showing clearly in ocher yellow. I saw more dark shapes lying there, but frankly I didn't have the fun I had promised myself; ship, after all, is ship.

I climbed away, and the sea became opaque again, a woven cloth spread over the corpses. From three thousand feet I spotted seaward, almost invisible in the reflected glare of the sun, the Cape Hatteras lightship. It was anchored several miles beyond the shoals, and it was the very outermost spot of habitation—if an anchor makes a ship a habitation. For good measure, I decided to circle out over it, too, still climbing. Beyond the lightship, I saw a tank steamer coming north, and also a passenger steamer with large superstructure; it looked like a Havana boat. It was a view well worth the risk. Hatteras in action, the Cape sticking out, the shoals foaming and hiding things, the lightship warning, and commerce giving the whole thing a wide berth. My altimeter now showed seven thousand feet, and beyond the ships I could see the region where the Gulf Stream flows and a horizon that was a hundred miles away, though veiled in sea haze.

But the wind was stiffening, scattered clouds had begun to drift in below me, and when I looked landward again, a solid layer had slid in between me and the Cape. There was now nothing to see but the Atlantic. Wait a minute, I thought, I am only a tourist, and I stuck my nose down and left the throttle well open and shot her home past the edge of the cloud layer in a whistling fast power glide. At the Coast Guard Station, the latest weather forecast was in, and was for local thunderstorms and rising winds. I decided to retreat to Norfolk and a hangar without delay before the weather should break.

But first I had to borrow a car to fetch gasoline from the pump, and then stowing luggage and leave-taking took a while. When I got upstairs again and was well on my way, there were thunderstorms rearing up inland over the Carolina swamps; tall anvil-shaped beings of cloud.

Still I was not worried. A thunderstorm is much more local a threat than it usually appears to observers on the ground. Once you go up and look around you may see two or three of them around and still be able to pick a clear route between them. I was confident that I could fly out along the beach in front of the storms, like a car beating a train to the railroad crossing; if I could not make it I might still let a storm go out to sea first, and fly through behind it, like a jaywalking pedestrian crossing a busy street. I would let the storm have its precedence by sitting down on the beach and waiting. Another thing one might ordinarily have done, I did not want to do over this sea-country; I did not want to cut through behind it by flying inland over the lagoons and swamps.

Half way back from the Cape, I came upon the wrecked ship again. This time I circled her twice for a good look. The bowsprit was still on her, and even her name was easy to read from the air: the *Kohler* of Baltimore. It seemed that in her lee, I might be able to wait and have some protection in case the wind rose. And though I wanted to get away quickly, it seemed the best policy to land and wait now rather than have to sit down on the open beach later. There was also this in my mind, that it was the only time I had ever seen an interesting sight from the air and had a chance to land right on the spot. I decided to land. I touched down a thousand feet from the wreck. There were no obstructions, except half-buried pieces of driftwood, and so I kept her rolling and taxied right up to the big hulk. That, I thought, was an all-time high in aviation, and I thought how I was going to brag about it to the airport fellows: "Like a goddamned tourist driving up in a hack!"

With my wing tips almost touching her tall black side, I cut my switch, and again the rhythmic thunder of the surf took me by surprise.

I felt excited from all the low flying and the uncertainty of the weather and the thought of what might overtake my little ship out here on the Cape, and my knees were a bit shaky from the tension of landing and taxiing on the soft sand. By contrast, the wreck was dead. She was high, too high for me to scale. Her boats were gone, the ropes still hanging from the davits. There was really nothing to see but a mood, the melancholy of a dead ship high on the beach with all hope gone. It was driven home to me all the more because I was myself the captain of a little ship. I must get away.

I poured gasoline out of my cans into the tank, started up the engine, climbed in, buckled on my safety belt, and gave her full throttle.

She did not move.

I could lift her tail up to flying position with the controls, but she still just stood balanced on her wheels and roared. It was not that her tires had sunk in; but the sand here was rippled into many tiny dunes, and the tires, because of their softness, could not squash through those mounds, flimsy as they were. And to pull the ship up-and-over even a five-inch obstruction, the propeller had not enough pull, now that the ship had once come to a standstill. I tried all my arts on the controls and kept on full throttle until I had the engine almost burned out; then had to cut back to idling, and acknowledge that I was stuck.

"You must beware of Hatteras." The old ill-reputed Cape had trapped me here; it had put the wrecked ship here as a decoy. I cut the switch and climbed out, and I tried to pull the machine on to smoother ground by my own effort, but could get no foothold in the yielding sand. As for help, the coast guard station was a three hours' walk away, and the nearest village, a two days' walk. I would have to work my own way out, and do so in a hurry, before the thunderstorm caught me here.

I got out my coal shovel, and packed down and smoothed a pair of tracks for my wheels, working frantically. If a thunderstorm did catch me out here on the beach, the black hulk's protection wouldn't help me: I was jammed between it and the surf. I would lose my ship either to the wind or to the tide or to the blowing sand.

I threw my equipment into the ship. I tried again; she moved not all all, but again stood on her wheels, tail in flying position, and roared.

The whole western sky was a dark towering wall of cloud.

I walked the rudder, giving full right and left kicks alternately in slow rhythm, while I watched my wheels. I could move her that way, one side at a time, foot by foot, the left wheel squashing forward, when the tail swung over to the left, and the right wheel when it swung to the right the way a station porter walks a trunk. It was not much like a take-off run, more like the walk of a goose; but it gave me new hope, and I kept walking her, throwing first one side forward, then the other one. The engine meanwhile must be overheating fast, but I was getting to the approximate speed of, say, an academic procession.

Then she refused. She had done ten yards or so, and gradually she came to a stop.

I had made the run on a slight upgrade, up the slant of the beach, for the wind was blowing from the land out to sea; but that had made it extra hard for her. There was nothing to do but to build another runway, cross wind but level. I climbed out again, and went to work, frantically trampling and throwing sand.

At last it worked.

On the next try, she got up to real walking speed, and that was enough. She now had momentum enough to roll over ripples of sand, and kept picking up additional speed. At the speed of a fast walk, she reached a smooth patch. At the speed of a trot, what breeze there was began to take hold of her wings. I kept her tail low to give the wings plenty of attack and take part of the load off the wheels; and a moment later she speeded up into a regular take-off run, bounced a few times, and was off.

12. Key West with Lady

"That's the kind of touring more people ought to do," said Al Bennett when I brought the ship back and reported.

I knew now that I could fly from A to B with fair precision. I was now ready for a long trip, and ready to carry a passenger. There is something about experience that demands to be shared. There also is something about expense that demands to be shared: by dividing the cost, you could multiply your radius of action.

That was not so easily arranged. It must be admitted that one's best acquaintances were the ones that showed the strongest tendency to back out; in my case anyway. They knew you. They had seen you back the car into a hydrant and spill a cocktail because you happened to have jittery hands. They thought of piloting as an awesome art, close-coupled with sudden death; and they could not reconcile the man with the art.

Then again, when you measured flying against the more usual pursuits, it was still a bit expensive—a man who wanted to spend so much on flying, would just as soon spend it on flying lessons, and become a pilot himself, though a woman might not. Then again there were those incredible people who simply didn't care: "Want to fly up to Boston this afternoon?" "I haven't anything to do in Boston."

And there were those people who had no idea what a small airplane could or could not do; you might ask some girl to come flying,

thinking perhaps you might circle the Statue of Liberty or perhaps
Jones Beach—and likely as not she would say: "Let's fly to Bermuda!"

After all these experiences I was able to decide what my passenger must be like. In the first place, probably a woman. Seeing
that it would be poor etiquette for a woman to go off flying for weeks
alone with a man, she must be not only a lady, but so much of a lady
that she could afford a breach of etiquette. In addition, she must
represent certain traits of temperament and of upbringing, which in
my mind I vaguely described as being O.K.

Having thus worked out the specifications of an aeronautical
dream girl, I let my mind run back and forth over all the people I
knew. To my surprise, it stopped every time at an architect whom I
had seen only a few times at a mutual friend's house. I sat down to
write her a glowing prospectus. How about flying to Key West and
back, during Christmas vacation? I set forth the exact degree of risk,
of inconvenience, of hard work possibly involved; and next morning
I had a wire saying, "Count me in."

We worked hard over the luggage question. The ship's official
luggage allowance was only ten pounds. We needed a shirt and a
razor and their feminine equivalents; also, a spare pair of shoes
because of the airport mud and a sweater for the higher altitudes; a
lot of maps, a protractor, and the airport directory. I also carried an
extra pair of spectacles. We decided to take a camera. When we
added a thermos bottle and a pair of duffle bags to hold it all, the
luggage allowance was badly overshot. But in aeronautical law the
weight of a person is a hundred and seventy pounds regardless, and
since we both weighed far less, we figured out ways to hang a good
deal of clothes and utensils on our persons.

Only the front seat controls could be dismantled in the Cub we
were to fly. I did not like the idea of carrying a passenger in front, for
in case of a landing mishap the front occupant is more exposed to
risk. The farther back in an airplane you sit, the safer you are. On the
other hand, except in case of a real accident, the passenger can brace
himself against the instrument board with both hands during landings; and any ship is easier to fly with precision from farther back—
which in turn was a safety factor.

My passenger's interest being water-color sketching, we designed an airgoing studio outfit—consisting of water bottles and pouches for brushes and pencils that could be hung from structural members of the cabin. Then we went to work laying out our courses, working in unprecedented comfort on an architect's drafting table, instead of the usual hangar floor.

On the morning set for our departure, the weather broke into a series of winter storms. There was nothing to do but go home, phone the airport weather bureau every few hours, and watch our vacation time trickle away. On the third day, a great big "High" came swimming along on the *New York Times* weather map, soothing as a spot of oil on troubled waters, and we got away.

But with winds still high, and the short days of late December, it took us a day and a half to negotiate Richmond, Virginia. That evening, I calculated the average speed we had made since the time of departure originally scheduled. It came out at 2.5 miles an hour, or a brisk walk.

By Christmas Eve, we made Charleston.

Now Charleston is not the kind of place one can do by airplane, and our sightseeing there does not belong in this story. But what does belong is the flavor it gives to Charleston—or any other town— to have gone there by air. Not on an airliner, of course, behind two engines and two uniformed pilots and on a radio beam and an underslung wing that shields you from the view below; but the way we did, behind a putt-putt, on one's own responsibility, and slowly, with time to worry, time for the country to get under one's skin. In the case of Charleston, one felt much less "mellow" that way and much less patronizing, much less like a tourist, and much more proud, much more the way the people must have felt who first built that town; not because the houses and gardens were beautiful or because they were old, but simply because they are there. Any work of man seemed a proud thing just for being there, on a coast that hardly seems habitable.

We had flown, for instance, across Cape Fear. Flying south from Richmond, we hit the Atlantic Coast just north of it, and on our way further down, we short-cut across it: as concentrated an upcropping of geographic nastiness as you will find. It is bad enough for a Cape to be a hazard to navigation and to bear a bullying name—but what gives that Cape its nasty character is that even inside it is all soft and gooey, one brown expanse of swamp; even as land it is bad. You don't necessarily see that right away; when I first approached it looked to me more like some sort of prairie, hard and flat and treeless; wonderful country to fly over, you could land on it anywhere anytime, but when we were over it I happened to look down over the side and I saw the sun glistening between the grass leaves, and the clouds and the blue sky mirrored up to me. After that we went up to five thousand feet to cross it and still kept watching our oil pressure with some uneasiness. And after country like that, the gardens of Charleston make their real point.

Or take the way we first laid eyes on Charleston itself. We were still flying high, almost at the level to which the fear of Cape Fear had driven us, and still for the same reason: that we were afraid of what was below. It was forest then, nothing but forest, the blackest forest I had ever seen, no landmark to steer by, no trace of human settlement, not even a cabin, not even a road. In clear weather we might have seen its ends, but the air was filled with watery haze and shot through with slanting rays of sun. Actually, of course, we had our compass course to steer by, but we seemed to stand even stiller than one ordinarily does when flying, and as the minutes went by it felt as if we would never get out of the forest again, as if it were a fairy story; we seemed lost in the deep dark forest, and night coming on.

Eventually, I saw a stream, and across the stream there was a bridge. How nice, I thought; one of the forest people has laid a board across the stream and built himself a little bridge; and I wondered if I would see his cabin. And even while I looked we were coming closer and the light shifted a bit, and instead of a cabin in the woods, I saw the houses of Charleston. And with my sense of scale set right, I recognized the little bridge as the huge steel-structured suspension bridge that leads from Charleston to the Charleston navy yard. A few minutes later we landed on one of the finest airports in the East. All the next day, while sightseeing in the old, urban civilization of Charleston, all that was still under my skin.

It was much the same with Savannah.

We had an early morning conference with the commercial pilots at the Charleston airport. We found we could fly to Savannah along the outer beaches, which were hard and good to land on. But in case we really ever should be forced down out there by engine failure, it would be days before we could be got out, and we might never get the ship out before the next gale and high tide would break it up. We could also fly along the landward edge of the coastal region, along what farmers and motorists would consider the coast line. But to fly over country firm enough to support, for instance, railroad tracks, would have meant a wide swing landwards, and then only more forests under us. So we did what one usually ends up by doing: fly the shortest route by compass and try not to look down.

That compass course took us again over a country neither land nor sea. The Atlantic and the outer beaches were just barely within sight on our left, by comparison looking nice and clean. But under us were mudflats and rivers, swamps and salt marshes all mixed up.

My passenger, who was sketching hard on this hop, was drawing something that looked like a diagram of blood vessels in an anatomical cross section; and the colors she was mixing on the margin, as a note for later execution, were neither green, nor blue, but gray and silver.

I was still a well-brought-up young pilot at that time—well-brought-up never to trust my engine—and there is nothing like hanging over a piece of land on an engine you don't trust to develop an almost physical feeling for that piece of land. You can't help looking down. Landing would not have been a catastrophe, it would at worst have meant a slow somersault, well-cushioned by the morass—you could feel its softness up at one thousand feet. But then, what of the modesty of a 40 h.p. pilot? I hadn't had myself teletyped ahead to Savannah as I might have, and nobody would miss us. It would mean trying to walk out, and that in turn would mean our slightly ridiculous and very slimy end.

Our engine, of course, kept running.

Once or twice a fisherboat on one of the inlets made a nervous stepping stone; then there were fields—those last morsels of the continent are the Sea Islands where a famous kind of cotton once grew. St. Helena Island, with the village of Beaufort, looked solid enough under its trees. There was an emergency field nearby which looked inviting, and also a naval airfield, but we proudly passed them up. The country became drier and greener, though still empty and treeless and without roads; and at the calculated time, on the calculated heading, we hit Savannah right on the nose. There was an oil tank in the distance, then the river; a steamer we knew from the New York waterfront; then a pattern of friendly roof tops with breakfasts cooking out of every chimney. It seemed again quite a feat of civilization to have a city here, and civilization seemed wholly good.

The beach of Florida we first saw while we were technically still over Georgia. It was the same beach that further down becomes famous as Daytona Beach, and Palm Beach and Miami Beach—but up here it was just plain beach, unpublicized and empty of people. It stretched out all the way to the horizon, almost straight, a smooth ribbon of sand, with the inviting expression of a highway. There are some types of scenery that one cannot look at without wanting to take some action: mountains, for instance, ask to be climbed, snowfields, to have tracks made on them. Seen from an airplane, that beach seemed to ask for action, and we gave it action. We really did.

We flew it low, lower than I had ever flown before, as low as an airplane can fly and not be an automobile—or an airplane wreck. Flying low is what every pilot sometimes itches to do, for it is one of the Forbidden Things. Only if you fly very low can you have a taste of both flight and speed—and together those two make a very strong drink. It is called hedgehopping; and if you hedgehop across country that really does have hedges, fences, and ditches and your engine quits, you crack up.

We lowered ourselves carefully at first, staying at the fifty-foot level for a while to watch things. Seen from that level, the beach moved along at a pleasant dog trot, and even that was exhilarating. The tide was half out, and there was just room enough for our wing span between the surf on one side and the dunes on the other—with the necessary margin to spare. The sand itself was smooth. Any time that the engine might quit, one would merely have to pull a normal landing. Things looked as if for once we might mix ourselves that stiff drink.

I wound the stabilizer back a few turns until the ship became slightly tail heavy and wanted to climb, and had to be held down with some forward pressure on the stick. That way, I figured, I only would have to let go of the controls, and she would lift herself away from danger. Then, carefully and gradually, I forced her down onto the beach.

At ten feet or so, she became lively. Seventy miles per hour may not sound so fast to a motorist, but both of us were accustomed to the suspended feel of an airplane—and then, it wasn't highway we were speeding over, but open country. At six feet, she became down-right fast. Dunes, palms, pieces of driftwood began to flow, and the ground under us—that same ground which so often seems to stand still—moved so fast that it began to blur.

It was easy flying, though, and my pilot's conscience was merely prickling pleasantly without actually hurting. The air was smooth, as it usually is very near the ground. The dunes seemed to stow up the sea wind, for she shot straight ahead without any sidewise crabbing. Her flight felt solid, as if on tracks. Even her sound had a reassuring note. The sand seemed to absorb some of her usual overtones and to throw back others, and the resulting tone was much deeper than usual and had a periodic throb in it, a monotonous rhythmical beat that made me feel like a railroad train. And though it may be a peculiar commentary on the air age that a pilot should enjoy feeling like a railroad train, I did like it.

The view was a railroad train view. What's more, it was like a train view in a place where the track runs through a deep cut. We were so low that the dunes, just off our right wing tip, cut off all view inland. It felt comfortable and homey for once not to look at the world by states and counties, but to take it piecemeal; to be personally present, even if only for one roaring instant, on some nice warm spot of ground.

For half hours, we saw no people. It was the old Atlantic loneliness again.

Once we rumbled past a colony of slapped-together houses that stood on the crest of the dunes, higher than we were, and out of the corner of my eye I had a glimpse of a lot of electric poles and of fluttering wash and of a girl in a red dress. I thought how convenient it would be to have one's heart interest living in Florida; diving on your lady's house no longer cuts any ice, but flying past under her window still might. That was the last of human company for a while. Sometime during that hour we passed near Jacksonville, but we saw no trace of it; we were too low.

Instead, we had birds. They sat on the beach in great numbers and fluttered up on our approach, and were quite a hazard; for they were big substantial creatures. Birds must take off against the wind, just as humans must, and we were flying against the wind. Furthermore, some of them seemed to underestimate our speed, and to make up their minds too late. Thus, instead of getting away from us, they were forced into moments of close formation flight with us, with the relative motion greatly slowed down, and the danger of collision greatly prolonged. More than once, I had the finger on the ignition switch ready to slacken the propeller speed instantly if one of them should get into our way. It would not have saved the bird, but it might have saved the propeller. I have an almost personal memory of one big fellow who flapped along beside us for a few of the slow, powerful strokes of his wings. He looked across to me with a raised-eyebrow expression on his face which conveyed to me that he considered me a noisy and ill-mannered bird; the Dirty Look of highway traffic translated into the air. Then, just as he seemed about to say something, he thought better of it; he turned away, and was left behind.

Once we came upon a few fishermen who stood in the surf in high boots and were casting. It may have been the fascination of fishing, but more likely it was because for them the surf drowned out our noise—at any rate, we noticed that we came upon each of them by surprise, and their heads jerked around toward us only when we were within a stone's throw. It made you feel wonderfully like a ghost to come floating up to a man, silent and scaring. We had fun looking them in the eyes during the few moments each of us had in which to react. We were keyed to so much faster action than they were. One of them shook his fist at us; but his timing was sluggish, and he succeeded only in threatening the place where we had been a few moments ago. Most of them smiled, in answer to our smiles, but it seemed a delayed-action smile that was going to break out in full, we could see, only after we would be well away.

Then we came upon a party of bathers on the beach. We were at six feet, and we were going to climb higher to avoid scaring them, but they saw us from afar and scattered, clearing the road for us as if we were a miserable automobile honking its way. Then they stood aside and saluted us as we shot past.

Thus we shot South.

Salt spray collected on our lips and on the wind shield. My face began to burn from the mere reflection of the sun in the waves and the sand. Beyond the monotonous noise of the ship, our ears learned to distinguish the swishing of the waves as they rolled up on the beach—but only the swishing part; the thundering part of their sound was drowned out by our power plant.

We were getting deep into Florida.

In the end we put the ship all the way down. I nudged her down carefully, foot by foot, with small motions of the stick, then inch by inch until, I honestly believe, we had but a couple of inches of altitude. Our eyes were closer to the ground than they would have been in an automobile, and her speed became ferocious. It was as if a horse had suddenly made up its mind to run and really extend itself, *ventre à terre,* belly to the ground.

It took precision work on the controls, though, for the beach slanted upward from the surf toward the dunes, and thus our right wing tip rode almost as close to the ground as did our wheels; hooking it into a piece of driftwood or even only sliding it on the sand would have meant a bad crack-up. I edged her out over the surf to get away from that hazard, and I kept my head well out to the right to be able to see ahead past her nose and watch her ride. Our mild-mannered Cub rode like a ramrod come to life—I hadn't thought she had that in her.

I opened her throttle from cruising to full power, and she wanted to climb, but I held her down and she speeded up still more; 90 m.p.h. was her top speed. The way I held my head cocked, her two right side cylinders were just before me, the two short exhaust stacks now blasting away staccato. So often high up in the air, this same type of ship had sounded to me as if it were frantically trying to drill a hole in the air and getting nowhere. Now she was like a firecracker that blasts itself along the pavement by the force of its own explosions.

But our time was up. By dead reckoning we must be there. I let her have her head and she zoomed to three hundred feet before all her excess speed was spent. Things quieted down, and we got a look inland. There were sand flats and subtropical shrubbery and in the distance the lagoon called Indian River. Beyond that, sure enough, the water tank of a town, high on a tripod, and we went to look for the airport.

The little landing field was sandy and hot. No car was available, and the nearest eating place was a mile down the highway. An airplane will do that kind of trick to you. It will take you and dump you into places where the tourist trade has not yet lubricated things with soft soap. It will make you, instead of a tourist, an old-fashioned stranger, eyed with suspicion. That morning in Charleston I had put on my bulky flying suit once more, and my passenger wore a ski suit and ski boots; down here it was now really hot. We walked down the highway; it was U.S. 1, the main highway from the North, and all the tourist traffic bound for Miami flowed past, old cars, shiny cars, trailers. They forced us off into the rough, and they gave us the nasty eye one gives the penniless and the queer.

The eating place turned out to be a roadhouse with an all-day night club inside, artificially darkened and electrically lighted, with a dance floor and a three-man band. The waitress called my passenger Honey. At the table next to ours were two salesmen in white knickers and two girls, drinking cocktails. We hadn't spoken to anyone since Charleston except to two gasoline pump men at two airports; the last hours spent flying the beach might have been anywhere along the edge of the world's oceans; but now, we were suddenly in Florida and felt very strange.

The flight further down the coast was smooth—even aloft, life in Florida seemed effortless. For navigation, all one does is to follow the coast; for forced landings, if one should ever be necessary, here is always the beach. Also, Florida is one state which has an adequate state-run airport system (the other being Michigan). Flying at five thousand feet or so along the East Coast, one is rarely out of sight, in fact rarely out of gliding range, of an airport.

Brilliant white cumulus clouds came drifting in from the Gulf Stream—not at four thousand and five thousand feet as in the North, but at fifteen hundred and two thousand feet; the shady chasms between them made good flying. We passed one more Cape, Canaveral, the last one down the coast, dark in a rain squall. Then Palm Beach, where a Vanderbilt-owned air yacht sat on the airport, big as a house, too big to fit into the hangar; and then in the twenty-first hour of our flight, Miami.

Now for the last hop. Like a couple of romanticists, we wanted to go down the Atlantic coast as far as one could go, and that meant Key West. It also meant trusting the little ship across considerable water. The famous sea-going railroad had been put out of commission by a hurricane. Ground travelers at that time could reach Key West only by repeated transfers from road to boat and back again to road, and that made it seem a little adventurous to fly out there. It is strange how long it takes your mind to rid itself of ground considerations. Actually, of course, it makes no difference: air is air, regardless of what is beneath it, hungry lions, "no admittance" signs, water, national boundaries, or whatnot—as long as the engine runs.

Again the local airport people advised us not to fly, seeing that we had no business there. But we took a day off, had the engine given its regular twenty-hour check, and then had a slightly ridiculous conversation across a restaurant table in which a man explained to his lady what to do in an airplane that is forced down into the water: namely, unlatch the door, keep one hand on the safety belt buckle and the other to brace yourself with against being thrown forward after hitting, unbuckle and get out backwards, behind the wings. And then we flew.

We went out over the Hialea race track, where Miami borders on the swamps, and assumed our compass course. We picked up our next check point, thirty miles away, in thirty minutes: Homestead, the last town on the mainland, complete with cannery chimney and water tank. The Atlantic appeared high on the left horizon, and on the right the part of the Everglades known as the big cypress swamp: a khaki-colored, deadly soup. It was the most horribly flat country I have ever seen, if you want to call it country; too thick to make waves, too liquid to have even the slightest mound. Under us in the next few minutes passed a few last orange groves, a bit of pine woods, then flat green tundra, turning into marsh, swamp, pools of water, tidal flats: a continent petering out. A railroad shack was the last thing that was man-made, upright, and dry.

Low in the water to the south were the Keys.

The railroad and the road went out there on trestles, each making straight for the nearest point of land. We went out, too, but shortcut-ting on a compass course, and with a pronounced feeling of superi-ority. For nothing this side of a flying dream will give you the sensa-tion of flight as keenly as will the moment when you slide from land out over the water. After the first few hours of one's flying experi-ence, one's nervous system sets to work to take the edge off this unaccustomed thing. And very soon ordinary flying feels no more thrilling than a walk, a special sort of walk to be sure, on giant stilts across towns and country, but still a walk that somehow has always one leg on the ground. You know by lifelong experience that the ground can be trusted. But when you fly out over the water, that same earthbound imagination tricks you into expecting—with some tiny corner of your mind—that now you will get a cooling and will have to gasp for air; that at least you will have to labor to keep from sinking; and when nothing of that sort happens you are suddenly reminded that you are really flying, that nothing is holding you up but your wings' plowing through the air. It feels fine.

We became quite lighthearted—she had run all the way down here from New York, she would probably keep running a little longer. We picked up Key Largo after a quarter-hour over water, and also the railroad again. We were now in the middle between the Gulf of Mexico and the Atlantic. It seemed quite a place for this little piece of New Jersey property to be, and she was still headed outward. The view was almost wholly sea. The wind out here was stiff and gusty. Looking out over the blue from our height one could understand why the older writers used to write of the winds, rather than simply the wind. One could actually see the winds, many of them; they appeared as dark shaded blotches that ran over the surface of the sea in packs, like wolves.

Sixty more miles. The islands were all strung together by that absurd railroad, and because of the wind we went low and followed it along its laborious dams and across low uninhabited islands. We stuck closely to it the two times when it bridged ten- and fifteen-mile gaps of open water. It has since been re-fashioned into a highway, but that winter it was abandoned. The rails themselves still held together but in places the hurricane had swept them off and they hung down loosely beside the road bed. It looked much like a shoulder strap slid off a woman's shoulder, and it gave you the same feeling; it irked you and at the same time it was nice to have things for once not so prim. It reminded you that here was the edge of the temperate and Anglo-Saxon zone. There were other bits of scenery to bear that out: a palm having its head mussed by the wind; a piece of tropical seashore.

Most of our attention was taken up by the sea, or rather the two seas—how large they were, how blue, how intensely lighted.

Then the island of Key West, and the end of this flight.

Key West, the town, low in the water, stony and treeless and fortress-like, grim in spite of all the blue and silver in which it lay. Whatever mellow and leisurely flavor life there might have on the ground—from the air one could not see it. It made you think, not how warm these waters were, but of the hurricanes.

An outpost station: there were two high radio towers, rather heavily built, and a lighthouse; an airway radio beam station whose beam was trained, according to my map, on Havana; a fort, unused but still looking military rather than merely romantic; an airport; a Coast Guard base, and a seaplane ramp. It was clearly one of those places that live by being the last stop. The railroad stopped and the United States themselves didn't go any further and the Atlantic Coast itself just ended. Even the fishing boats kept close to the town, and beyond them there was nothing but open sea and winds traveling in hordes.

13. Adventure in the Forest

And now I must confess that I finally dropped the lady and the ship into the woods.

That such a thing might happen had been part of my sales talk to her. A light ship such as the Cub, I had explained, was in a way safer than the most expensive twin-engined ship with ten thousand dollars' worth of the safety gadgets.

If worst should ever come to worst we could always rely on the slowness of our glide, pull a deliberate crash landing. Thus, I had explained, our ultimate risk was reasonable. For according to the laws of physics, the Cub, touching down at only half the speed of a heavier ship, would hit only one-fourth as hard—no harder than a car slithering into the ditch at twenty-five miles per hour.

That was the theory.

Its practical test took place in the pine forests of Georgia, just north of the Florida state line, between Okefenokee Swamp and the Swanee River. It happened on the second morning after our return from Key West, shortly after we had left the last Florida town at daybreak. We should have put in a long distance call to Jacksonville for weather reports and the forecast. But the sky was clear, and we were by that time well routinized and somewhat tired; and anyway, where would you go to use a phone in a small fruit-growing town before daylight? That's the mixture of which most accidents are concocted: not the dangers of the air itself, but sloppy ground work.

In the airport dawn, we saw tiny wisps of mist floating among the tree tops and just above them. We had seen the same sort of wisps the morning before, and had seen them burn away under within an hour after sunrise: dew, the natives called it, somewhat unscientifically. They were no bigger, each taken by itself, and no more substantial than what a good cigar smoker could produce with one lungful; but they were fog.

We took off and set our course for three hundred and fifty degrees which is almost due north. The sun was up, but not yet clear of a bank of clouds low on the eastern horizon, and something in the mood of the landscape suggested the north and winter and that our days in the tropical Gulf vintage of air were over.

It was a forgotten region far off the main traveled air route, except for some railroads that cross it on the way from somewhere to elsewhere.

Almost immediately, we were lost over the pine forests with nothing to see from horizon to horizon but trees; no houses, no roads, no clearings. Even our own port of departure had been swallowed up by the trees when, after a few minutes, I gave my customary look back over the tail to etch into my mind the port's appearance from this side so that I could find it again quickly in case of need. There was not a single landmark except far away an observation tower for forest fires, like a lighthouse watching over a dark ocean of trees.

After negotiating the Keys, it was not necessary to watch that cageful of lions quite as closely as might have befitted a less experienced crew—or so I thought. Our tanks were full, our next hop an easy hundred and twenty miles, and the wind was on our tail. We simply went. Flying seemed more like driving a car than it ever had before. I neither kept track of my exact position, nor of my angle of drift, nor of the exact direction and strength of the wind. I was trusting two railroad lines to catch me up eventually funnel-wise and lead me into the next airport.

Because there was so little chance of a successful forced landing in case of engine failure, I stayed at five hundred feet; anyway, I had come to trust that engine.

After ten minutes, the sun at last rose clear of that bank of clouds and shone prettily on wisps and the crowns of the trees, and we could feel it also shining into our cockpit. The forest was presumably getting the same radiation. The mists would now burn away.

We started our breakfast.

After half a sandwich, the rising sun disappeared behind another cloud, to be gone, from the looks of it, for twenty minutes. The day turned cool again and a bit grayish, and I threw away my sandwich. Below us the wisps of smoke seemed to solidify. But at our altitude, the visibility was still twenty miles or so, and I went on wishing I had seen a weather report and knew dew point and temperature. It would obviously not be so good if the temperature sank back much closer to the dew point.

Ten minutes later, I saw in the distance, lying across our course, a solid pool of white that wasn't dew or mist or any other fancy Floridian form of condensation. It was downright fog.

To strike the proper balance between one's caution and one's determination to keep going—that is the essence of flying judgment. Caution one hundred per cent doesn't work: you could never get away from the airport. I kept on my course, but climbed to two thousand feet to look around. Behind me, the mists, now thickening, still left plenty of the ground uncovered—my retreat was not yet cut off. Before me, the fog might be some local condition of which the other end might presently come to view. I decided that I was not likely to get caught, and I kept going.

When you get too afraid, you turn around; but there is also something in turning around which brings out your fear. When I finally banked around steeply to run back, the whole adventure had suddenly turned grim. The sky had by degrees clouded up, and the patches of fog underneath us were coalescing fast into a solid layer. I had waited too long. I was some fifty miles in the forest with my exact position unknown. There was no reasonable chance now of flying a direct course back to the last airport by dead reckoning.

The only chance now was to fly one of those reasoned-out courses, so as to intercept a certain railroad track which eventually would lead me back. It was a detour that would cost me half an hour extra, for it was uphill work against the wind. Meanwhile, the airport itself might fog in.

It was one of those cases where all you can do is to sit it out; absolutely nothing could help now, no amount of skill; simply the passage of minutes. I kept nudging forward against the stick to make more speed and lose altitude; against a headwind, one makes better speed down at lower altitude.

After ten minutes, I was down to two hundred feet, flying in the clear air just above the stuff, and looking down through the holes at the forest, waiting for the railroad track to appear.

The holes were coming less and less often, and I was watching them sharply. It was, of course, elementary that I must fly contact. I must not allow us to get caught atop the stuff, out of sight of the ground without full radio and blind-flying equipment and fuel for several hours. For if a pilot is thus caught, he is bound to hit hard when, eventually through lack of fuel, he must come down blind.

At intervals, I was now getting loads of the stuff in the face. It was a foretaste of what I half knew would come next: that I would have to go down into it entirely. It was like swimming in a ghostly sort of surf that rolled over you. It was not cold and was gaseously soft, and it did not hit hard and it could not throw you. But it blotted out all vision, and gave you a sense of choking that was ugly.

I burst into another one of those ghostly waves and I did not burst out again; it seemed endless. With well-trained reflex action, I tried to capsule myself up against so shifty an outside world, the way I had taught myself in all those hours under the hood; I turned to my instrument board. But it was almost bare. There was no turn indicator on this ship, not even the rolling ball of the bank indicator, not one of those instruments by which one can fly blind; it was like stepping on the brake in an automobile and have it go all the way to the floorboard with no effect. I must fly contact; and the only way to do that was to go all the way down.

When at last I came out again, I waited in vain for the next hole and the next glimpse of the ground. I pulled up a bit higher to see ahead. It was all a solid floor of fog. For a moment I thought I had missed my last chance to go below, and I was half glad. It was more to one's instinct to keep in the clear as long as one could. But then, better judgment prevailed; I turned back, a retreat within a retreat, to find one of the holes that I had passed up.

It was only a minute before I found one, dark trees showing up through it. I cut my power, and gave one last look at the gray clouds high above. I jammed the stick over to the left, rammed my right foot forward, and let her sideslip silently down into the fog.

Below, the light was dim, a whitish gray, through which the tree crowns showed indistinctly, then disappeared again and reappeared. There was a cloudlike structure to this fog. The stuff was resting on the tree tops; there were not even the ten feet or so of clear air I had half hoped for.

The horizon now was a hundred yards away; the world was a mat of pine tops, emerging out of the fog and rushing past ten feet under me the way a road surface rushes past a driver.

I put on power again and settled down to wait for the railroad tracks.

Fortunately the country was flat. But somewhere in the fog, I knew, that observation tower must be lurking, and I would have no warning. For that matter, watch towers, like rattlesnakes, seldom come alone: they are usually arranged in pairs, so that between them they can take cross bearings and determine the position of a forest fire. I kept rehearsing in my mind what I should do if one of them should loom up: I was too low to bank without hooking a wing tip in the trees; yet I would have to bank if I wanted to turn. You can't make sharp turns in an airplane without banking; if you simply kicked rudder you would simply skid along broadside but in the old direction. Thus I deliberated that I would first pull up to get enough altitude, and simultaneously, in proportion to the air-room thus gained, I would lean over into my bank, thus making a climbing turn. But I would have no decent horizon to guide me: if one of the towers did loom up, the chances of crashing were fifty-fifty.

I expected my passenger presently to turn around and act up with questions or complaints: What was the matter, or what was going to happen now, or how much longer, or what not? If she did, I thought I would never take another passenger, and I would never look at another woman. But she sat rigidly, looking down and watching the fog with a neutral sort of curiosity. Was she so stupid, I thought, or was she such good stuff? She was Radcliffe plus M.I.T.; she couldn't be stupid.

I was waiting for the railroad track. I knew it would be easy to miss, for it would only be for seconds, and only when we were directly over it, that the dark forest would open and show us dark rails and dark cross-ties; and we must not miss it. Yet I must also keep a lookout forward for those towers, or other unknown hazards. Hills? I hoped not.

My passenger had by that time become expert with landmarks; I shouted to her: "single track," which was instruction enough.

After a while, I could no longer deceive myself: the stuff was still thickening. I thought of the sun. For two hundred feet above us was fog; for two thousand feet above that, clear air. Above that, a layer of gray clouds; above that, I hoped, the sun, rising higher, burning away at the stuff.

But it better come down to us soon. The gasoline gauge was noticeably lower now. The horizon was constricting itself around us like a noose.

The minutes dragged.

We had made the railroad track, we were feeling our way along it, boring through the stuff back southward, with only thirty more minutes to go when the fog finally became overwhelming. What I had thought could be no thicker, thickened again. It came in thick clouds, clouds within clouds, as if someone had opened the door to the devil's wash kitchen. To go still lower and keep the ground in sight I didn't dare; it was only a matter of feel before I would hit some extra high tree.

A chair, or a table, needs at least three points of support before it will stand. So does a pilot's sense of knowing where in space he is, and how to steer: a pilot must be able to see at least three known points outside his own ship. With a skilled pilot, those three points can be quite close together, just as a floor lamp may be standing precariously on a narrow base; the same way, a skilled pilot can keep himself oriented if he sees perhaps only a narrow circle of ground underneath him. The three points of support need not be present simultaneously; they may come into action in rapid mutual succession, as they do when you balance a stick on a finger, the finger first acting as one point of support, then as another, then as still another. The same way, a very skillful pilot may keep flying straight and level if he only has an occasional glimpse of the ground under him, then perhaps a short one of the sun, then perhaps another one of the country to one side. But if a pilot's mental picture of his own flight hasn't those three points of contact with the outside world, it collapses within a few minutes.

I knew all that, both in theory and by experience. I had found it out in instrument flying practice. I knew that a pilot who tries to fly by neither outside vision nor proper instruments staggers around for a while, winds up finally in a terrific spiral dive whose force will break the ship in midair unless it buries itself in the ground first. I had felt the force of that diving spiral, experimentally under the hood, with instruments before me and a knowledge of how to break the ship out of it, and a safety pilot outside to see that I got out promptly. But now the stuff thickened, and for seconds in a stretch cut me off as effectively as a hood, and I had no instruments.

I wobbled around in a wide turn, picked up the track again, and began fighting my way northward; it was sixty miles that way, to an airport, and my fuel range would only narrowly suffice; but it seemed the only chance.

The stuff thinned out a bit. But the forest deepened. On aeronautical maps, forests are not marked; I was half hoping that I might come out into open farming country soon. But no luck.

We passed over a group of roofs at the railroad side; some settlement, but apparently not a farming one; the forest stood all the way into the backyards of the houses.

Five minutes later, the thick stuff again came rolling through the thinner stuff, clouds within clouds, blotting out all my contact with the ground except for one point, which was a pinetree top, hastening past me at a slightly wrong angle.

Have you ever stepped on ice and had your legs slide out from under you? That was the feeling I now had, in horrible slow motion. I knew it and knew what it meant: I couldn't fly anymore.

We were finally caught then.

My choice was clearly between a full-size crash very soon, or the best landing I could pull off in the forest.

I turned back, regained the thinner patches of the fog, regained the cabins. I circled, looking for a landing spot. The plane was observed over the village of Hamlow "circling low as if looking for a landing." I had once ridiculed that newspaper phrase; as if you could see more landing places from low down than from higher up. But now, there it was: and a man could really be reduced to a position where he needed to go down low and look closely, because all he wanted was a decent place to crash. The street between the cabins was clear, but not quite broad enough. I made another wide circle over the forest, low over that racing mat of tree tops.

I saw an opening slide by, not a clearing exactly but at least a bald spot in the forest. I cut the gun for a moment and said through the sudden silence, "Watch your head. I'm going to land."

My passenger made some small sound, it seemed a whimper. But the engine, re-opened, drowned it out. I hated to risk smashing up a woman's face, and I hated to let the ship go, but it couldn't be helped now. I was already thinking of the prescribed telegram to the authorities at Washington: "Damage considerable, injuries slight."

I had lost the spot, and maneuvered around in a certain pattern George Adams had insisted on teaching me, a right turn followed by a left turn which brings you out so that you can double back exactly on your track. It had seemed to me like useless parade-ground stuff. But now I needed it, hoping to pick that open spot up again, headed against the wind.

I throttled back to half power and wound the stabilizer all the way back to help me keep the nose up and the glide slow. The ship slowed up and the controls felt soft, her lift was almost gone. It was now a matter of statistical chance. The steeper I could let her sink, the less likely we were to hit a tree or a stump. The more slowly I could bring her in and still not drop or spin, the less it would hurt if we did hit something hard.

I kept the ship barely flying with small bursts of power just clearing the crowns of the trees hoping the maneuver had been properly gauged and the clearing would appear again.

Then it opened up under me.

I cut the gun. She stalled and mushed down like an elevator; out of the corner of my eyes, I saw the trees grow up beside us. Halfway down I gave her another blast of power so she wouldn't drop entirely out of control. Two tree trunks loomed up dead ahead: the crash.

I gave a fast kick on the rudder and jerked the stick over so as to stick the ship's nose through between the two. This way the wings would take the shock and shear off, rather than the ship's nose and our heads. My hand was on its way to the ignition switch. But before we reached the trees, her wheels brushed through some flimsy greenery, with a noise as of a deer breaking through some under-brush, and she stopped almost on the spot.

The forest was quiet except for the slow throbbing of our engine. I switched it off. Then it was even more quiet, and it was green and almost motionless. Where there should have been the cracking noise of a crack-up, and shaky-handed work with the first-aid kit, there was nothing catastrophic now. It was simply a dull gray day. All the hurry had stopped; except in myself. I climbed out; and even while I did, I reached forward and shook my passenger's hand and somewhat aggressively congratulated her on being alive and unhurt—this to forestall any recriminations, for I didn't know her so well then.

The bushes and the grass were wet. I fingered the propeller, and it was whole. Incredulously I grabbed the wings and shook them; they were rigid as ever, and were not touching anything but soft branches. I looked all over the ship; it was intact. It looked normal as if it were standing in a hangar, instead of deep in a forest. Ten feet before us were some high tree stumps. Ten feet behind the tail were some young pines, double man's height. All around was forest.

My passenger climbed out, and I discovered what the whimper

had been about; it wasn't that she had been scared. She had merely meant to report that she was ready with her hands propped against the instrument board, to brace herself like a good girl.

I can't deny that I was pleased with myself. Naturally, it had been entirely chance that we had not struck some hidden stump. But the same approach, made a shade faster, a shade less steeply, would have meant breakage. The old reflexes, I thought, had worked O.K.; my training, having contained that item about the switch back, and that item about the power stall, was O.K.

But what now?

We were in the forest with a dead object weighing six hundred pounds, measuring thirty-six feet across and almost as much fore-and-aft, and as vulnerable in most spots as an umbrella, consisting as it did of fabric held in place by wooden ribs of matchbox thickness. A take-off from this spot was unthinkable. To detach the wings and cart the ship piecemeal to the nearest airport would be terribly expensive, and likely to lead to much minor damage.

First of all we sat down on the soft tires of the Cub and finished our breakfast. Fittingly, the next thing that appeared out of the depths of the forest was a hunter with dog and double-barreled gun.

I still felt so high that I got up and walked to meet him and shook hands, with the purpose of accepting his congratulations. "Are you hurt?" he asked. "Is anybody hurt?" He was the superintendent of a lumber mill in the village. We exchanged names. His third question was a ground man's; one that among air folk would have been perhaps the seventh or eighth in importance: where were we from? New York. We were from New York. He was articulate, and proud in the rôle of host to New Yorkers. "How are you going to rise again?" In Southern speech airplanes don't take-off; they rise. And with that, he pushed us back into our problem: what next?

More men came out from among the trees, wood cutters, in overalls, their once-a-week shaves now in their second day. They were shy, standing off at some distance. They felt free enough to inspect the ship, but not to talk to the pilot. "New York." It is hard to say just how one can tell such things, but one could tell we were to them not two people in an airplane in the forest but two people from

New York. That was the first thing newcomers were told as they straggled out of the forest: ". . . New York, . . ." And the other thing was: ". . . going to rise again."

But where? Sometimes a road will do.

It was half a mile to the road. Pine forest is loose anyway, and around the bald spot in which we had come down it was extra loose. It seemed possible, with perhaps a tree chopped down here and there, to get the ship to the road. At airports one soon learns not to open the heavy hangar doors more than necessary, and to switch a ship through gates so narrow that at first they seem mathematically impossible. I went to inspect, leaving my passenger sitting in the forest with the ship, the white men standing respectfully around in one semicircle, the dark men in another.

On the way, walking through the dripping grass, trouser legs wringing wet below the knee, we met the women, steering through the forest, about a dozen of them, hardworking, drab, a column of battleships. "Nobody hurt," called out the hunter.

"There is nobody hurt," one of them repeated in turn to the next group behind her, with a wave of the hand that said quite clearly, "It is all off." Part of the column turned back.

We broke out into the road. It was a third-grade road, gravel; it was straight and would have done beautifully as a runway, but the pines on both sides were too close and high; there was no reasonable chance of getting clear. Another group was coming down the road on their way to see the accident, and had to be apprised of the situation: nobody hurt, and from New York, and looking for a place from which to rise again.

There was a council.

We plunged into the forest on the other side of the road; the trees were standing close together there. We climbed a fence that was disconcertingly solid to keep out the hogs. To get the ship across would mean undigging fence posts or chopping them down and presumably paying heavily for it. The clearing itself turned out to be a small farming patch, long since abandoned; they had never bothered to undig the stumps and already the pines were growing back on it. Anyway, it was too small.

New council.

Was there any stretch of road, anywhere, where the trees stood a little back from the road?

An old car wheezed up, hitting on two cylinders, an open car with most of its coachwork worn away and rusted off, the hunter's son at the wheel. An idea crystallized, and we got in. We went to look. Into the village, out by another forest road, five miles or so. We came out, of all places, at the forest observation tower (its top was still in the fog). I must have passed it fairly close by. There was also a narrow clearing on either side of the road though cluttered up with some Negro cabins.

When I started flying, I had picked up a mental habit which can become tedious and actually tormenting and which many pilots have: I can't look at any flat piece of land without considering it for imaginary landings or take-offs. But it still is a different thing when you do it in earnest.

This spot was not inviting, but provided we succeeded in moving the ship to it in the first place it seemed possible. There were those cabins, but they were low. There were some of those self-invited young pine trees, but they could be chopped. There were some fences that came close to the road, but at that point, my wings ought to be safely above them. There was the tower itself, set only a dozen yards or so back from the road. There was a telephone line on poles which led to the tower, but all that could be avoided by careful steering. I thought of those early take-offs with George Adams, his insistence that I climb away in a straight line, and of Ellen's impatient taps on the rudder. What wind there was blew slightly across the road; it would do more good than harm.

I decided to try it.

We drove back. Walking to the ship, I noticed that the forest was drying out and the fog was lifting. The wind was also picking up, which would help. People were still standing around, both Negroes and whites, at a respectful distance from my passenger who was talking to some women. She was talking about different types of kitchen ranges, of all things.

I will say this for the men of Hamlow: they didn't wait to be coaxed. I did not even finally announce my decision to move. The ship started to move as if by magnetism. A few small pine trees had to be laid low; they laid themselves. The ship moved through the forest smoothly and almost without shouting. The men caught on to that system of switching and twisting surprisingly quickly, and all I could do was to trot from wing tip to wing tip and guard their passages past the rough barks of the trees.

The ditch of the road was the last serious hazard. In an effort to roll her out, the men started pushing on her vulnerable parts, and a fist or two went through the fabric. Still, that could be patched at the nearest large airport.

Now for the road. Its official width, including the ditches, was thirty-five feet. Our span was thirty-six feet, and there was nothing official about that; it simply was so in solid spruce-and-fabric struc-ture. We started out in a long caravan, the old car leading; the ship, tail first; then all the men spectators; then the women.

By this time, the day had turned hot and humid, with the sun just unable to break through bad weather for hard work. It was growing toward noon by that time. We had no hats. Our first stop came almost immediately. Pine trees had encroached on the clearance from both sides. To get by, we had to head the airplane across the road and switch it back and forth much as one wiggles his way to the curb in a narrow parking space.

There were to be five miles of this. Then the column began to march again, with much yelling and with many hands pushing. Shots of corn liquor here and there increased the enthusiasm. It was my first try at an art which a man should know; namely, to keep saying "stop," "wait," "easy," loud enough and sharply enough so that it is obeyed immediately and yet in such a way that your crew will not wind up jumpy and excited and impatient, and that the effectiveness of your commands does not gradually diminish.

I noticed that our stopping distance was gradually lengthening; several times the delicate tips of the wings wedged themselves be-tween trees. I expected any moment to hear a wing spar crack.

My passenger had thus far been successively promoted from

mere payload to luggage stower, timekeeper, purser, and flight stew-
ard. She was to finish the trip a navigator, assistant engine starter,
and co-pilot. At this point, she was detached to walk fifty feet behind
the ship while I took a position where I could jam myself against the
ship and stop it sharply. She was to use her architect's eyes to judge
whether the wing tips would clear, and her woman's voice to yell if it
seemed that they would not—a yell which I could distinguish from
the raucous bellowing of the column—for the local women were
keeping strictly quiet.

It was noon by the time we got to the village. We worked down
the village street—and picked up still more of a following, especially
women and children.

Being responsible for both a lady and an airplane I might have
been in a bad fix—if the airplane or the lady had been different. As it
was, the lady was next utilized as a trailer coupling. Sitting in the rear
seat, along with the gun and the bottle and the hunter, she held the
ship's tail skid on her shoulder, cushioning it with a leather jacket,
and holding on with both hands, bravely taking the jerks when the
hunter's son let in the clutch too hard; ready to let it slip at a signal
from me.

We went awhile that way, the car in second gear, myself trotting.
Most of the crowd gradually fell back, except the children. Then we
met a tractor. To let it pass, we twisted the airplane around and
pulled its tail into the forest, and the branches tore some triangles
into the fabric of the steering surfaces. If we kept on thus reducing
the ship, there was little point in the whole march; we would be
unable to take off. We resumed our march, half trotting. We had
gradually acquired experience, and now a new method invented
itself: where the passages were too narrow, all the children swarmed
up the offending tree, hanging onto it like bunches of grapes, bend-
ing the soft stem away by the critical few inches.

Once more we got stuck between a telephone pole and some
trees that were too rigid to bend. The left wing tip failed to clear by
four inches. The Negro giant, getting impatient, simply reached
down, grabbed the Cub by its landing gear, lifted it and shoved it

over sideways, all the six hundred pounds of it. The right wing tip bashed itself against a tree and cracked.

It was all over.

We pulled the ship with the tail into the forest again, to clear the road. We sat down in the shade—by that time I would have been glad to sit down in the shade for almost any reason. The rest of the caravan also sat down and waited. There seemed nothing to do now but to take off the wings, get a truck, and move the wreck to the nearest large airport and licensed repair station, which might be Jacksonville or Atlanta. It would cost hundreds of dollars of next year's salary, for by now it seemed highly dubious that this type of damage was included in my contract with the owner; and it would cost my reputation as a pilot—the man who came home without his ship. The first job, anyway, was to wire for information where the job could be done. The hunter said that could be done at a town thirty-five miles from here.

There is something about literature: for me, things in print are just as good as things in reality, and sometimes a bit better. Flying a real Cub, I had nevertheless picked up at Miami an article in an aviation magazine that discussed among other things the structure of a Cub wing, and pictured it with the fabric stripped. I now remembered that, and dug it out of the luggage compartment, and went away quietly to study it. Then I went back to the ship to compare, wiggled things, felt things, poked a stick into things, shook things: it turned out to be not a vital part structurally but only a "false rib." The dent and lacerations would disturb the air flow at the wing tip, which is a critical point; but I did not see how it could be disturbing enough to be dangerous. I might yet rise.

We resumed our march, and ten minutes later broke out into the clearing.

My passenger would not be able to fly out with me. That was understood. It is one of the entries I find quite often in my log book: "the passenger proceeds by train." We hired the hunter's car to drive her and the luggage some thirty-five miles to the nearest airport, and went to work lightening the ship.

We took our luggage in amazing armfuls: all our northern clothes and flying suits and all the maps. The gasoline cans went out and the fire extinguisher, and the first-aid kit, and the tool kit; every pound less would help. The front stick had been taken out to begin with, and now I took out the front pedals and the wires. It was like gnawing the last bits off a chicken bone. I unhinged the window flap and even unscrewed the compass—I could find my way to the airport without it. Out went the front seat cushions; then the whole side enclosure came off; and on top of that, I changed my shoes and put on the light pair. I had not quite three gallons of gasoline left in the tank, at six pounds a gallon. I drained another gallon onto the ground, planning to use up another portion during the warm-up: altogether, when I got through, I had lightened ship by almost three hundred pounds.

Meanwhile, my passenger had the luggage all stowed away in the car. She had been invited by one of the women to lunch in her house, and was eager to go; it seemed that she was on the scent of something called "Kitchen Arrangement, Low Cost Rural House." Then she would follow in the car to the airport, and we would fly on, and by next evening would come out at Aiken and have easier flying from there on, weather reports, emergency fields, established airways. But first I must get off.

We pulled the ship as far back as we could, not only to the point where the road came out of the forest, but still farther back into the forest. The trees were forming a tunnel, with their branches almost touching over the road. It was narrow, but with careful footwork I should be able to make the first part of my take-off run in that tunnel without hooking a wing, and thus I might build up considerable speed by the time I reached the clearing itself.

I warmed her up. I gradually put on full throttle, the engine roared mightily in the confined spaces among the trees and I could see in the bystanders' faces how the rising noise level was drowning out all levity.

I was worn out, and had by that time more than a touch of the sun. But I would still have been willing to pay with a complete collapse if I could only get this ship back to its home field in good shape. I switched off once more, clambered out and walked down the length of the road to warn everyone to keep out of my way. They were already lined up on both sides, behind the trees, sheltered by the fences, hoping, I suspected, to see some excitement. They took up the word willingly enough. He is going to rise. Stand back while he tries to rise again.

Nothing could be gained now by any more preparations. I started the engine up again, kicked away the chocks, shook hands with my passenger, and climbed in. It was time to push full throttle. In twenty seconds she would either have crashed, or be free.

I gave her full power, and charged down the narrow runway, holding my head, my ship's head, low like an angry bull. It felt good to have the ship again by its throttle, stick and rudder, instead of dragging it around by its tail—to throw yourself once more against the air. She felt buoyant even before she had come to the end of the forest tunnel. I had never flown a ship so light before, and the battle seemed half won. But I kept her down, and let the landing gear pummel from below and the trees flash by on both sides; for to an airplane, speed and lift are the same thing, and the more speed she could build up, the more lift she would have at the end.

I broke out into the clearing, still rolling her. It is easier for a ship to gather speed while rolling than it is while hanging on its wings; making a close take-off is therefore much a matter of the pilot's nervous attack, and I knew it. I charged at the cabins and the fences as if I wanted to smash my ship and myself to bits there. It probably looked as if I could not get off; and I was itching to show the people whose presence I could half see, half sense among the trees. "Wait, you people. I shall rise yet."

Then, with my right hand, by barely an inch's motion, I let her wings bite. The pummeling ceased, her feel became soft; she was hanging on. The wing tip worked all right, and my confidence rose.

Once more I held her down. Instead of letting her climb, I threw myself forward again now against the wall of trees at the end of the clearing. Aiming at a point about half their height I attacked them, the left hand clamped on the throttle to make sure it would stay wide open: more speed. Fences and young pines flashed by close under my wings; the trees were growing up before me. Out of the corner of my eyes I saw the last I ever saw of the people of Hamlow, a pair of white eyeballs turning anxiously in a black face as I shot by.

Then it was time. With a two-inch backward pull of my right hand, I demanded from her all the lift she had stored up. She rose up against me from below and like a horse jumping, lifted me up, lifted me away from the road so that the rush suddenly slackened. The trees seemed to have buckling knees and gave way and sank down out of my line of sight, and beyond them the far horizon came up.

14. My Kind of Flying

When I did my navigation the next evening in the hotel at Aiken, working on the further homeward route, I realized that my personal conquest of the air was now accomplished.

I was now no longer merely training, no longer merely playing at something which at some future time I might perhaps do in earnest. I was doing the real thing right then and there, and I had been doing it right along, for the last three thousand miles or so, the miles flown in the small ship, both of good going and bad going. Out of those weeks of airport waiting and those twenty-five-cents-a-minute hops and the first timid pokings cross-country, and all the scheming, a new kind of flying had finally crystallized for me; a kind of flying that in its own way was as clear cut as airline flying or military flying or record flying or show flying were in theirs. You might call it personal flying. And the same kind of flying has held good, since that time, for many thousands of miles of air touring.

True enough, this kind of flying is all small-time stuff. Flying a rented air flivver at seventy miles per hour falls perhaps somewhat short of the kind of thing one envisages in adolescent dreams; piloting in shirtsleeves and hat, instead of flying suit, helmet and goggles; and the glorious roar toned down into a rattle. It may also be perhaps less glamorous than the sort of thing that is being glorified in the newspapers and on magazine covers: I still can't beat the trains; I cannot even beat the Greyhound bus. Four hundred miles is a good daily average. It has the disadvantage furthermore that it cannot be used to impress one's best girl; when she sees you sitting in your little airplane, you are likely to appeal less to her capacity for hero worship than to her maternal instinct.

It is small-time stuff, but it works. On the financial side, it works out so well that I spend no more on my flying than many a business man spends on his golf, though perhaps I can less afford it. You get more than twenty miles to the gallon of fuel. That was one of the things I figured out that evening in the hotel: from New York to Key West, over some 1350 miles of flying, we had spent for fuel and oil, plus hangars, plus one 20-hour engine check exactly $21.50, or $10.75 per person. Thus once one owned a ship, he could travel by air more cheaply than by hitch-hiking. But even a hired lightplane will get two occupants from A to B at the same cost as an airliner, which in turn is about the same cost as first-class train travel: about 4 cents per seat per mile. It takes longer, and it is less comfortable. Statistically speaking it must also be admitted that it is less safe. But it is more fun.

People sometimes ask me: "But can you see? When I do have time and money to travel, I want to see the country." I have traveled by almost every means known to man, on foot, horse, mule, bicycle, automobile, motorcycle, ski, boat, canoe, river-steamer, hitch-hiking, train, airliners—but in my memory the stretches of America over which I have piloted an airplane stand out the way some gadget stands out sharply in black and white in an advertisement where the rest of the photograph is retouched to look hazy and pale.

The country lies below you, mercilessly lighted, flat, without foregrounds and backgrounds, without mystery. You see the bend in the river, but also what lies around the bend; the range of hills, and also the country beyond them. The same glance that takes in the lake front of Chicago and the parks, also sees the laundry hanging in a thousand backyards. It has a slightly sour flavor, this view; but it is habit forming.

You know America, and you know flying. There is no need here to try to describe America from the air, and there is no hope that I could do it. What needs telling here, particularly to people who have had a few trips on the airlines, is not what you can see from the small personal airplane, but how you see it: the air tourist's particular way of seeing a country.

The most important thing, then, is that bluntness. The face of the earth is honest to the flier. For most of the country, this bluntness is good. It makes it look sounder, more dignified, more hopeful than the strips one thousand feet right and left of the main highways would make you believe it is. Discouraged intellectuals should have regular treatments by airplane. That is one thing about which I could go on for hours: simply how much country there is of which one never thinks. This bluntness is bad, on the other hand, for some spots: all glamoured-up locations, all staged and landscaped effects. Whether that be some expensive residential real estate which looks, when you see it within its surroundings, like a touch of chocolate sauce on a steak, or whether it be some place in New England which tries to persuade itself that it is really still quite the old stuff when the actual factories are merely hidden behind a hill.

As an example, take parks. You are bound to pass over one whether you come out of Chicago Municipal, or out of the old Northbeach Airport at New York, or most anywhere else. And you get that slightly sardonic feeling of being behind the scenes at the opera: you know it's make-believe, and you see exactly how it is done. They have built themselves a poor little artificial paradise of winding roads and wooded lakes and skillfully staged scenery. But the rowboats on the lakes seem to be sitting on mud, for steam shovels cannot scoop out a lake as deep as God can; and the winding roads actually go 'round and 'round. Poor ground travelers drive and drive and think they are traveling deep into romantic lands; but seen from up here, the joke is on them.

Thus romance—in the sense of the travel ads—escapes the flier. But instead, he sees other things, new ones that have never yet been catalogued in literature or guide books, let alone the ads. Those big swamps of the Carolinas for instance; you could never even have got near them by automobile—the roads just turn quietly away. Or any one of the big cities of America, as one whole thing, how it sprawls, how it smokes all over heaven, how it crawls in all its streets at once. What one can see from an airliner is only a weak foretaste of what the private flier sees; for in the private airplane one's vision is incomparably better—forward, to both sides, downward. There is generally no wing under you to obstruct downward vision; one generally flies much lower and more slowly. One flies where one pleases. Think about that one thing for a minute: *one flies where one pleases.*

And it is not true what one sometimes hears, that the flier feels divorced from the ground, isolated from it, and might as well look at a photograph. The air tourist can feel the country and he sometimes can smell it; and he also gets it through his nerves direct. The country sends up its bumps. Once three thousand feet over the West side of Chicago, where the cool air from Lake Michigan heats up and rises, I met a front page of *The Chicago Tribune* flapping lazily around on the thermal up-currents. Around the South end of Lake Michigan, one can navigate by smell alone; there are three different streaks of smell, one from the oil refineries, one from the Gary steel mills, and one from the Chicago stockyards. In Massachusetts, there are certain ponds, mentioned in history books where the Yankees cut ice and sold it at a profit to the West Indies. I flew up that coast in the spring, and the once valuable stores of coldness could be felt clearly. They sucked us down so hard that my watch jumped out of its pocket.

Here is what I mean by getting the country with one's nerves direct. It happened to me along the Atlantic Coast, over Maine, in early spring.

A barometric "high" was drenching New England with sun. Visibility, for once, was unlimited. We saw windowpanes glistening seventy miles away and there would have been all sorts of famous sights to see—country and settlements straight from the history books, the White Mountains, actually white, off my landward wing, the surf and rocks and islands under my seaward wing. But my departments of beautiful thoughts wouldn't get going. All I could think was how ridiculous my ship looked, holding out its little wheels against the watery seascape. All I could think about over that noble old region was that I wanted pontoons under me instead of wheels;

and, while flying, I began to design them in my mind: lines, attach-
ments, and all; and a lovely pair of boats they were.

All the time, though, I was slightly annoyed at myself, thinking
how barbarously machine-minded flying had made me. When we
had arrived at Mt. Desert, all I could do was to look over our hostess'
beach for imaginary mooring places for an imaginary seaplane on an
imaginary next visit. Only much later did I understand that there
was really nothing wrong with that; that I was getting, not too little
but too much of the Maine coast, that all that boat designing was
merely an old trick of that country; doing to an airman, in airplane
tempo and in airplane terms, what it had been doing to its people
from the beginning—turning a man's mind to the sea.

Or, another example of getting the country with one's nerves
direct. There is a widely believed libel to the effect that mountains
are, so to speak, wasted on fliers. This is simply not true, even as far
as visual perspective goes. The Alleghenies, for instance, are for the
motorist merely a series of grades and they are for the small-plane
flier a very fearful mountain range. Nor is it true in this other respect. Here is what a mountain pass felt like the first time I made
one.

The ridge was guarded with clouds, not a solid layer, but big
towering cumulus formations that floated before the entrance to the
passes like jellyfish, pawing me, sucking me in. I kept close to the
tremendous mountain slopes, and hunted for a pass. I had calculated that I had fifteen minutes' gasoline to waste in hunting. After
that, I should have to turn back.

I climbed up into the canyons between the clouds, curving in the
narrow clear channels, trying not to get caught. Once I slipped out
from between two big fellows just as they closed in on me. A few
times, for seconds, all vision was blotted out by dazzling mist. Once,
the shifting white curtains uncovered, for just a glimpse, a rocky saw
tooth, close and terrible; a reminder that the ridge was near. I felt
the wind, spilling over the top from beyond the mountains, falling
down on me in gusts. I had to trust my ship's own stability; I couldn't
guide it by these ghosting nothings.

I was just about to give up and fly back, when a new perspective opened, and I saw the ridge, and in the ridge, a gap, a quarter mile away and about my own height. That was a pass, and through it, far away, I could see a sunlit blue-green forest. It was clear to the west. I pressed the throttle all the way forward and went for it. Two rocky slopes closed in beside me. A gust tried to turn the ship over, but I caught her with hands and feet. The passage was narrow, and a strong downdraft forced me into the deepest, narrowest point. A dead tree stood there and stretched out its nasty arms for me. But I cleared by a hundred feet; I slipped through. There was a lifting surge from below; that was the west wind, blowing up the slope. I slid out over the deep valley, the mountainsides now falling away from under me.

I looked back; the gap had closed again. I was alone, high up over the sunlit forests. Twenty miles ahead was the next ridge I should have to cross.

There, too, all clouds were hanging around the moutains; but one pass was open, a triumphal arch of two mountainsides, and a cloud across. It was far away, and it was small as the camel's ear, and it might still close. But when I pointed my ship's nose at it, I felt quite unreasonably high and mighty.

I am not the only one, of course, who has found out these things. Leaving aside the commercial airplane owners and the traveling they do; and quite a few rich older men and women with private, fast and heavy ships and air yachts, there are hundreds of amateurs in America who have discovered for themselves the same kind of flying—inexpensively, slowly, in rented small ships. And the way the small flying fields are now buzzing with students there will be thousands soon, both men and women.

Already there is emerging a certain routine of lightplane touring, something which is for the airways what the detour and the tourist camp and the hot dog stand are for the highway. It is much the same wherever one flies in America. It is also much the same whoever does the flying. If you did the flying, it would be much the same. And here is how it works.

You fly until you are tired. It's wonderful! When you think how

Flying Time used to be doled out, in half hour hops at a time, never enough to let you hit your stride, let alone get your fill of it. But now, you fly until you can't fly any more. Five hours of actual air time is enough, seven hours is a good day's work.

How quickly one gets tired depends mostly on the roughness of the air, in a lightplane especially, because the light plane is more wallowy in bumps and gusts and requires more steering. On cool cloudy days, the air is sometimes so smooth that the ship lies in the air for half hours in a stretch as motionless as if it were standing on the airport. Then again there are those sunny calm spring days when every plowed field and every hay field and every country road sends up a current of warmed air, and when every river and every lake and every bit of forest cools the air, sucks it down, and creates a down-draft. On such a day the ship is much like a child before the age of reason; it won't stay put. On such a day, the pilot must relax, or the ship wears him out. A disciplinarian puts the wings level and the nose onto the course for the thousandth time, but they won't stay. In the next gust, they go swinging off again, and at the two thousandth time the disciplinarian begins to slam the controls around as if he could teach her a lesson by cuffing her. At the three thousandth time, he is just about ready to dive the ship into the ground and crack it up viciously—and then finally he makes up his mind to relax.

By late afternoon, the noise of the engine, which in the morning was a smoothly blended roar, has long since dissolved into its ele-ments, the four beats of the exhaust, the howling hum of two pro-peller blades, the grinding and tapping of the valve action, each separately. The exhaust beats themselves are coming in an acoustic sort of slow-motion; at three o'clock they were coming out singly, like pearls on a string, and by evening they are individual puffs, lagging more and more: "Putt," says the ship, and it begins to lean over to the left. "Putt-putt," she says while her nose swings off-course to the left. "Putt-putt-putt," it says while you bear down a bit with the toes of your right foot and nudge the stick a shade over to the right. "Putt-putt-putt," it says while the dipped wing comes up again from the fields.

That is the time when one begins peering out forward through the propeller blur for the airport.

There is nothing ever as beautiful as the airport of one's destination, seen from afar, waiting there with its runways long and broad and flat. The familiar pattern of three runways crossed, the final O.K. sign to all your dead reckoning. Sometimes it is executed in concrete-on-grass, sometimes in cinders-on-mud, sometimes in dirt-on-grass, sometimes inconspicuously in mowed grass on unmowed hay field. A pilot gets so he will recognize it where his passenger will see nothing but farms.

You fold up your map, and put it away, and cut your gun. The noise stops, and the control feel slackens, and the wing lift goes soft, the ship sinks down forward against the stick in your hand. I like to arrive over my field high, and have a long glide down: for after a couple of hours of steady cruising, a slow glide somehow feels wrong and dangerous. One thinks one is stalling one's wings when they actually are still holding on briskly, and one has for the first minute or so a tendency to let the ship glide too fast. A high arrival gives you time to come down leisurely in a wide circle, getting accustomed to the limp feel of the ship, and at the same time looking the field over.

During the glide, there is often the same conversation between myself and my passenger: "Which way is the wind down there?" The passenger must help look. Half the time on small fields the wind sock is missing or is hard to see; this, incidentally, is about the only occasion I can think of in flying where a pilot can make any real use of his governmentally tested and certified vision. "See anything?" "There is smoke coming out of the farmhouse over there." "There is a flag over in the corner."

It is on days with gentle winds that those clues are hardest to read for flags and wind socks won't string out. Yet, even with gentle winds, if you misread the signs or if your fatigued brain interprets them the wrong way 'round and you came in down wind, the wind pushing instead of holding you back, you would come in like holy fury, and very likely overshoot and somersault. It is one of those things over which pilots crack-up.

You make up your mind, and choose your runway, and then comes the day's last job: a last precision approach. Not that it is necessary, with a whole airport to land on; but a sloppy one, using too much field, would grate on your self-esteem all evening. One last nice wide turn away from the field, during which you check the wind once more; one last finely timed turn towards the runway; a last slow glide with the nose held up to an almost level attitude and the wings almost dead, and then—stick back, and plunk.

Airports are not yet standardized. In the essentials they are becoming much alike, with runways, hangars, and the usual collection of airport men and of ships. But they differ in atmosphere and in the way you are received. At some fields you are treated like a steamer captain registering at the harbor master's: all the details and grave courtesy. At other fields a uniformed attendant comes loping with registration blank and sharpened pencil, though in my case slightly patronizing of so small a ship. Some fields are more like a yacht club landing, with introductions first, a cigarette after, and business only then. I have also been thrown out, or given hell for coming in with a private ship and no radio; that was at airports which cater mostly to airliners. Only once, in Key West, have I paid a landing fee. Then again, there are airports run in cafeteria style; you help yourself, roll your ship into a hangar which is provided, and a large sign announces that the city of Xville is not responsible for any harm that might befall. Sometimes you are given a check for your ship and you leave everything to the attendants; as for a car in a parking lot. Then again you are the half-personal guest and intruder of some flying service operator's hangar.

The whole style of lightplane touring is against any sort of swank. Which is just as well, for it keeps expenses down.

The airport itself usually lies on the cheap side of town, grouped, for reasons of real estate values, with the cheaper golf courses, the gas works, and the big cemeteries. The downtown district is usually one or two dollars' ride away by taxi—if taxis can be got. More often the tourist hangs around until after sundown, when most airport activities close down, and is taken to town free in some mechanic's jalopy. Sometimes a high school kid will drive you to town and out again the next morning and be your personal slave and fetcher of things in exchange for a few minutes' hop with a couple of steep power-turns thrown in.

You and your passenger arrive at the hotel with miniature luggage, muddy shoes, and sunburn, looking like not-quite-broke hitchhikers, and thus they sometimes make you pay for your room in advance. This is one of many occasions when you may feel called upon to explain how you got here, anyway. Or sometimes you will be asked where your car is or why you want a vacuum bottle full of coffee when there is a road house every two miles along the highway. But don't try to explain. The public mind simply has no niche for you yet, neither for pilots who wear spectacles, nor for private plane tourists who look like hitch-hikers. People are quite likely to think you are lying or crazy or spoofing; I pretty nearly got arrested once for telling the truth to a policeman.

You get a meal at last, and at the dinner table you do your navigation for the next day, drawing straight lines on maps to the amazement of waiters and other guests. Then you take a walk up and down the main drag to look at faces, and then you can turn in.

I no longer make allowances in my plans for whole days or even half days of local sight-seeing; I have found that I never use them. After flying, there is little point in sight-seeing on the ground, unless it be for architectural detail, or for the insides of factories, or for the night life. In one large swing over town before landing, you can see all that which the terrestrial sightseer must scramble for days to see bit-by-bit: the harbor and all ships therein, the new bridge, the old fort, the slums, the downtown skyscrapers, the big residences along the lake front—the whole lay-out; and, what's more, as in the case of Charleston, the whole surrounding country too.

In the morning, some airport helper on his way to work can usually call for you with his car, and the earlier the better. In flying, and especially in lightplane flying, there is actually very little of that barbarous killing of space and time which the casual newspaper reader would gather is the essence of flying. Even a pilot still works his way, and the old rules for travelers still apply: if you want to make haste, make it slowly; and if you want to get there, get away early.

The first early-morning chore at every airport is to roll open the heavy hangar door, and if you want to get your ship out and get away, you put your shoulder to it like a Volga boatman and push.

You help the airport helper extricate your ship from among the wings and tails of the other ships jammed in the hangar—a delicate and expensive game of jackstraws. Meantime, I like to send my passenger out with paper and pencil to collect the weather dope, from whatever sources there may be; if we are lucky, from the office of the airline, or from the airport radio complete with "Hourly Sequence," "Six-hour Forecasts," and "Winds Aloft." If less lucky, by phone from the newspaper or the weather bureau, and in the back country sometimes from the hunches of the local experts.

You wind up the time recorder, and fit a new disc of waxed paper into it, as a mechanical log of the ship's flying time, for the owner. You start the engine, whatever fuss that may imply. You warm it up, listening carefully, while you think how it will pull you across the forests, the swamps, the hills, all day long.

Meanwhile, the passenger comes back with the weather slip. You pay the ship's hangar bill—a dollar usually, sometimes one and a half, once in a while a nickel per foot of wing span (a system some hotel ought to adapt to beds)—and the fuel bill, which eventually will be refunded to you by the ship's owner since airplane rental rates are calculated on an all-inclusive basis.

While you wait for your receipt, you stow the luggage, carefully so that no shawl or sweater can be sucked out in flight and catch in the rudder or the flippers, and get in. And I usually start mumbling to myself as I figure out the compass heading I am going to hold, doing mental arithmetic with figures from the "Winds Aloft" slip, and figures on my map, and the compass error table on the instrument board, and all the time the staccato puttering of the idling engine adds a note of going-away excitement.

The helper hands in the receipt, and there is sometimes a bit of farewell advice: which runway is the smoothest to use, or which of the fields further up the line is most convenient to its town, or what not. Or sometimes an airline dispatcher comes at the last moment and puts two fingers on his cap and asks would you mind waiting a few minutes—an airliner is just about to come in, and one likes to let those big fellows have the air uncluttered. Or sometimes he sends word that an airliner will come behind you on the same course, and where will you be flying and at what altitude?

You nod, and the helper kicks the chocks from under your wheels, and holds onto one of your wing tips, letting the ship pivot around it as you let the engine pull, until it points toward the open field, and then you taxi out and get the map ready, and buckle on your safety belt, and ask:

"O.K.?"

"O.K." And only then, you swing around into the morning wind, and run.

When I sit up there now, that constricted feeling in the stomach region is pretty well gone; as the old textbook would have put it, "relaxation has been achieved." But even after tens of thousands of miles of cross-country piloting, the air is still air: thin, treacherous, pathless. The country is still out to get you, and piloting still takes a certain amount of action. This whole business of navigation by which one schemes one's way across the country, compass headings, gallons of gas, minutes of elapsed time, miles to the airport, degrees of drift, and the fingering of one's slide rule. It may sound like unmitigated machine age, but it is still a matter of the human heart, as you will know once you have been out there loaded down with a passenger's trust in you and with the trust of the ship's owner, alone over the rivers and forests, and in a lightplane, without radio and blind-flying instruments and long-range tanks.

So you work your way across the country, watching it for all sorts of small signs, and reading in it as in a book. Most of the cows on the pastures, to take an example, are facing northeast. That means the wind down there is probably from the southwest, and that again means that in case of a forced landing I shall know exactly how to shape my approach, even if I can see no smoke. It also may mean that I can gain speed by coming down into a more favorable wind. Or it may mean that the weather is about to change.

Or, take a calm, hot day, somewhere in the high country of the West, when the thin air and the calm in combination make for extra long take-off runs and shallow climbs. On such a day, you may get off, but immediately afterwards, over the tree tops and fences, you may have a feeling of drowning: not enough buoyancy to get you away from the ground. But once you have learned to understand the ground and the air, you bank over toward a plowed field which lies dark and hot in the sun; and an updraft carries you up.

Or, the water in some river below is green and clear, while all the other rivers have been muddy. That means there must be a dam and a stowed-up lake somewhere upriver in which the water clears itself, and that in turn means that your position on the map is somewhere between that dam and the point where the river's next large tributary muddies up the water again; and that sort of aerial scout lore sometimes provides wonderful short-cuts in navigation.

As for the routine of touring, after two hours or so it is time again to land, for it is not good policy to be out over the country with too little fuel. In fact, fuel shortage is directly or indirectly the cause of many accidents: the dangers of the air are not so mysterious as the public thinks. There is a laugh or a derisive snort in almost every air accident.

But quite apart from that, I am forever coming down, for weather reports, for rest from cramped seats, because of darkness or because the head winds are too stiff, and because I'd feel more comfortable with a couple of gallons more in my fuel tank. I seldom pass up an airport, and if there is no other reason for landing, there is always the amateur's itch to test my precision in yet another strange-field landing.

Those wayside stops of the air: the small airports of the country. When the sun is high and the air filled with shimmering dust and haze, it is the black yawning gate of a hangar you see first, sometimes long before the rest of the town and the runways emerge.

Again there are fields where, when you arrive and circle, the hangar looks deserted, no cars are parked, no ships are visible. Perhaps there is not even a hangar. Then the thing to do is not to land immediately. Instead, you first fly over the business section, turn a few curves to attract attention and make suggestive motions with stick and throttle, cutting the gun and gliding away toward the field. That is the only way to reach and alert the attendant whose main job might be that of garage man or courthouse janitor, and it will bring him driving out from town with the key to the gasoline pump, or with a barrel of aviation gasoline, a funnel, and chamois leather.

Yet again, some fields are hard to see even when you are over them. Then you may have an anxious time, thinking that they did plow their airport up, or that your navigation did go wrong and that this is the wrong town altogether; but then you look the land over once more, scanning the farms and suburban lots systematically with your eyes, and you see it. It has been there all along grinning you in the face, like one of those death heads that jump out of pictures of beautiful girls when you look long enough—only more pleasant.

You fill up, stretch your legs, have a cup of coffee from the thermos bottle.

Once down, the old habit of airport watching and waiting takes new hold of me; it seems there is always some reason why one could hang about the aerial waterfront. Student flying to watch for instance; some poor fellow, harassed by factor X, making stab after stab at the airport; or some new ship to look at; or talk. I seldom can resist a little hangar office where the stove is going, and it is nicely dirty, narrow, dark, and stuffy.

That's what I like between hops. The airport dog is there, sniffing at me, and the men are there who make their living in the air. A touch of local color, whatever that may be, Western, Southern, New England; a touch of mechanic; and, yes, a touch of horsetrading and county fair, heritage of those twenty years when flying was not yet a salable commodity. There is airport talk, the never ending airport talk; you pick it up at a Colorado field just where you left it at a Michigan one. I say cain't and ain't, I spit in the fire, and I am proud if they think that the "itinerant pilot" of the little ship is one of them, some pilot trying to build up his Flying Time for a commercial job, a factory pilot delivering a ship. On and on we talk; about ships, about the dangers of the air, about pilots and what they did right and what they did wrong, until the weather sequence begins to come in over the loudspeaker, droning but yet like a fanfare:

"Cheyenne, Cheyenne. Ceiling unlimited, ceiling unlimited; high scattered clouds . . ."

And I get going.

15. American Air

I used to think of the United States as one thinks of a golf course. It was simply terrain on which to practice your technique. The technique was "Cross-Country Flight"; XC for short, when you wrote it up afterward in your logbook. Flight was *much* newer then, in the early thirties. Merely to circle the airport still filled you, every last cubic inch of you, with a sensation that was like nothing else. And to quit circling, to head out straight cross-country—that was Flight, raised to the Second Power. Boy!

I used to look down, in those ancient days, and watch my fat little rubber tire hang idle over the depth. It went across somebody's roof: no jolt. Treetops; a highway; then a river. You flew out from over land to over water: no sink. No coolness. Imagine that: walking on land and water like a god. What a machine! And what a pilot! (Me.) Bring on your skyscrapers, so I can top them. Bring on your hills, so I can cross them. Bring on your distances, and I shall eat them up. Bring on your country, and I shall ignore it.

Well, you find out.

I remember my first flight over New England. Ignore it? I wished I could. Instead, I thought: "What horrible country!" You see, the thing about XC was—that fat little tire was always looking for a field

From Wolfgang Langewiesche, *A Flier's World* (New York: McGraw-Hill, 1951). Reprinted with permission of The McGraw-Hill Companies.

to roll on. The engine might quit anytime: That was official doctrine. It never did quit, even then—much less now. But the fear of it was carefully drilled into you. Any time at all, in the midst of the most delicate figure-8, when you were trying to make some farmer's barn hold still off your wing tip, bang! would come a tremendous silence as your instructor pulled back the throttle and said: "Forced landing!" Then you quickly picked a field (really, you were supposed to have one all picked out: "Always Have a Field in Mind.") and you went gliding down in a long S-turn—through the "Key Position"—down across the trees—down into the field—down until the grass began to tickle your tires. Then he was kind enough to open the throttle for you and let you climb out. To shoot a good Forced Landing was considered about three-quarters of the Art of Flying. And so you judged country mostly by its fields.

New England rated low indeed. Those gloomy hills, all wooded. Those nasty little pastures, with the naked rock poking up right through the middle. Those ugly stone walls around every plot of land—just imagine you overshot and rolled into one of *those!* "Horrible country. Not a decent field in sight." Then I caught myself: "What *are* you saying, man. You are supposed to find this charming. Don't you have any education? This is the cradle. . . . Hell, you *know* it's charming. Look at that white steeple nestled in the green. Trouble with you, you can't take it; you're scared!" But of course I was right in the first place: it *was* a horribly tough country they picked to settle; there *was* no decent field, nor a flat place to put one. They themselves called it a Howling Wilderness, and it very nearly starved them to death. Besides, most of them left it, first chance they got, for points west.

How different North Dakota felt! I had spent a week flying in the canyons of Idaho—a mountainside off each wing tip, a wild river below—with the thought of engine failure strictly repressed, of course: no use thinking about it where you simply can't afford one! I had flown down into North Dakota through night, a black night, with nothing visible but the beacons along the airway; and again the forced-landing idea had been switched off—there are lots of badlands on that route. Toward morning, not to get too low on gas, I had sat down on an Auxiliary Field to wait for daylight. It was deserted. (Those fields are not built to serve a town, but to serve the airway— they sit there, every hundred miles or so, their boundaries outlined by lights, just in case.) Parked there under the beacon tower, I had fallen asleep right in the airplane.

I woke up, and it was daylight. I started her up, and took off. Still dull in mind, I cleared the fence. There it was: Landings unlimited. You cleared the fence, and you had cleared everything. As far as the eye could see, big fields—flat as a table and bigger than airports. And smoothly cultivated: where farm machinery can roll, an airplane tire can also roll. It was fall, and most of them were stubble. The nice, combed-looking stubble of machine-sown wheat: a guaranteed surface, along with unlimited room.

"This," I thought, "is 100 per cent O.K. This is the rose without the thorn; this is the meal that is all dessert; this goes in easy." In fact, I swear I had a strong sensation as if I were a little boy again and had just been handed a dish of whipped cream with chocolate.

"I think I'll just roll my wheels on that one." I had only flown a minute, but why not? "I'll fly straight for exactly three minutes, and then close my throttle." Nothing to it—just glide straight ahead. I thought it would be fun to roll up to a fence and jump it and sit right down again, so I did. Why not? "I think I'll spiral up to 1,000 feet and cut my ignition and stop my prop." Done.

Now, I don't claim it is a red-hot and brand-new idea that North Dakota is different from New England. I tell it to show you how a pilot reacts to the country: he does react; he can't help it. And not as a tourist; he is not ever "just looking." He has business with the country, and the country with him.

I once had a piece of business with the Missouri River. I had undertaken to fly a small seaplane from Coast to Coast; up the Missouri, down the Columbia. Don't ask me why—I guess it was to prove it could be done. It was a short-range ship. You had to gas up often. Each time, you became boat. For a little while, you were a river pilot, back in Mark Twain's day. True, Mark Twain piloted on the Mississippi. But he himself says that the Missouri is twice as tricky, and a Missouri pilot twice as much of a pilot.

"The river was an awful solitude, then," wrote Mark Twain in 1883, as of the early French explorers' day. "And it is now, over most of its stretch." It *still* is, old man. Flood plain, with willows; for miles on either side, it's empty. I would always land near a bridge, because only for a bridge would a road come to the river; and only on a road could I hope to get to a filling station—a 5-gallon can in each hand. But a bridge is an obstruction; and near it may be that fearful seaplane-trap: an electric wire strung across the river (hard to see). So I would land a little way off, or what looked from the air like a little way. Once on the water, I would be deep in that solitude, the bridge out of sight around the bend.

The water was silent, oil-like, smooth, a very thin mud. How muddy it was! You got your hands wet, handling the ropes; then the western air would dry them, and they were suddenly caked with a thin layer of dry mud; you'd rub your hands and it would come off as a fine dust.

Now to get back to the bridge you had to "read the river." But from 5 feet up, not from the lordly pilot-house atop the Texas-deck. Those ripples—did they mean a puff of wind, or a shallow place? This upwelling here—that was a log, stuck under the water. It might rip your pontoons open. (You call that a "Sleeper.") There was also the kind of log that is caught on one end; the other end slowly comes out of the water, and then the current pushes it down again. (That, you call a "Sawyer.")

My pontoons drew about 8 inches of water—about the same as the old river steamboats. I ran aground many times. The old steamboats did, too. They would then walk—put a spar overboard and stem it against the bottom and push. I did much the same—rolled up my trousers, waded out, and lifted on one wing tip to push one pontoon forward a few feet; then waded over to the other side and pushed the other one forward. Hard, wet, slow work. "Mark Twain?" I used to think: "Mark o-point-twain!"

So, deep in the twentieth century, air age and all, you personally met this continent: its mountains, plains, rivers. You were an emigrant, thinking about decent fields. You were a river pilot or a canalman or a wagoner or a mountain man. You walked down Fifth Ave-

nue thinking—hey, you people, I know a way to get across the
Rockies with one single hump that you can clear at 6,000 feet.
(Maria's Pass, up near Glacier Park—I had dragged that seaplane
through there.) Of course nobody cared—you were a hundred years
out of step.

For instance, about the Alleghenies. To us they still were what
they once had been to everybody—a big barrier. They are not high,
but if there isn't some weather cooking on one side, it's cooking on
the other, or on the ridges; they get moisture from the Atlantic and
the Great Lakes and the Gulf. In those days, few pilots knew how to
fly blind; none of us small fry did. So, when the clouds were down on
the ridges, the barrier was closed.

I remember my first trip over the Hell-Stretch—where the New
York–Cleveland airway goes across the ridges. (The early airmail
pilots had called it that.) That day, a low, gray, ragged ceiling kept us
low. In the low perspective, the valleys and the towns are hidden.
You don't realize there are really quite decent fields down in the
river bottoms. All you see is an endless forest, coming at you in
waves—a green-blue, melancholy. Some of the waves were high. We
tried to climb, and bits of cloud started slapping us in the face. It was
Not Good.

Well, it's not supposed to be good! I found this later in a book.
Talleyrand had once traveled this same stretch. He had crashed
through these very woods under us. The branches slapped him in
the face as the clouds now slapped us. He lost sight of his servant.
He called out: "Are you there?" And the fellow answered: "Unfortu-
nately, my lord, I am." That seems to be the built-in feeling of that
country. I now looked at my passenger, saying, with my eyebrows:
"Are you still with me?" He pointed down, he pointed all around,
and then held his nose.

You discovered anew, for yourself, things that had once to be
discovered. For example (still talking about the Alleghenies), that
you could fly at water level from the Seaboard to the Middle West:
you got right on top of the historic Erie Canal. That way, you could
squeak through under clouds that were solid on the hills. Another
bad-weather route went through Pennsylvania. Up the Susque-

hanna River to Lock Haven; up another valley to Altoona. This far, you could fly even if perhaps it was like a tunnel, valley sides with the ceiling across it: there were nice long fields along the river. At Altoona you sat down. You had now only one ridge between you and Johnstown, which is the headwaters of the Ohio. So, you sat and smoked cigarettes and watched the ridge. When it came out of the clouds, you hopped into your ship, spiraled up at wide-open throttle, and went for that ridge. On top, you picked up the main line of the Pennsylvania Railroad. You got right on the quadruple rail and scooted down the incline into Johnstown. There, you got on the river and wound your way out to more open country. Clever, isn't it? Well, I found out this was exactly the idea of the old Pennsylvania Canal— an engineering wonder that flourished just before the railroad age. They took the barges to the very same spot. Then they had a marine railway that hauled the barges bodily up that same ridge, and down that same incline on the other side. There they could float away to points west. It goes to show: a place sends out something like a magnetic field—a field of ideas. You fly through there, and those ideas generate in your mind.

Now flying has changed. You have more speed, more radio, perhaps two engines. Even with only one, the forced-landing obsession has faded out. You try again to treat the country with contempt. You try to think of it as pure expanse—graph paper, yours to make lines on. But it still doesn't work out that way. The country still makes itself felt. In fact, speed sometimes makes you feel it more. It's like a phonograph record: the needle has to slide to bring out the tune.

I like to see East change to West. I like that moment, on the New York–Pittsburgh–St. Louis route, when you get to the last ridge, called Laurel Ridge. There, at the end, the dislikable Alleghenies are almost real mountains. On the brow of the ridge, facing west, there is a bald, stony strip, scoured clean by the west winds and the sleet and the rain. An airway beacon stands up there, alone. Then the stuff falls steeply away under you. You slide out across there, and you enter the Middle West. It feels different. It feels easy-like. Not that the country turns nice right away. Right around Pittsburgh, it is a tortuous jumble—small, steep hills, slag fields, deep-cut railroad tracks, lots of smoke. But you know it will calm down. A pilot gets the habit of "think ahead of the airplane." The Now and Here is no longer so important in the faster airplane: now and here, the engine percolates, the weather is O.K., the gadgets work, you have lots of gas. What's ahead is what matters. And so you study cloud shapes, listen to weather reports, and feel out the situation ahead. And there, you know, comes flat country, come open fields, come comfortable cities, big airports, runways with clear approaches. The squeeze that makes the Easterner elbowy and unfriendly squeezes also in flying. In the East, airports are small, obstructed by power lines, hills, gas works, squeezed in between the cemeteries and the insane asylums. West of the Alleghenies, they give you room.

So now, if the ceiling is low, you can stay under it and push on; you know the terrain gets better all the time. Or you can go on top of the overcast; you know that when you want to get down, no hills will stick up into a low ceiling. And so you feel, ahead of time, way up in the air, that certain ease and plenty of the Middle West.

Presently, you pick up the section lines. Now *that* is something. It is really one of the odd sights of the world, and it is strictly an air sight: a whole country laid out in a mathematical gridwork, in sections one mile square each: exact, straight-sided, lined up in endless lanes that run precisely—and I mean precisely—North-South and East-West. It makes the country look like a giant real-estate development: which it is. One section has 640 acres. A quarter section, 160 acres, is the historical Homestead. You sold your goods, you crossed the sea somehow, and they *gave* you *that!* "Land-office business" used to be done in this matter, and no wonder.

Get this right. These section lines are not something that an attentive eye can distinguish in the landscape. They are the landscape. Compared with this gridwork, the natural landscape—flat here, a little rolling there, a river valley, a pond—just can't quite catch your attention. In fact, the natural landscape has long fitted itself to this scheme. A man has a woodlot, his neighbor a cornfield; the boundary between woods and field is of course the fence line; but the fence line is part of the grid. More than people know, all their coming and going is channeled by that grid. Their roads—except for the biggest highways—run along the grid. In fact, from the air, the lines are mostly marked by roads.

For flying, the section lines are wonderful. They make this country in reality just what a pilot wants country to be—graph paper. You can time your shadow with a stop watch across two lines, and get your exact speed. You can head the airplane down a section line and check your compass. But you hardly need a compass. You simply draw your course on the map and see what angle it makes. Then you cross the sections at the same angle. You can't miss. If you want to go exactly west, you get on a fence and follow it. The fence presently leaves off; the line becomes a highway. The highway curves off, but the line goes on as a fence again, as a lane between fields, as a farm road, then perhaps as the main street of a town, a highway again. It is easy on the brain.

It's true what the foreigners say—it all looks pretty much alike. A town comes out of the haze, moves through below you, falls back—only (you sometimes think) to run through some secret passageway and plant itself again in front of you!

Flying, you tell these towns apart as you tell stars—by constellation. This one, of about the fourth magnitude, with a smaller one to the north of it—that must be this one on the map. Those three-in-line, that's those.

What is it like, this American town? Well, it isn't crowned by no castle, that's for sure; and by no cathedral either. By an insurance sky-scraper, more likely; or by a hotel, perhaps; but most likely by nothing. It is not fortified, and never was: no crowded Old Town, no ring-shaped boulevard where the Walls used to be. And it is not a village.

It is always a small city. It is laid out with streets at right angles, and has at its center a little Downtown, perhaps only two streets crossing each other, perhaps a few blocks. In there, it's naked and stony; it achieves a certain businesslike ugliness. There a well-developed parking problem. And at night, that downtown core glows with bright lights and red neon signs, where the seller entertains the buyer and the boy the girl.

The rest is quiet streets with little houses and lots of trees. It fades out into the farmland in an indifferent way—streets and avenues already marked out on the ground, but still empty. You can tell—it expects to grow. Add a few blocks on the outskirts, and the downtown gets a bit more stony. Keep adding, and Farmerville becomes Bloomington, Bloomington becomes Springfield, Springfield becomes, say, Indianapolis.

There is always a Wrong Side of the Tracks to the town. In the thirties, when the price of paint made a bigger difference, this used to show up plainly. There is always a giant high school, and certain other standard furniture—a gasoline bulk plant, race track, "institution" (maybe a Veterans' Hospital, maybe a teacher's college, maybe a county poorhouse). These things are marked on the flying maps, not because it is remarkable that a town should have them, but it helps you tell the towns apart. This town has its high school at the east end. If this is the town I think it is, there should be an institution on the north edge. Sure, there it is. You make a pencil mark on the map and fly on.

Somewhere now, about a third of the way across the country, you notice something has changed. The fields are bigger; the air is clearer. Things have opened up. There is less junk around the landscape—I mean by junk, I guess, things of which a pilot cannot immediately see the sense and purpose: a clump of trees here, a different-colored patch of field there, an old abandoned factory building—that sort of thing. The landscape is tidier. Each farmhouse sits on its land as if it had just been set there; each fence shows straight and strong, as if it had just been strung. Each town seems to say: "Look, I am a town." Things have a sharper edge to them.

What's happened is that you have crossed the line between the forest and the prairie—the line that was there in Indian days. The white man has cleared the forest and plowed the prairie, and has made them both superficially alike—both farmland. But still the difference shows. Maybe it's the different color of the soil. Maybe it's that up to here, the country has been darkened by the last poor remnants of the old dark forests—a clump of trees, a woodlot—and here the trees leave off. Maybe it is simply the drier, clearer air. At any rate, you have moved one more notch west.

Here, in the less cluttered country, your map reading must change. A town may be so small that it would rate only a circle, o, farther east: here, it gets the full treatment. The map shows it as a yellow area, shaped like the town's built-up area. A town may be so small that farther east it wouldn't be on the map at all: here it gets at least an o, and a name. This, I like. It reminds you of the way each person counts for more out west. Go west, young man, and put yourself on the map.

And I like the names of those towns. It used to be that a prince would graciously call a town after himself—Williamstown or Fredericksburg or Charles' Rest, or what not. Out here, the ordinary man sat himself down, founded himself a town, and named it, by gosh, after himself. I like to check them as I fly: here comes Charlie. Howdy, Riley. *Wie geht's,* Hoehne. Hello, Kline. Landusky, Henderson, Milliken, Goessel, Weir, Swink, McPhee: how are you doing?

Or the man would name the town after a woman of his: Beulah, Maybell, Dolores. I had often flown over a town named Beatrice, Nebraska, and I had thought: "Poor Beatrice, whoever you were (farmer's wife? railroad president's daughter?)—that really wasn't much of a present to give a woman." It is a nice town and all that, but it isn't exactly—you know—it hasn't got *glamour,* out here in the sun-blasted country between Omaha and Wichita. (It hasn't got glamour if you were over Manhattan yesterday and will be over the Hollywood hills tomorrow.) Well, I came over Beatrice again one night. Now people don't know that, but a town at night is the most beautiful thing made by man in the last hundred years—especially an American town, where they don't spare the current. A brave sight, too—out there, where towns are far apart, with a lot of darkness in-between. People went out into this vastness, built a home town here and lit all those lights. A proud sight, just by being there. And I thought: "Beatrice, wherever you are now, you ought to be proud. It looks real nice."

Now, halfway across the country, come the Great Plains. It happens fast, in a matter of minutes. A grassy butte sticks up right through the fields. A bit of badlands shows up. The pattern of the farms opens up to detour around it and comes together again. A gully shows up—Grand Canyon in miniature. You know the signs. You are getting west another notch. You hitch yourself up in your seat and take new notice.

Ahead, the country rises a step, and the step is a bluff: its face is eroded; it grins at you like the teeth of a skull. As you pass over, the farms fall back. The last you see of them is a mile-square wheat field draped over some hump, abandoned. It reminds you of a wrecked ship on a beach—tried to go where it should not be, and got in trouble. Ahead are the vast khaki plains, rising toward the West. There's nothing to see but vastness, clarity of air, distance. The sun glistens on a window of some ranch house, 50 miles away. A train, very far away, is a small black thing under a smoke plume, like a ship at sea.

You head straight out there, and the world fades out: badlands; the dry, bare hills. That fellow yammering about the "Lone Prairie"—he's been there. You suddenly remember you have no water aboard, no strong shoes, no big hat. You are lucky if you see a ranch, hidden deep down in some secret canyon, in a patch of green. More likely, you see next to nothing: a barbed-wire fence; some cattle; a windmill pumping beside a water hole.

You fall in line and follow the railroad. Everybody and everything else does, in that country; even the Civil Airways. Now the United States slenders down to a mere strip—river-plus-railroad-plus-highway. Along this strip are the irrigated fields, the towns, the airports. And the railroad is the great sight—doubly great by default of everything else. It's long straightways and mathematical curves, the way it goes on and on through empty country up toward the West.

Finally these bright yellow-green plains rise under you like a wave about to break; over the crest comes a white spot that turns out to be snow. There, between two high mountains, is a gateway, where the river comes out. Toward this gate, you have been steering all

along; so was the railroad; so was the highway; so were the radio
beams along the Airway. You go in through that gate, and East has
changed to West.

The air view is an honest view: "You can't kid *me*" is your attitude as
you look down. "So *that's* how it is." For example, the great, famous
dams—Hoover, Norris, Grand Coulee. In the ground view, the thing
you marvel at is how big they are. The glamour photographs show
them that way—small human figures, dwarfed by this gigantic wall
behind them. Well, from the air, it's the other way round. It strikes
you how small they are. Hoover Dam especially—it's actually hard to
find! The eye sweeps all over the naked rock and the shores of Lake
Mead before you find it—hidden down in a gulch. It makes you
smile. Some boy has jammed a rock into this stream at just the right
spot—and has managed to dam up one hell of a big lake. Small
cause, big effect: clever little devil. And that, I'm sure, is the correct
view. An engineer would say so. He would always try to build the
smallest possible dam, not the biggest.

Or, New York City. What's it all about? On the ground, why you
know: *Time, Life, Look, Quick,* and *Harper's;* Batten, Barton, Durston and Osborne; Merrill Lynch, Pierce, Fenner and Beane; NBC,
CBS, ABC; words, ideas, paper of all sorts. But, from the air, I regret
to state, New York looks like a place where steamships tie up to
piers. The piers catch your eye, not Radio City or the Wall Street
skyscrapers. Manhattan, with all those tentacles sticking out into the
water, looks like some biological exhibit—some organ specially developed to draw nourishment from the sea.

The foreground doesn't hide the background. Looking down at a
place from the air, you see everything, literally, that's there. You may
not notice everything; you may not understand the half of it; but at
least you've seen it. What's this? Why does it look so odd? It's been
amusing, for example, to watch the college campuses: the old fake,
ivy-covered Gothic; the stadium with its vast parking space; the new
research factory; the rows of Quonset huts. 'Tain't Oxford, brother.
You run your own private census all the time. This thing—why do I
see more and more of this? Not much can happen in the country

that you don't notice, often ahead of the papers and magazines. For example, much will be written soon about our cities, how they have grown in area, not to say exploded; how the FHA town, way out on the potato fields, is taking the place of the tenement; and so on. Why sure: pilots have seen that grow for years.

Everything people do, and perhaps everything they think, makes its mark sooner or later on the ground. (That's what Reconnaissance is all about.) I used to amuse myself, looking down at Washington, by tracing the idea of Checks and Balances in the city plan and the shape of buildings. I've seen, in the South, a little country church with a swimming pool behind it: a fine point of theologic doctrine—baptism by total immersion—clearly written into the landscape! That is the kind of writing you try to read.

The American landscape is a palimpsest. Underneath what is written in it now, in concrete and barbed wire, there is older writing.

To bring out old writing, a man might photograph a document under trick light. The same in flying. Over the forests of New England, winter light is best. The trees must be bare, so the eye is not stopped at the treetop level. There must be snow on the forest floor, because that lights up the inside of the forest and makes it easier to look down into it.

Then you see, underneath the present-day forest, the farms of long ago. They did have decent fields there after all! Not decent to land on, but lovingly made, cleared out of the forest, carefully fenced by stone walls. Each rock once was picked up by hand, carried out of the field, carefully placed. It's said they made their children do that, to make them hard-working and God-fearing. Stern stuff. It's all under the forest. The forest is still only scrubby; but already it is full of dead trees helter-skelter, like virgin forest. The 1938 hurricane put them down, and nobody cares. History did a high-speed job here.

The second layer in this palimpsest is in strong plain writing: those section lines are the main part of it.

I believe this was written by Jefferson and perhaps Rousseau, but I don't know. About this, the main feature of the United States landscape, it is curiously hard to find anything in books. But I have often admired this scheme. Remember, it was drawn up on paper before the country had ever been explored. The lines were run before the people came: so it was literally a blueprint for a future society. I think it is a diagram of the idea of the Social Contract: homestead by homestead, men would sit each in his own domain Free and Equal: each man's domain clearly divided from his neighbor's.

I mean, it wasn't the only way they could have parceled out the country. They could have gone out there with manor-houses, each with a bunch of cottages around it. (You do see some of that in the South.) They could have built villages nestling around a commons and a church. They might have built forts. Today, I think, we would build a headquarters first. There would be a row of houses; a communal water tower, "housing" for bachelor workers, a hospital, a recreation area. Radiating out, I imagine, would be roads, and off the roads would be the fields. The whole "development" would be star-shaped, and right in the center would be of course the Administration Building.

But they picked the layout where every man is his own boss. Even now, this is the main feature of the American landscape: the square-cornered parcels, big in the West, small in the East, big in the country, small in the cities, of which each means a man. I realize they rent 'em, they are mortgaged, they grow the stuff by government subsidy, all that; but it is still true—the *design* of the landscape, seen from the air, is a design for independent men.

In the years I've been flying, I have seen the American landscape being redrawn. A third set of lines has begun to show up on top of the others—a new style. Contour plowing is an example. It makes the marble-like pattern of fields and furrows, dictated not by property lines, but by the terrain. It is a new thing—and the new thing goes right across those straight, right-angled fences. Two farms that are divided by a section line are drawn together by this joint pattern. You can tell—two men, one plan.

Strip farming, too. I remember one evening on the Montana prairie. The whole plain—those parts that were tilled at all—was in a strict rhythm of dark strips of fresh-plowed earth, yellow strips of stubble, alternating bing-bong. The sun shone on this pattern, and it almost dizzied the eye—like some fantastic checkered fabric.

That does not just happen by the chance judgments of independent operators. You could see a marshaling force at work. It was, in style, like those newsreel shots you used to see before the war, from countries since gone under, where "The Youth" was doing calisthenics on the parade field. "One," and an acre of humanity was heads; "two," and it was tails. I hurry to say that I have nothing against contour plowing or strip farming. Flying gives you too vivid a view of erosion, of blowing dust, of destroyed land. I remember the first time I saw really eroded farms, out in Nebraska, in the dry years. I said practically out loud: "Well, this, of course, has to stop." But that's just it—you see these changes in the landscape, you understand why they are made, and you can't mistake the meaning. New ideas of society are cooking here, and a blue pencil works, redrawing the old designs.

You see the same thing going on in cities. Those "housing projects"! You can tell someone thinks the "human resources" should be stored in bins more orderly, more manageable. And bins is all they are. But the funny thing about such architecture or city planning is: it makes a lot of sense in the air view. Seen from above, straight down, the dreary mass takes on a certain rhythm, an order, even a wit. This block here, this block there, the star-shaped thing in the middle. This building brackets that one which brackets that.

The reason is, I think, that such things are conceived, sketched, approved, by someone who looks at humanity in a perspective much like a pilot's: he is way up, on the Policy-making Level, and he looks down on a desk.

What kind of country is this, anyway?

There is always a lot of fresh dirt dug up, wherever you look. Old Alexander Botts gets around with his Earthworm Tractor and fixes the place up to suit himself. The whole country bears the tracks of the Caterpillars, the bulldozers, the listers, the middle-busters, the ditchdiggers, the power shovels, the dredges, the pipeline-laying outfits.

A superhighway goes hell-bent. I mean, you can see it go. It's got this far with actual pavement, actual traffic; for another 70 miles, it is fresh-dug dirt. For still another hundred miles, it is a trace through the farmland; it's started pushing over trees, moving houses, cutting hills in two: look at it go! It gets to a river, 10 miles broad—really a branch of the ocean: you can see, it's going to walk right across. The stepping-stones are already laid.

Even the farms are all power and precision; nothing yokelish, nothing idyllic. I like to watch the plowing as I fly over. The plow moves fast—faster than any animal could pull it. The fellow rides on it! He leaves six furrows at a time! You see results even during the brief minute that you can keep a field in sight. A brush seems to be drawing fresh brown paint across the green. The other day, 3,000 feet somewhere above the corn belt, we smelled something peculiar. Hot wire? Insulation searing? Quick now, check switches, check fuses, check meters, check the map for the nearest airport—Shucks, it was pigs. Must have been *lots* of pigs, somewhere below. That's how they operate. When they raise pigs, they raise pigs.

They make mistakes too; they make big ones—and are not afraid to write them off. Witness those dead wheat fields on the plains, those ghost towns, those abandoned railroads. There's a canal across Florida—a big, deep, ship canal. Only it doesn't really go across: it exists only in sections. They changed their minds.

They get big results. At least they get big production. I remember India from the air. India is one of the few other places in the world that has any real farmland. (Most of the world, after all, is desert or mountain or jungle or ice or ocean.) Well, it was all there: the fields, vast plains of them, just like here. The furrows, weakly scratched perhaps and a bit wavy, but just the same, it was careful, painstaking farming. It was all there but the product. No corrals full of cattle; no grain elevators; hardly any roads to carry the stuff away: most of the stuff gets eaten right in the villages; there is not enough net production to make visible signs in the landscape.

Over here, you can see the stuff: the wheat of the prairies shows even in upstate New York, along the St. Lawrence, in huge grain elevators with steamships docked at their base. Through much of the West, grain elevators stand like skyscrapers. Cattle? Acres of cattle, brown and white mottled, in the corrals and stockyards. Fruit? By the trainload, going east from California. Cotton—bales in huge piles. Iron ore: all the railroad tracks near Lake Superior are covered with the rust-colored dust, spilled off the cars; on the Great Lakes, the ore boats make a steady procession all summer long.

It is a shirt-sleeve country. "Gracious living," so-called, has made few traces in the landscape. You do see places on the Eastern Sea-board that make you think: "Hey, Mack, who do you think you are?" "Come out from behind that Chateau. I knew you when you used to eat down at Joe's Diner." Well, half an hour west of tidewater, all nonsense stops, and it doesn't start again till Hollywood.

The cities, too, such monsters as Chicago, turn out to be, when you fly over them, still mostly earth, with light, wooden, modest houses on it. Sometimes this still strikes me: If you had asked me when I was a boy in Europe, I would have said that the Americans (such as are not cowboys) must of course live in some superurban way, all in penthouses among the skyscrapers. Somehow it pleases me that they don't. Those factories that glow from inside at night with bluish light; those highways—the masters of them live in little houses up some tree-lined street.

About the Authors

Wolfgang Langewiesche was born in 1907 in Germany, in the very morning of the Air Age. Intrigued with the notion of America, in 1929 he emigrated to the United States, where he learned to fly as a means to explore the broad land. At a time when few people flew, he made the airplane and the typewriter his tools. He crossed this country innumerable times and flew the skies of three other continents. His keen powers of observation of the topographic, physical, mechanical, and sociological worlds, combined with his simple and elegant style, led to five books and countless national magazine articles about flying. *Stick and Rudder,* "an explanation of the art of flying," is the book for which he is best known and has been in print for nearly sixty years. Mr. Langewiesche died in California in 2002.

Drake Hokanson is an author, photographer, editor, and educator. His books include *Lincoln Highway: Main Street across America* (Iowa City: University of Iowa Press, 1999) and *Reflecting a Prairie Town: A Year in Peterson* (Iowa City: University of Iowa Press, 1994). He has exhibited photographs coast to coast and has lectured widely about roads, the American landscape, photography, and literary nonfiction writing. He teaches at Winona State University in Minnesota and has been a pilot since 1977.

Carol Kratz is an author, editor, educator, and physician assistant. Her work includes the first editing of *Lincoln Highway* and *Reflecting a Prairie Town,* co-authoring book chapters, and writing a forthcoming book about America's county fairs with co-author and husband, Drake Hokanson. She has been a pilot since 1977.

William Langewiesche is the son of Wolfgang Langewiesche and the author of four books including *American Ground: Unbuilding the World Trade Center* (New York: North Point Press, 2002) and *Inside the Sky: A Meditation on Flight* (New York: Pantheon, 1998). He is a national correspondent for the *Atlantic Monthly* and a commercial pilot. He lives in France.

Other Books in the Series

Siftings
Jens Jensen
with a foreword by Charles E. Little and
an afterword by Darrel G. Morrison

This Hill, This Valley
Hal Borland
with drawings by Peter Marks

On the Shore of the Sundown Sea
T. H. Watkins
Illustrated by Earl Thollander

The Desert: Further Studies in Natural Appearances
John C. Van Dyke
with a critical introduction by Peter Wild

*The Friendship of Nature: A New England Chronicle
of Birds and Flowers*
Mabel Osgood Wright
Edited by Daniel J. Philippon

*Illustrated Sketches of Death Valley and
Other Borax Deserts of the Pacific Coast*
John Randolph Spears
Edited by Douglas Steeples

*The White Heart of Mojave: An Adventure with
the Outdoors of the Desert*
Edna Brush Perkins
Edited by Peter Wild

Printed in the United States
30431LVS00002B/1-57